Experiential training

Experiential Training: Practical Guidelines explores how to train people in areas which are particularly emotionally, and therefore intellectually, challenging. The majority of people recoil from death or dying, from frank awareness or discussion of sexuality, from seeing the limitations of their own ways of communicating with others or how they try to manage their own stress.

This book adopts an experiential, or participative, learning approach. This is a powerful tool in helping people integrate their own emotional and practical experiences and competence, whilst learning considerably from others in group settings. It enables them to come to appreciate realities which previously they had not been aware of, often blinded by deeply ingrained beliefs, attitudes and values.

Detailed descriptions of training workshops explain why such training is necessary and provide a wealth of clinical experiences which vividly convey the flavour of these workshops and the personally vulnerable and challenging position of the trainer.

Experiential Training: Practical Guidelines will be invaluable to all professionals employed in health care, personal social service and education.

Tony Hobbs is Senior Consultant at the Centre for Crisis Psychology, based in Skipton, North Yorkshire and an Honorary Tutor at Birmingham University. He works with individuals and organisations experiencing, or at risk of experiencing, major psychological trauma.

Experiential training

Practical guidelines

Edited by Tony Hobbs

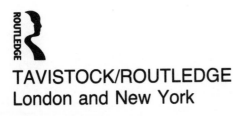

TAVISTOCK/ROUTLEDGE
London and New York

Revised Edition of *Running Workshops*
first published in 1987 by Croom Helm

Published in 1992
by Routledge
11 New Fetter Lane, London EC4P 4EE

Simultaneously published in the USA and Canada
by Routledge
a division of Routledge, Chapman and Hall Inc.
29 West 35th Street, New York, NY 10001

Phototypeset in Times by Intype, London
Printed and bound in Great Britain by
Mackays of Chatham PLC, Chatham, Kent

British Library Cataloguing in Publication Data
A catalogue record for this book is available from the British Library.

Library of Congress Cataloging in Publication Data

A catalog record for this book is available from the Library of Congress.

ISBN 0–415–07438–X

This book is dedicated
to
Frank and Peggy Hobbs
and
Elizabeth-Anne Cooke

Contents

Figures

Contributors

Tony Hobbs is a Chartered Clinical Psychologist and Senior Consultant at the Centre for Crisis Psychology. The international work of the Centre, based at Broughton Hall, Skipton, North Yorkshire, England, involves provision of psychological debriefing, training, assessment and consultancy to individuals and organisations experiencing, or at risk of experiencing, major trauma and catastrophe. He began his professional life trained in counselling psychology.

Stephen Murgatroyd is Professor of Management and Applied Psychology and Dean of the Faculty of Administrative Studies at Athabasca University, Canada. An experienced counsellor, consultant and teacher, Stephen is the author of fourteen books and over 100 academic papers.

Richard Pates is a Principal Clinical Psychologist and Co-ordinator of the South Glamorgan Community Drug Team; he also provides psychosexual and marital therapy. Formerly Richard worked with children and adolescents. He has run workshops on sexuality for several years with a wide range of people.

Sylvia Rhys is a counsellor and course tutor in the Faculties of Social Science and Education in the Open University. A researcher at the Institute of Health Care Studies, University College, Swansea, she also runs classes for the Extra-Mural Department at the University of Wales College, Cardiff. In addition to writing several journal articles, she is co-author with Stephen Murgatroyd and Ray Woolfe of *Guidance and Counselling in Adult and Continuing Education*

Mike Shooter is Clinical Director of the Child and Adolescent Psychiatric Service in South Glamorgan and a former journalist and teacher (amongst many other jobs). He heads a multidisciplinary, community-orientated team, working out of the Preswylfa Child and Family Centre and Harvey Jones Adolescent Unit in Cardiff. The team believes in helping people with problems as the people concerned see them, and in the context in which they live; it aims to tailor help to the clients rather than the other way round! Mike has a particular interest in working with chronically ill, dying and bereaved children and their families. He has facilitated hundreds of experiential workshops for front-line contacts in many countries.

Ray Woolfe is Senior Lecturer in Health and Social Welfare at the Open University. He is an experienced counsellor and trainer and has written widely on counselling and helping skills. His books include *Coping with Crisis, Helping Families in Distress, Guidance and Counselling in Adult and Continuing Education* and *Handbook of Counselling in Britain*.

Preface

In 1979 Stephen Murgatroyd and Ray Woolfe founded the Coping with Crisis Research and Training Group within the Open University in Britain. Its aim was to develop further the existing understanding of how adults and younger people cope with stressful life events. Membership comprised interested members of staff of the Open University and concerned practitioners from clinical psychology, psychiatry and social work.

This group collaboratively ran a series of training workshops over a five-year period, learning together and refining the training formats adopted. *Running Workshops: a Practical Guide for Trainers in the Helping Professions* (Croom Helm 1987) reported the group's initial findings but then went out of print.

Subsequently, the Coping with Crisis Research and Training Group was dissolved as individual members moved on from its Cardiff base to fresh posts. Yet each member remained dedicated to the model of participative, or experiential, learning. This is a model which, through a process of collaboration, provision of structured exercises, periods of reflection and minimal direct teaching, powerfully aids participants' learning in areas which are both intellectually and emotionally challenging. These areas, such as death and dying or sexuality, are those in which people hold strong attitudes and beliefs which impede their receptiveness to learning.

No longer learning and finding their way together in the collaborative enthusiasm, mutual support and intellectual stimulation of the original group, each original member continued independently to develop the model for this kind of training in his or her own area of expertise.

Experiential Training: Practical Guidelines, the successor to *Running Workshops*, while retaining much of the original material has been completely updated to reflect this individual experience. It also includes two important new chapters on evaluation of change and development through workshops and the guidelines necessary for effective workshop practice, with the intention of making the book useful to the very wide range of people for whom this method of training is now relevant.

In effect, the early venture has 'grown up', and the contents of this volume are the fruits of experiences gained over the years by competent practitioners, now recognised as experts within their chosen fields.

Introduction

This book is written for those who are seeking an introduction to experiential learning, who wish to discover what this model is about and how it can best be used. It is written also as a resource for those considering starting to use the experiential model, who are looking for ideas, guidance on proper practice, and a check-list to ensure that important preparatory and practice issues are not overlooked. It will also be useful for those already experienced in such a style of working as a source of further ideas and as a comparison to their own practice.

The book presents details of training workshops on individual and organisational stress management, communication and basic counselling, working with sexuality, and coping with death and dying. Additionally, introductory and concluding chapters consider broader issues of principle concerning experiential learning, its effective practice and evaluation of workshop impact.

Each chapter is written by a competent practitioner, experienced in their respective field. The stylistic differences between contributors, both in workshop practice and in writing about it, have been preserved, as they will add to the readers' appreciation of the practical reality of such work. Recognition and acceptance of such differences is crucial; each time people come together to learn, the experience is a new one for the participants and trainers alike. The trainers' flexibility and competence have to combine quickly so as to respond to the fresh challenge presented by the current group. Description of this enables a strong flavour of what it is like to run these workshops to be presented, alongside description of the evolved structure of the sessions.

Experiential learning, sometimes known as participative learning, is a process which directly acknowledges, welcomes, values and uses the existing knowledge and competence of those being taught. Its use is particularly appropriate where the subject matter under consideration touches on people's deeply held beliefs and attitudes, involves emotionally charged or value-laden material, or is just plain difficult in human terms! The topics dealt with in this book, dying and death, sexuality,

ways of coping with stressful experiences, and basic styles of communication, have been chosen because they present a deep challenge to most
people.

Didactic teaching, where a person presents information to others in
lecture or lesson format, almost invariably results in learning taking place
solely at an intellectual level. It has been described as being based on
the 'mug and jug' theory of learning (Rogers 1983; Hobbs 1986). Put
simply, the recipient of the lecture is like an empty mug waiting to
receive information poured into it from the source of knowledge, the
jug. This method of teaching involves a predominantly passive form of
learning in which students are not required to examine their own
emotional response to the subject material. They are able to remain
personally unaware either of the intensity or the effect of their own
emotional response to the subject material on themselves or on other
people. This can on occasion be a basis for later damagingly inadequate
application of knowledge. For example, when student nurses or doctors
are being 'taught' about management of dying patients or their distressed
relatives and information is imparted solely didactically, the future practitioner will not have the necessary opportunity to examine the manner
in which their own fears of death affect the quality of their being with
such people.

Experiential training therefore aims for a qualitatively different degree
of learning from that resulting from 'didactic' teaching methods. The
intention of this book is not to devalue use of the didactic teaching
process in other settings, but simply to promote recognition that, as with
the experiential learning process, it has its appropriate place and it has
its limitations.

The different quality and nature of experiential learning lies in its
involving as many different aspects of the participant as he or she is
prepared to invest in the learning process. Learning occurs at intellectual,
emotional and behavioural levels in an integrated manner, resulting in
real attitude and behavioural change as influential early learning is effectively re-evaluated. Our early learning is influential in determining how
we view the world, our place and that of others within it. Much of this
will have occurred before we learned to think independently and decide
for ourselves (Berne 1964; Malan 1979). As such, the experiential learning process has to be a collaborative venture between teacher and learner. It involves all participants, teachers and learners alike, in a process
of mutual vulnerability and risk taking, of personal challenge and
learning.

Considerable skill is required to be effective as an experiential teacher,
and it is with this that this book is directly concerned. The person needs
to be competent in their subject. They need a high level of comprehension of the theoretical background in addition to considerable practical

experience gained at first hand working with these issues with a wide range of people. They need to be sensitive and responsive to the nuances of the learning process within individuals, confident in managing emotionally charged group processes, flexible within necessary structure. They need to be able to use their knowledge and practical experience confidently, yet with an appropriate degree of humility which respects the learner's current knowledge and enables them to work together to build on this.

The process of experiential learning is both exciting and challenging. Its underlying philosophy is that of student-centred learning (Rogers 1983), and it closely comparable to that of 'helping' and 'caring' as described by Søren Kierkegaard:

> If you really want to help somebody, first of all you must find him where he is and start there. This is the secret of caring. If you cannot do that, it is only an illusion, if you think you can help another human being. Helping somebody implies your understanding more than he does, but first of all you must understand what he understands. If you cannot do that, your understanding will be of no avail. All true caring starts with humiliation. The helper must be humble in his attitude towards the person he wants to help. He must understand that helping is not dominating, but serving. Caring implies patience as well as acceptance of not being right and of not understanding what the other person understands.
>
> (Kierkegaard 1849)

REFERENCES

Berne, E. (1964) *Games People Play: the Psychology of Human Relationships*, Harmondsworth: Penguin.

Hobbs, T. (1986) 'The Rogers interview', *Changes: Journal of the Psychology and Psychotherapy Association* 4: 254–8.

Kierkegaard, S. (1849) *Sickness Unto Death*, Harmondsworth: Penguin (1989 edn).

Malan, D. H. (1979) *Individual Psychotherapy and the Science of Psychodynamics*, London: Butterworths.

Rogers, C. R. (1983) *Freedom to Learn for the '80s*, Columbus, Ohio: Merrill.

Chapter 1

Experiential learning in workshops

Ray Woolfe

THE NATURE OF EXPERIENTIAL LEARNING

Experiential learning has been defined elsewhere by one of the Coping with Crisis Research and Training Group (Murgatroyd 1982) as having four main components:

1 the learner is aware of the processes which are taking place, and which are enabling learning to occur;
2 the learner is involved in a reflective experience which enables the person to relate current learning to past, present and future, even if these time relationships are felt rather than thought;
3 personally significant experience and content: what is being learned and how it is being learned hold a special importance for that person;
4 there is an involvement of the whole self – body, thoughts, feelings and actions, not just of the mind; in other words, the learner is engaged as a whole person.

These principles result in the following concrete propositions:

1 Experiential learning is concerned with the experience of individuals, not just with their participation. Participants are asked to consider and utilise their own experience as a basis for self-understanding and assessment of their own needs, resources and objectives.
2 The individual participant is regarded as an active rather than a passive participant in the process of defining and putting into practice educational agendas and methodologies.
3 Through this process, power (locus of control) is shifted away from the teacher in the direction of the learner. Another way to put this would be to say that the nature of the teacher–student relationship is usually asymmetrical; the former has more power than the latter. In the workshops described in this book, this asymmetry is reduced. Learners are planning, carrying out and evaluating their own learning. The 'expert' and the learner engage in a process which is concerned not with the former transferring facts into the latter but rather with

facilitating an active process of learning in the student. It could be described as a move away from a model of education in which the learner is seen as an empty vessel to be filled full of facts towards one in which the latter is seen as a candle to be lit; a potential to be developed.

4 The participant becomes responsible for his or her own learning. The expert is a resource and a provider of structure, but learning is seen as taking place when the learner is trying actively to assimilate external knowledge into his or her own internal frame of reference.

I would like to elaborate these points by saying something about how they are reflected in each of the chapters which follow. Chapter 2 explores the experience of running workshops on the subject of coping with stress. The author draws a distinction between stress perceived as an objective phenomenon and stress perceived subjectively; that is to say, how each individual comes to identify, understand and experience stress. While there are many similarities between individuals, each individual experiences stress in a unique way. The author describes how the focus of the workshop is concerned with helping individuals to understand, through sharing, what stress means to each of them as individuals. The structure of the workshop reflects this emphasis. The basis of the workshop is established by a series of linked activities through which individuals are enabled to gain insight firstly into what it means to say that stress is experienced, secondly into the source or origin from which they see this stress as deriving, and thirdly into the ways they have of reducing stress. Formal knowledge is seen as generated by the participants' own work. Thus, for example, the idea of types of coping strategy derives from the workshop itself and the efforts of the participants to understand what stress means to them. The author describes how more formal academic structure can be arrived at as a result of using the participants' own experiences and sharing. In other words, knowledge is constructed through the workshop rather than being seen as a product presented by an expert to the unknowing. The experience of the participants is regarded as an asset through which his or her understanding of both self and the external world can be increased.

Chapter 3 is also concerned with stress, in a specific context, work, but this time with an organisational rather than an individual focus. It can be described as seeking to promote an understanding of the interactive relationship between experience, reflection and learning.

Kolb (1984) describes a four-stage, cyclical process of effective experiential learning which embodies these dimensions (see Figure 1.1). Kolb perceives experience in the present as the basis for reflective observation. Out of this emerges a conceptual analysis which can then be tested in an active fashion. This testing generates a new experience, and so the

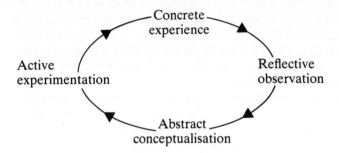

Figure 1.1 Cyclical process of experiential learning (Kolb 1984)

cycle begins again. The model allows for the possibility of preferred learning styles. Some people, for example, prefer to reflect, whilst others prefer to act. The implication is that the effective learner is able to employ a range of learning styles, while the effective organisation embodies the whole range of skills within its workforce and allows for the deployment of these skills at appropriate points in the organisation's work.

The model developed in this chapter places particular emphasis on reflection through, firstly, structuring the person's reflective experience of stress at work; secondly, providing a model and a language through which experience can be reflected upon; and thirdly, providing an opportunity for participants to engage in the reflection/learning process together in a spirit and climate of mutual support. The barriers to experiential learning that arise in this workshop are of two kinds: those that relate to the personal pain of learning; and those that are about the difficulty of accepting responsibility for learning about self in front of others. In order to overcome these problems the workshop design moves from 'safe' activities to increasingly unsafe ones. Throughout this process the teacher is seen as needing to exercise monitoring functions so as to maximise learning and minimise undue distress.

Chapter 4 is concerned with training in basic counselling and communication skills. An important aspect of this particular workshop is the use of role play, through which the idea of experiential learning is translated from a theoretical concept into reality. The author describes how participants experience at first hand aspects of what it feels like to be involved in a therapeutic encounter. They are also intimately involved in evaluating the experience. This is concerned not just at the end with looking at what changes the experience of the workshop has brought, but also with encouraging participants to evaluate their own previous experiences of communication or failure to communicate and effectiveness or non-effectiveness in helping relationships. In other words, individual self-evaluation is an integral aspect of the ongoing process of the work-shop. While every workshop account emphasises the need for a clear structure, this one makes the point most explicitly. The objective is to teach specific skills in a defined manner. What is offered to participants can be defined as freedom within structure; self-expression within the limits of clearly signalled parameters.

Whereas this account emphasises the area of skills basic to communi-cation and counselling, Chapter 5 is concerned with the more diffuse concept of helping skills. Moreover, unlike the other chapters, this is concerned with a specific occupational group, health visitors. Neverthe-less, the principles behind the workshop are similar. The leader describes how she used the workshop as a personal learning project, and the chapter illustrates how principles of experiential learning were employed. The approach adopted was again one of freedom within structure, a perspective which was explored with the students at the beginning of the workshop. The issue of the power held respectively by leader and participants receives attention. The author makes it clear that learning is a risky business for all parties concerned. Students were reluctant at times to accept that they were active shapers of their own experiences, as opposed to being the object of influences external to them. The chapter offers a somewhat original conceptual structure of the leader as decision maker and the process of running the workshop as a series of connected decisions. The account of student motivation indicates that it is a multifaceted phenomenon. Although students were expected to come to the workshop as part of their Diploma course, the enthusiastic way in which many joined in the activities indicated an intrinsic motivation to learn more about helping skills as a topic in its own right.

The workshop account on sexuality (Chapter 6) emphasises the need for an experiential base because what is being learned and assimilated is not information primarily, but ways of dealing with problems. This cannot effectively be done by didactic teaching, but through an exami-nation of people's attitudes and perceptions. This involves looking at early learning experiences of sexuality, becoming immersed in the lan-guage of sexuality and sharing of thoughts and ideas with the group about different aspects of sexuality.

The aims of the workshop are seen as follows:

1 to increase the awareness of participants' own sexuality;
2 to increase awareness of others' sexuality; and
3 to be able to discuss sexuality with others.

If one looks at the role of the trainer, it can be seen that this type of workshop, involving discussion of a sensitive subject, is risky for the trainer, as the group can take the subject where it wishes; this freedom is an important one for successful workshops. The trainer, therefore, cannot predict what will happen and has to accept or acknowledge the group's feelings.

The chapter exemplifies some of the problems experienced in sexuality workshops. The need to have co-leaders is important because of the defended areas involved in sexuality work. The potential for destructiveness by a leader via a group is certainly present, and co-leaders can take the heat out of this, but the relationship and degree of comfort between co-leaders needs to be established prior to the workshop. Confronting resistance within the group is vitally important, because this is a mirroring of what participants may be experiencing within their own work situation, and if it is not resolved then workshops will not play any useful purpose in these participants' experience.

Experiential learning is seen as actively challenging people at an emotional level. Without such challenge no change is possible. Given that this is so, it has been important to make clear to potential participants exactly what they might expect from a workshop. The account of the workshop illustrates – as do all the chapters in this book – that helpers cannot remain emotionally aloof from the experiences of the event. It follows that there is a need for there to be more than one leader if this is at all possible.

Shooter's chapter, on coping with death and bereavement, begins with the question, why is a workshop setting necessary? The answer provided is that people seeking help require not words of advice, but an opportunity to express emotional pain. An experiential workshop offers precisely this opportunity. The chapter emphasises the overall aim of providing a good experience of sharing within safe boundaries.

Every chapter helps to establish the practical relevance of experiential learning and the key assumption that it makes: that learning about a subject (death, sexuality, stress, communication and so on) cannot be divorced from the process of learning about self.

The point is clearly made that learning places the self under the microscope and exposes all kinds of feelings. Some participants may dislike what they see and deny feelings which emerge by externalising them. They blame the teacher or the book or the system rather than examine aspects of self which have emerged. But for the student who is sufficiently open to look at self, learning offers a big opportunity for re-evaluation, to put the self into new relationships with the world.

What participants learn through studying stress or bereavement or counselling and communication or sexuality is taken out of the workshop into a complex social matrix or network of existing relationships. This may well produce lasting changes in relationships and life-styles. This applies not just to intimate personal relationships, but also to very traditionally defined professional relationships. Indeed, our experience has been that participants who have joined workshops ostensibly stressing their role as emotionally neutral, 'white-coated' professionals in order to develop skills or expertise and who explicitly initially disavow any interest in personal change, find that the experience of participating in an experiential learning event generates all kinds of feelings of which they had previously been only dimly aware. It is difficult to ignore such feelings, which by their presence provoke the subject to looking at herself or himself. To make this point allows us to stress that experiential learning is more than just the physical act of participation. It involves the whole being of the participant, his or her active intellectual and emotional participation.

THE ROLE OF THE TRAINER

The four principles set out above have a number of implications for trainers. These are:

1 Control of the nature and content of learning is shifted away from the trainer towards the student. This may involve the tutor in feelings of personal and professional risk and uncertainty with which he or she may not be familiar.
2 The trainer has to allow students to make mistakes. Making mistakes is traditionally perceived as providing feedback about the tutor's skills and competence as well as about the student's performance. Experiential learning, however, is based on the notion that all experiences are learning experiences. The tutor, therefore, must be clear about who is responsible for the students' learning and what taking or accepting responsibility means. Some tutors accept hardly any responsibility for the student – certainly not the lecturer who walks in, talks and walks out. The facilitator does take responsibility in so far as he or she works to develop an awareness of when there is an apparent lack of understanding and, as far as possible, seeks to provide a variety of opportunities for students, if they wish, to remedy their lack of understanding. The tutor assumes that different people have different ways of learning and, therefore, need different types of opportunities. To this extent the tutor can be said to accept responsibility. But in the final resort, responsibility lies with each individual student for the success or otherwise of the learning enterprise in which they are engaged. Unless the tutor is able to accept this fact and to let go, the student is maintained in a position of dependency. This is as unhelpful to the student as the abrogation of all responsibility.
3 Groups need structure, but in experiential learning many boundaries may have to be negotiated with the participants. These may refer to time, the nature of activities, agenda items or the relationship between tutor and students. Negotiation is not a greatly used skill in more

conventional didactic methods, but in experiential learning it becomes crucial.

4 The trainer has to be prepared to become redundant. This may involve learning how to cope with feelings of being unwanted.

5 Sometimes groups coalesce and form an identity through the process of identifying an outsider, against whom they can react. This outsider is frequently the facilitative leader. The trainer has to be able to work through this process and to be sufficiently self-aware to acknowledge that the rejection may have more to do with the needs of the group members than with any personal inadequacies in himself or herself.

For all these reasons, running an experiential group involves the leader in taking risks. Instead of being the all-knowing expert, the leader deliberately places himself or herself in a vulnerable position, in a situation where the idea of expert (akin to the knowledgeable parent telling the naïve child) is replaced by a process in which the expert becomes facilitator. Integral to this process is the tutor's involvement in it as a whole person with his or her own personal feelings. Awareness of these feelings is certainly a necessary, even if not a sufficient, condition, for effective workshop functioning. It involves acknowledgement of areas of self that are potentially frightening and painful, such as that one sometimes gets angry or that one has sexual desires and fantasies or that one sometimes dislikes people for reasons which are irrational. It is not that the trainer is expected to be the perfect human being, but that she or he must have a commitment to understanding themselves. A trainer cannot expect participants to look at themselves in depth unless he or she is prepared to do the same. Without such a commitment, the tutor will not be able to disentangle what is happening within a group of people in terms of differentiating between their needs and his or her own needs. The tutor is, therefore, up-front, aware, exposed, not attempting to defend himself or herself with the structure (or shroud) of expert status.

The notion of facilitative leadership as a necessary but not necessarily sufficient condition of effective group functioning was referred to above. It should be made quite clear, that facilitation is not a euphemism for anarchy or for a policy of *laissez-faire*. The term (often used as a synonym for the idea of 'enabling') implies a commitment to a client- or student-centred form of relationship or to operating from within the other person's frame of reference. This is not the same as non-involvement or non-participating, or withdrawing from responsibility for establishing a structure, framework and boundaries within which a group of people can work. Indeed, as each chapter in the book testifies without exception, the workshop in question is carried out within a clear and well-defined structure, the responsibility for whose establishment lies with the facilitator as well as the participants. Indeed, that is one of their primary tasks. It is not enough, therefore, just to describe facilitation as a form of student-centredness without a prior acknowledgement of the fact that this must take place within defined limits. This is necessary for the well-being of both trainer and participants, and the success of the training venture.

What these limits are is a function of how a group of people came into being, its chosen methods of operation and ground rules for member interaction, as well as what tasks (if any) it has to achieve. In a sense we can describe the answers to this set of related questions as forming a contract (sometimes explicit, most usually implicit) which group members have with the group. In the groups described in this book, the goal or objective or task is usually well formulated: to learn how to help people to cope with stress, bereavement, sexual problems and so on. All group members acknowledge these objectives by the very act of joining the group. For the facilitator to ignore these expectations and simply to run the group as an open-ended encounter group would be to invite disaster and is certainly not what is meant by facilitation. In practice, members' expectations represent a critically important dimension in the practice of running any workshop.

EXPECTATIONS AND CONTRACTS

People are motivated to come to workshops for a variety of reasons. These include: (1) to increase their own knowledge of subject area; (2) to hear what experts have to say; (3) to improve their skills; (4) to be better able to help the people they work with; (5) to become more self-aware; (6) for personal therapy; (7) to share ideas; (8) to express fears and anxieties; (9) because they feel it will be instrumental in the process of gaining promotion or a better job; (10) because their line managers expect them to attend; and (11) because they are representing an organisation. This list is by no means exhaustive, but it does illustrate the problem faced by the facilitator in meeting everyone's needs. The person who comes to hear the expert is likely to have a different set of requirements and a different kind of personal commitment to the workshop from the person who is motivated (for example) by a desire to increase self-awareness and to promote personal change.

We can refer to motivation as falling into one of two categories, either intrinsic or extrinsic. In the latter case, the motivation for attendance can be seen as deriving from outside the individual. So, for example, people come to the stress workshops described in this book because they perceive this as expected from them by their organisation or because it is seen as a useful pathway towards promotion or because an intimate friend has insisted on attendance as a basis for the continuation of the friendship. By and large it can be said that the individual's commitment to the workshop is likely to be greater the more intrinsic is his or her motivation. It should be appreciated that this is simply a rough model to help our thinking. In real life, variables such as motivation are often manifested as a continuum; many shades of grey rather than just two discrete black and white positions. Moreover, motivation (a person's desire to do something) operates at both a conscious and a subconscious level. So, for example, while at a conscious level a person may attend a workshop in order to assess how an organisation can adapt its organisational procedure so as to cope better with the stress of its members, at a less conscious level that individual may be motivated by a desire to cope in a more satisfactory way with the stresses of his or her own life.

In these ways, therefore, individuals bring to workshops many different expectations, and it is important for the trainer to assess what these mean in terms of the agenda (programme) and the methods employed in the workshop. The need to check out expectations cannot be overstressed. If this is not done, the trainer can easily get into what could be described as the 'bosses and workers' syndrome. What happens typically is that the trainer comes to the workshop with a set of expectations derived from prior discussions with those managers responsible for organising it, who frequently are themselves not active participants. Participants' needs may have been interpreted (for example) as to run a workshop on counselling skills, or the nature of adult learning or how to cope with stress. However, when one asks the participants themselves what their needs are, one frequently discovers a considerable divergence between their expressed needs and those needs as articulated by their organisers and managers.

One example concerns working with community education development workers who were said to need a workshop on adult learning needs and group dynamics. When this was checked out with the participants, what they were really concerned about was the management expectation that the prime criterion of job performance would be the number of groups successfully established. What they wanted, therefore, from the workshop was some understanding of how communities operated, so that they could more accurately assess community needs and thus initiate new groups. Another example concerns a group of teachers concerned with in-service education, whose managers thought they needed a training course in resolution of conflict within groups. However, the workers themselves were more concerned with the lack of definition inherent in their job description and wanted to use the workshop to explore the potential and the limitations inherent in the job.

The expectations which participants bring to a workshop refer not just to their perception of their needs but also to how these needs can be met. There are expectations about pedagogy as well as about content. This often expresses itself in terms of the participants' desire to be given the 'facts', to be told the 'truth', to see the trainer not as facilitator but as leading expert. What is being referred to here is the reciprocal of what was referred to above as the risks inherent for trainers in adopting a facilitative role. Just as there is a risk for trainers, so there is a corresponding risk for participants. This is that they will not be able to remain hidden in a passive fashion but will actively be called upon to reveal aspects of self-experience about which they may feel vulnerable or defensive. This may not operate at a conscious level. There are dozens of examples of workshops where participants have been told beforehand, often in written form, that they will be expected to accept responsibility for their own learning, yet where participants have found this hard to come to terms with in practice. In such situations, participants find the idea of an active form of participation, in which they are expected to explore the interface between ideas presented and their own experience, too threatening to contemplate. The result is often resistance, directed usually initially at the trainer for not taking on the role of expert. Such experiences indicate that the idea of 'accepting responsibility for one's own learning' often means little to many participants at an emotional level. Although initially it may sound appealing intellectually, the first attempts to invoke the philosophy, to translate an idea into operational practice, may provoke strong defensive reactions.

I recently worked with a local authority group of eighteen managers, selected according to their potential for promotion to the most senior positions. The day workshop on coping with stress came some nine months into a one-year course. At the workshop it soon became clear that there was major resistance within the group to the idea of an experiential workshop; what they wanted were skills. They were not prepared, as a group, to consider the appropriateness of their request to the subject areas in question. What was clear to the trainer was that this resistance had developed over the nine-month period and during many meetings, yet the group and the organiser still persisted in the rhetoric that they were involved in experiential learning and accepting responsibility for their own learning. No attempt had been made to confront this fantasy.

COPING WITH DIFFICULTIES

This example raises the question of what the facilitator might do when conflict of expectations of this nature is experienced. Although there are no simple answers to this question and each situation must be assessed on its own merits, there are a number of guidelines which can be offered.

1 It is absolutely crucial to have a clear answer to the question of whether it is something about the facilitator or something about the

group that is causing the blockage. No matter how extensive their skills and experience, all facilitators have their own defended areas, and sometimes, perhaps quite unexpectedly, a group of people can activate these defences. In such situations it may be necessary to face up to the possibility that the problem lies with the facilitator rather than with the participants, and that progress is dependent upon acknowledging and responding actively to these defences. This is just one reason, though a critical one, why every workshop should preferably have co-leaders if at all possible. Between them, two people can check out against each other their perceptions of what is happening.

2 Sometimes, however, it becomes clear that the problem lies with the group participants, not with the trainer. In this case, a number of options are available. The first is to confront the group with its resistance. This is likely to involve the trainer becoming the recipient of angry feelings, as the calm and equilibrium that the group has established in order to defend itself from self-examination is disturbed. Clearly, 'confrontation' here does not mean banging the arms of one's chair or acting in an aggressive, frightening or threatening fashion.

3 It is often, however, difficult to confront a group in the manner outlined above. In the case of an example already quoted, this was a difficult option to take because of the expectations of the organisers, who were employing the trainer for the day. Their expectation was for a smooth-running event in which motivation was seen to be high and in which clear evidence of learning would take place and its implications for the organisation acknowledged. In the event, it became clear to the trainer that the contract he had with the organisers was an unfair one, in the sense that important details about the history of the group had not been revealed to him (though perhaps the organisers were not even aware of them) before he had agreed to undertake the task in hand. In this kind of situation, one may sometimes simply need to accept the reality of the situation as seen by participants and to don the mantle of expert. Whatever the decision one takes, the example illustrates that expectations and contracts do exist in the minds of organisers, participants and trainers. If there are any differences between the three sets of expectations, these will inevitably express themselves in the workshop. Clearly, the task of running a workshop begins long before the participants ever get together, and involves trainers in agreeing contracts which will ensure that they understand and are able to meet the expectations imposed on them. This sometimes means that trainers must be quite explicit about what they expect from participants in order to clarify existing expectations.

Although how to handle conflict in workshops has been referred to above, it is necessary to be clear that conflict provides a vehicle for learning and can therefore be highly constructive. Indeed, sometimes workshops may even involve the active creation of conflictual situations (as in a role-playing simulation about decision making) so that participants can constructively experience conflict in a structured, controlled context. Ideas for working effectively with conflict in groups are contained in Fewell and Woolfe (1991).

CONCLUDING COMMENTS

Experiential learning is not likely to be an easy option, either for the learner or for the trainer. Even in the act of engaging group members in what are often euphemistically called 'ice-breakers' or 'warming-up' exercises, sensitive personal areas are likely to be confronted. A seemingly innocuous activity like being asked to think about one's first name by itself often provokes strong feelings about self-image and relationships with parents. But paradoxically it is the fact that experiential workshops *are* concerned with both thoughts and feelings which provides the energy and the potential through which learning is facilitated. The experiential workshop openly acknowledges that people feel as well as think, and their concern with the whole person is their primary characteristic. This, above all else, is what identifies every workshop described in this book.

As we have also seen, the enterprise involves risk both for the participants and the trainers. The latter can no longer rely on handing down tablets of stone. Indeed, he or she must find methods of sticking with the needs of participants as they are exposed to the awful uncertainty that there may be no tablets of stone, or absolute truths, and, therefore, no experts. The trainer must, therefore, be prepared to work with the dynamics of a group as it comes to terms with the full implications of this fact; as it begins to experience the implications of accepting responsibility for its own learning.

When these risks are practised in the context of the settings described in this book, they can be seen to be both significant and real. No trainer or participant can be expected to engage in a workshop on stress, death or sexuality without being prepared to explore these areas in the context of his or her life. The results may be painful or creative of anxiety and uncertainty as old defences are exposed. It is hardly surprising, therefore, that each author, without exception, emphasises the need to tread cautiously, to be sensitive to what is happening to self and others, to display the quality of immediacy (stay in the here and now), and to work whenever possible with a co-leader (or leaders). In short, an experiential workshop can be represented as a process in which people come together to learn not just about subject content but about self. Each workshop described in the book can be seen as an attempt to facilitate this process of self-development.

REFERENCES

Fewell, J. and Woolfe, R. (1991) *Group Work Skills: an Introduction*, Edinburgh: Health Education Board for Scotland.

Kolb, D. A. (1984) *Experiential Learning*, Englewood Cliffs, NJ: Prentice-Hall.

Murgatroyd, S. J. (1982) 'Experiential learning and the person in pursuit of psychology', *Education Section Review* (British Psychological Society), 6 (2): 112–17.

Chapter 2

Coping with stress[1]

Ray Woolfe

MODELS OF STRESS AND COPING

Traditionally, stress has been perceived as a force (or forces) which exists externally to the individual, somewhere out in the world and which exerts pressure upon the individual. The model is analogous to that used by engineers to describe a situation in which a force acts upon a physical object and generates a strain in that object. Stress is thus essentially seen as an input measure of an event external to the individual. One result of this approach has been the generation of a number of scales designed to measure the stress potential of particular events, of which the best-known is that of Holmes and Rahe (1967). In this particular scale, to give only a few examples, the death of a spouse is given a stress value of 100 points, divorce 73, marriage 50, retirement 45, down to change in residence 20, Christmas 12 and minor violations of the law 11. Although this approach clearly has some value – without any doubt death, divorce or house moving clearly have the potential to be stress-producing events – it is also equally clear that no two individuals react in exactly the same way to any given event. An event which is perceived as a challenge by one person may be experienced by another as much more of a threatening experience.

Other writers, therefore, have focused upon output as well as input in asking how an individual responds or adapts to an outside stressor (a stimulus-response model). An important worker in this tradition is Caplan (1964 and 1968), who emphasises the individuals' desire to maintain balance in their lives (he calls it 'homeostasis'). Stress arises when the individual is unable to cope with a situation which generates arousal, with the result that levels of arousal continue to grow. This produces anxiety or stress. More accurately, as the discrepancy between desired arousal and felt arousal increases, the feeling of tension the individual experiences also increases.

More recent work emphasises the importance of examining the inter-action between environmental stimulus (stressor) and the reacting individual. In fact, the notion of a stimulus or stressor must be seen as part of a reactive or, more accurately, an interactive situation. This model is essentially the one followed in this chapter, in which the emphasis is on stress and coping as a subjective rather than objective phenomenon.

Although we do not deny that some people may be more prone to experience stress than others either because of personality type or because of the environmental context in which they live, our concern is phenomenological: with how people come to understand, experience and cope with stress. The model is associated with Lazarus (Lazarus and Launier 1981) and perceives the individual in a transactional relationship with the environment; a person–environment relationship in an adaptational encounter (Lazarus 1978). Stress occurs when there is a misfit between the characteristics of the person and the environment. Coping is the process of working towards a state of fit between the two. The model can be described as cognitive as well as phenomenological. By this, we mean that emotions (and stress) are seen as products of cognitions, through the way in which individuals appraise the situation in which they find themselves. Appraisal, in fact, is a key concept. The individual works through a process of appraisal, by means of a 'how am I doing' set of questions and thereby makes decisions about the adequacy of coping mechanisms employed.

Coping is seen, therefore, not as a fixed structural property of the person but as a transaction which itself transforms the person–environment relationship. Put simply, we are suggesting that stress resides neither in the environment nor in the person, but in the interaction between the two. This view has the important consequence of investing emphasis upon the individual as an active factor in both creating and coping with his or her experiences.

This model has a number of consequences for workshop practice. In particular, it informs the need to facilitate a situation in which each individual can be allowed to make a self-appraisal of his or her own techniques for understanding and coping with stress. Pedagogically, this sets clear limits on the use of didactic methods of teaching and emphasises the process of student-centred learning. In terms of content, it directs us towards examining the relationship between thinking and feeling as a central feature of the workshop. While Lazarus' model perceives emotions as a product of cognitions, it recognises that the relationship between the two is strongly interactive. Whatever the source of emotions, once experienced they clearly influence thinking and behaviour. Anxiety, for example, is consistently reported by participants as affecting thinking processes, often in the area of creating states of cognition confusion. This creates further anxiety, and so the interactive cycle continues. For this reason the structure of the workshop is strongly influenced by the concepts of thinking and feeling and their outcomes in terms of behaviour

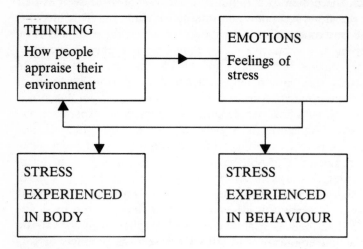

Figure 2.1 The relationship between thinking, feeling, behaviour and body

and body (physical states). This can be represented diagrammatically as shown in Figure 2.1.

WORKSHOP STRUCTURE

The remainder of this chapter outlines the experience of the Open University's Coping with Crisis Research and Training Group in running workshops on the theme of coping with stress. The framework described represents the distilled result of some three dozen workshops ranging in length from an afternoon (one session) to a whole weekend (four sessions). In other words, the model has evolved and developed as the direct result of experience gained. This chapter presents the contents of a full two-day workshop (comprising four three-hour sessions), but in essence the shorter workshop follows a similar pattern. Although the amount of work covered may be less, the philosophy and the objectives remain largely the same. These can be described as fourfold:

1 to increase the awareness of participants of what experiencing stress means to them, using the thinking, feeling, behaviour and body dimensions:
2 to encourage them to explore the conditions under which they experience stress and the manner in which they create stress for themselves through the expectations they hold about themselves;
3 to help participants to focus upon their existing coping mechanism for dealing with stress;

4 to present to participants, through the experience of group membership, a range of coping mechanisms which offers them an opportunity
to increase their repertoire of coping skills.

The philosophy underlying these objectives is that there is a need to
attempt to reconcile two potentially conflicting approaches to coping with
stress. On the one hand, it is possible to approach the subject in the
primarily humanistic terms of increasing self-awareness without too much
concern about specific coping skills. On the other hand, it is possible to
approach it as located in a set of specific coping skills, without too much
concern about the level of self-awareness embedded in the practice of
these skills. The more experience we have gained in the workshops, the
more we have found it necessary to adopt an eclectic approach. Partly
this reflects the fact that participants come to the workshop with different
needs, and partly it reflects a degree of pragmatism which suggests that
the two approaches are more easily separated in theory than in practice.
It also, however, reflects our own personal philosophy that the presentation of skills without awareness is de-humanising, while a focus upon
awareness without attention to skills overlooks the value of the latter as
a practical helping mechanism. We have articulated this philosophy in
Murgatroyd and Woolfe (1982) as a 'commitment to both eclectic helping
interventions within the community and with individuals and to our
search for simple models of crisis, change and transition which help in
the understanding of the pain of personal crisis'.

More specifically, we would describe our approach as encompassed
within what Dryden (1984) refers to as 'technical eclecticism', as being
more concerned with practical rather than theoretical issues, and as
expressing our concern with the question, 'What technique works for
whom, and under which particular conditions?' Dryden suggests that
perhaps the best example of technical eclecticism is Lazarus' 'Multi-
Modal Therapy', which systematically covers seven basic modalities of
human functioning and dysfunctioning in therapy: behaviour, affect, sen-
sation, imagery, cognition, interpersonal relationships and drug taking/
physiological (hence the acronym BASIC ID). While we have not followed these modalities in the methodical fashion outlined by Lazarus
(1981), our work has been informed by this approach.

The participants

Participants have come from a wide variety of professional backgrounds.
Our experience has been that social workers, nurses (particularly health
visitors), teachers and psychologists have been forthcoming in large numbers, whereas other groups, such as doctors (particularly GPs) and clergy,
have proved more difficult to attract. Many of the workshops have been

mixed, but some have been provided at the request of particular organis-ations and occupational groups and, therefore, have been more homo-geneous in composition. Our practice suggests that a dozen is an optimum number, although we have operated with fewer and with more (if suf-ficient leadership resources existed). For the open workshops, partici-pants have by and large been self-selected as a result of local advertise-ment, more or less on a first-come-first-served basis. It has not been our practice to send any preparatory material to prospective participants, other than the information provided on the application form. This draws attention to the four objectives previously outlined and indicates the participative, experiential basis of the workshop. In the case of the single occupation groups, the leaders have some ideas of what needs partici-pants bring, and of their expectations of the workshop. However, even here caution is desirable. Experience suggests that what participants expect or want is often substantially different from what their managers suggest they need or want. So the first part of every workshop is always centrally concerned with gleaning information about what participants themselves expect and desire from it.

Of course, the more heterogeneous a group is, the more difficult this task becomes, and the more complex it is to balance what may well be conflicting needs. For example, many of the people who have attended the workshops have themselves been experiencing considerable stress and even crisis at the time, and have seen the workshop as an opportunity to work at resolving their immediate problems. For others, their primary motivation has been to discover techniques which they can use in helping their own clients.

Our approach to such potential conflict has been as follows. At the outset of each workshop, we have made clear to participants that all stress management begins with exploration of the individual, but that this poses a potential problem for the group. This concerns the extent to which the use of the group by any individual for the purpose of catharsis is likely to lead to the group as a whole being helped or hindered in the primary task for which members have contracted. We ask the group members to be sensitive to this 'problem' and to take some responsibility for determining the direction taken by the group. In practice, the leaders (of whom there have almost always been at least two) have, as one of their main tasks, a need to develop a careful understanding of both the expectations and contracts that exist within the group. For this reason the leaders have to be consistently concerned with simple questions of group dynamics – like who is in this group now, what brought them here, what expectations do they have, what are the dynamics of the group, who is strong, and who is in need of support? The extent of their ongoing concern with these and related questions will be a function of the leaders' familiarity with the group and the group's familiarity with one another.

Throughout the remainder of the chapter, the need for the leaders to remain cognisant of group dynamics will be treated implicitly rather than explicitly. However, this in no way should be taken as underestimating the importance of what is happening in the group. This involves such issues as

- acknowledging that the group has an emotional life and that understanding this is crucial to the achievement of a group's objectives;
- recognising that groups go through stages of development;
- being able to establish a safe environment in which people feel free to share aspects of themselves with one another;
- appreciating that conflict is a normal, not a pathological feature of the group process, and finding ways to work constructively with it.

Fewell and Woolfe (1991) address these issues in a training pack on group work skills produced for the Health Education Board for Scotland.

Group leaders have all been members of the Coping with Crisis Research and Training Group, and have come from a range of occupations (university lecturing, counselling psychology, clinical psychology, social work, psychiatry and sociology). However, they have all had a common commitment to an eclecticism which emphasises the importance of the question 'what works for whom and in what conditions?' and of acknowledging individual needs while working in a group setting. Workshops have been planned collectively and evaluated in the same way, thus ensuring an ongoing process of assessment, supervision and development.

SESSION ONE

The experience of stress

After an initial period of warming up, getting to know one another, and exploring expectations, the first of the four sessions (lasting until the end of the morning of the first day) has focused on three consecutive but linked activities concerned to develop awareness about three related issues:

1 What do we understand or mean when we say that we are experiencing stress? For each individual, the question posed is 'how do you *experience* stress?'
2 From where does this stress emanate? The emphasis here is on the *source* of the triggers which cause stress for the individual.
3 What *strategies* are available for coping with stress?

We have sometimes found it useful or even necessary to remind partici-

	FEELING	THINKING	BEHAVIOUR	BODY
MILD STRESS				
STRONG STRESS				

Figure 2.2 The experience of stress

pants, before getting into these activities, that the contract we have with them is not to provide a tutorial-like input. Rather, we have indicated that the experiences of those present are real for them and a rich source of sharing and interacting with others. Moreover, this is a workshop in which discovery and the processes of discovery are themselves tools for coping.

In the first activity, participants are asked to complete the grid in Figure 2.2 as a small-group activity. The overall group is broken down into sub-groups of three or four. People are encouraged to work with persons they do not know as well as those they do, and to change groups and work with different people as the workshop progresses. The task of the group in this activity is not to agree on a consensus list, but to ensure that the range of experiences which count as 'stress' for the participants are fully expressed. To this end, the grid is drawn up on a large sheet of paper and entries noted down in the most relevant cell. The technique of brainstorming is encouraged; that is to say, participants are encouraged to write down anything which comes into their heads before it is censored or filtered. Each group has its own chart, so that at the end of the activity a number of charts are available for comparison. There is no group leader. Each participant is provided with their own felt pen.

The activity usually raises questions about mild and strong stress as a continuum rather than as a dichotomy. It also raises questions about the links between cognitive, affective and physical states. Participants note that a pain in the shoulder is often linked to a lack of concentration or feeling of anxiety or inability to act purposefully. Related to this point is a distinction which can be drawn between 'pressure' and 'stress'. Without pressure, life would be bland and dull. It is when levels of pressure rise beyond a level with which an individual can cope that it becomes stressful. The aim of stress management programmes, therefore, is not to eliminate pressure, but to help participants to understand in what ways and at what points pressure turns into stress. We have found it useful, after the grids have been completed, to place them side by side on a wall and to hold a plenary discussion about the findings. The discussion can focus on such issues as what are the most common indicators of stress and what are its most common effects. The mild/strong distinction offers the opportunity to make the point that at low levels, stress may well be a positive raiser of adrenalin, a 'turn-on' or a motivator. Coping may thus be related to the individual's ability not to reduce stress to a zero level, but to maintain it at a low level of arousal.

So far as the content of the boxes in Figure 2.2 is concerned, participants find that although they may each experience stress in a unique fashion, there are many areas of overlap with the experience of others. The variety of material generated covers a vast area, though some topics tend to appear on almost every list. Below we have provided just a few examples of the responses offered.

Feeling: Depressed; frustrated; short-tempered; irritable; inadequate; angry; withdrawn; anxious; apathetic; humourless; disillusioned.

Thinking: Mental blocks; taking the easy option; diversification; daydreaming; not being able to switch off; inability to think straight; confusion; inhibiting creativity; rigidity; inability to understand new ideas.

Behaviour: Clock-watching; withdrawn from company; violence; inflexibility; attention-seeking; malingering; shouting and yelling; alcoholic excess; indecisive; wanting to talk; confrontation; smoking; exercise; more sex; less sex; insomnia.

Body: Tired; headaches; need to urinate/defecate; shaking; palpitation; muscular aches; spasms; skin rashes; twitching.

This is just a small sample of what participants identify. It is interesting to note that when we have asked groups of teachers to note down the characteristics of troublesome or 'maladjusted' pupils, their list bears remarkable similarities to the characteristics which our participants claim to experience when under stress. It includes such features as shouting at others, aggressive behaviour, withdrawn behaviour, lack of social skills, inability to concentrate and so on.

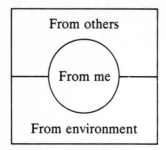

Figure 2.3 Stress and its sources

The origins of stress

By the end of the previous activity, we assume that participants have an understanding of the idea that stress is a subjective phenomenon; it is how each individual experiences it that determines what stress means to that individual. Given this, participants can be asked to focus on the next activity, which is concerned with where this stress emanates from. Or, to put it another way, what are the sources of the triggers which cause stress for the individual? Once again, participants are asked to fill in a pre-prepared chart in their small groups. This asks them to note down each source of stress and to locate it in others, the environment or self. The chart (adapted from Bond and Kilty 1982) is shown in Figure 2.3.

As before, individuals are encouraged to brainstorm. The aim is not to negotiate with others, but to log *all* possible sources of stress for each individual.

Participants should be encouraged to concentrate on the 'From me' cell. Although many people are tempted to externalise the cause of stress in other people or in their life environment, the maximum benefit of this activity derives from helping participants to see how they generate stress for themselves. In effect this activity is concerned with the psychological causes of stress. In fact, there is rarely any shortage of material for the 'self' box. Many participants recognise that it is their own desire to be loved, or for recognition by bosses or peers, or to experience excitement, or to satisfy unrealistic self-expectations, and so on, that causes them stress. Many of these inner needs derive from messages learned and internalised in childhood and carried over into adult life. The more that participants recognise the source of their need for love, approval, esteem and so forth, the more they have something tangible on which to work in order to reduce the stress they are experiencing in the present. A small sample of the material which emerges is reproduced below:

From me: Desire for control; desire to be loved/wanted; strong achievement motivation; need for reassurance; high personal standards; personal insecurity; inability to express feelings.

From others   Relatives or friends or workmates making unrealistic demands; the managerialist ethos at work; people being rude, aggressive, unkind, unpleasant, dominating, rejecting.

From environment: Dogs; cats; smoking; travelling on trains, planes, buses, cars; politics; vandalism and delinquency; unemployment; newspapers.

The issue of work as a stressor is one which may be particularly important as a discussion point. The contemporary emphasis on account-ability, auditing and throughput has generated a situation in which many workers, particularly in the helping professions, have come to see work as increasingly dominated by a managerial and accounting rather than a caring ethos. This has resulted for many people in a general raising of stress levels and a general lowering of satisfaction with work. However, within this context, a point which has emerged again and again is that the role in which professionals see themselves as cast, the white-coated, emotionally neutral person distanced from clients, which is supposed to shield them from emotional involvement, is one which paradoxically causes them enormous stress. Because they are supposed not to become involved in the client's problems, they report repression of feelings like pain, guilt and anxiety in their dealings with poor health, illness, accident, relationship difficulties and bereavement. The workshops have provided countless opportunities for professionals to acknowledge that helping other people is itself a stressful experience. Many who have come to workshops to find out how to help others to reduce stress find that an understanding of their own stress is a primary prerequisite.

Coping strategies

The third and last of the three linked activities for the morning session of day one allows participants to move forward positively from consider-ing the experience of stress to the experience of coping. This activity can be done on a small-group basis or by brainstorming with the group as a whole. While originally we provided a chart divided into adaptive and maladaptive strategies, we have gradually preferred to think simply in terms of coping strategies. This allows participants to elicit for themselves the fact that alcohol or sexual activity or shouting or exercise or creative activity or a thousand other ways of coping with stress are adaptive or maladaptive depending on the extent to which each individual employs them and the effect they have on that individual's self-image and relationships. Against each strategy, individuals may be encouraged to note, firstly, whether they have any skills in the area which they might wish to share with other participants, and, secondly, whether they have an interest in learning more about a particular strategy or approach.

The list of strategies is enormous. It includes such items as the following:

Strategies for coping: Shouting; swearing; hard work; physical effort; sport; sex (more, or less); violence; getting away; alcohol; absenteeism; day-dreaming; withdrawal from social life; complaining; knitting; talking; sharing; eating; head-banging; not eating; smoking; arguing; gardening.

The list is processed by engaging with participants in a process of clustering. An interesting way to do this is to write each item on a separate piece of paper and then ask group members to put each piece of paper into an appropriate cluster with similar items. Certain categories of strategy tend to emerge, such as:

- strategies which involve self and those which involve talking to other people;
- strategies which involve physical exercise;
- strategies which involve withdrawal from the stressful situation – e.g., holidays or absenteeism;
- strategies which involve confrontation with the stressful situation – e.g., being assertive with a boss;
- strategies which involve direct attempts at mood change – e.g., music or having a warm bath or running;
- strategies which involve emotional catharsis – e.g., shouting or swearing; this may involve shouting at partner even though work may be the major stressor.

Our view is that *every* coping mechanism has a survival value in so far as it prevents the individual being overwhelmed by what may seem like forces out of her or his control. Even smoking or drinking or shouting at other people can be seen in this light. However, they are survival mechanisms only up to a point. If individuals continue to avoid the emotional issues which lie behind their stressful feelings, the risk is that the coping mechanism becomes a part of the problem rather than of the solution. The aim of the trainer in this situation is not to break down 'ineffective' coping strategies, but gently and supportively to encourage group members to examine the advantages and disadvantages of the different types of coping they employ and to help people to become aware of the wide range of coping strategies which are available.

At this point, lunch is taken. Our policy has always been to encourage people to bring provisions which can be eaten on a sharing basis. At the very least, we hope that participants will eat in rather than go out. Group leaders have always taken part in this process with the other group members. At the same time, because we rely on flexibility, particularly in the remaining three sessions, we think it is valuable for the leader (or leaders) to find a certain amount of time on their own in which they can reflect on the previous session, assess progress, relax and unwind, and clarify the possibilities and the shape which the next sessions might take.

SESSION TWO

When we began the workshop, we played the remaining three sessions very much by ear, and this is still the case. We attempt to take account of our resources as well as the resources available in individual participants and the interests expressed, and generally to be sensitive to the needs of the group and of individuals within it. Already by this point in the workshop, particular individuals have frequently expressed a wish to explore further some aspect of their life, past or present, and we attempt to structure the workshop so that space can be found to meet these expressed needs. Beyond this, we have a wide range of techniques at our disposal which we believe are useful in coping with stress. These include relaxation training, assertiveness, cognitive restructuring, co-counselling, guided fantasy, *Gestalt* and meditation.

To begin the afternoon we regularly employ a high-energy fun game known as 'Mixed Veg' or 'Railway Stations'. Each person takes the name of a vegetable (or railway station). In a circle, seats are provided for all but one participant (a volunteer), who stands in the middle. This person calls out the names of three or more vegetables (or stations). These persons have to change seats without allowing the person in the middle to grab a seat. The essence of the game is speed. The person in the middle is allowed to call out 'Mixed Veg' (or 'all change'), in which case everyone has to change seats. The game is remarkable in raising the energy level, which is usually fairly low after lunch, so that participants feel more willing to work. It is a particularly relevant activity in a number of ways. Firstly, it demonstrates in action one way of coping with stress: namely, physical activity. Secondly, because it changes the atmosphere of the group, it demonstrates the link between physical and emotional states. Thirdly, it demonstrates the value of play in changing psychological states.

A theoretical framework for coping

At this point, we ask participants to sit down, and we begin to integrate the morning's activity with what is to come. If appropriate, we point to the paradigm of coping strategies suggested by Pearlin and Schooler (1978), which we find useful as an aid to our thinking. They begin by drawing a distinction between tactics and strategy. A strategy is the scheme a person adopts in order to cope with some specific stressful event, whilst a tactic is the person's way of implementing this scheme. Pearlin and Schooler suggest that there are essentially three strategies for coping. These are: (1) strategies aimed at preventing situations developing as crisis or stress – an 'anticipatory' strategy; (2) strategies aimed at creating a buffer between the person and the stressful environment, so as to prevent the full effects of the stress being experienced – a 'buffer' strategy; (3) the strategy of coping with a stressful event by learning to manage the feelings and thoughts experienced – a 'crisis-management' strategy.

Anticipatory coping is used by a great many people; for example, psychoprophylaxis (psychological preparation for the prevention of pain) is taught to pregnant mothers in order to ease pain during childbirth. Another example refers to a couple attempting to cope with a relationship problem by negotiating about it. Anticipatory coping sounds ideal, but in practice is difficult to implement for a number of reasons. Firstly, it requires the accurate identification of the potential source of stress. This is not always easy. For example, in relationships it is often difficult to find the specific feature which is creating stress. Secondly, even if a source is identified, individuals sometimes lack the skills to transform it. Thirdly, even if identified *and* transformed, resultant change may well generate problems elsewhere. For example, working harder to overcome problems at work may create stress in one's private life. Fourthly, some situations such as living with illness or handicap may simply not lend themselves to such forms of coping. Many methods for coping with stress focus upon teaching anticipatory coping. These include relaxation therapy and meditation, assertiveness training and transactional analysis. Reference should also be made to anticipatory grief work in anticipation of death, which doesn't lessen the pain of death, but does decrease the chances of the resulting process of coping becoming stuck and going wrong.

The buffer strategy aims to inhibit the effects of the stressful situation even though the situation itself has developed and does exist. In other words, what is involved here is the reinterpretation of an event so that its effects are perceived as innocuous rather than harmful. Perhaps the most common example is denial that a problem exists. For example, a relationship problem is pushed under the carpet with the rationalisation that it doesn't really matter. Denial should not be interpreted in a totally negative light. For example, it may be valuable in the short run in preventing an individual being overwhelmed by a crisis (see Murgatroyd and Woolfe 1982). Another example of buffering is repression or selective perception. For example, the pain of the death of a loved one is reduced by perceiving it as involving the end of the sick person's suffering. A third buffer strategy involves reaction-formation – that is, doing the opposite of what is thought or felt, but doing it unconsciously. This results in, for example, a sexually repressed person coping with 'dangerous' sexual feelings by actively campaigning against pornography, prostitution and so on. A short-term response to unemployment may be to reflect about the freedom one now has relative to ex-colleagues still in work. While the buffer strategy may be valuable in the short run, its use of defence mechanisms in the course of selective perception, denial and repression of painful thoughts and feelings may generate problems in the longer term. Cognitive restructuring of irrational thoughts may be seen as an example of this type of strategy in action.

The crisis-management strategy is concerned with easing the discomfort caused by stress. Such a strategy makes use of any tactic that seems likely to reduce the level of tension. Thus relaxation therapy may be practised for this purpose as well as to support anticipatory coping, thus illustrating the point that the activity itself represents the tactic, but that it is the use to which it is put which represents the strategy.

Thinking and feeling

This theoretical framework offers participants a conceptual scheme whereby they can attempt to locate the various strategies discussed in the previous session as well as the techniques developed in the workshop. However, the primary conceptual scheme around which we continue to work is the feeling/thinking/behaviour/body distinction. We have found that the links across the four areas are clear and apparent and that the relationship between thinking and feeling is a crucial one for the individual.

Over the years there has been a long-running debate within psychology and psychiatry about the relationship between cognition and affect in both normal and pathological states. Increasingly it is recognised that in both conditions the sequence is one of perception–cognition–emotion, though we prefer the notion of circularity. Beck (1971) points out that the difference between 'normal' and 'pathological' lies in the way the pathological state is characterised by internal processes which distort the stimulus situation. Although the humanistic tradition has tended to downgrade the role of cognition and upgrade the importance of the affect, we believe that there are good reasons for starting with the role of cognition in stress creation and reduction. This belief is rooted not just in the present state of our knowledge but also in the fact that in our society, the use of thinking as a primary tool through which to reflect upon our own actions is a dominating one. This chapter offers an account of the theory which underpins our actions, although in the actual work-shop the discussions of theory are much less explicit. The emphasis is upon the participants themselves making the links. If theory helps then it is relevant, and vice versa.

We move on, therefore, into the area of cognition and the idea of cognitive restructuring. If we can change the ways in which we think about things that cause us stress, they become less stressful.

Our aim is not to demonstrate rational or rational-emotive therapy, or even to suggest that we approve of its theory or methodology, but rather to draw from it some aspect which will enable participants to think about stress. We have found the 'ABCDE' approach useful, where 'A' stands for Activating Event, 'B' for Beliefs about this event (rational and irrational), 'C' for the Consequences of holding these beliefs, 'D' for Disputing or challenging the irrational idea, and 'E' for Alternative Thoughts.

How we tackle the activity varies from workshop to workshop, but typically we ask individuals to write down on a piece of paper the details of a situation which causes them stress. We ask them to describe the situation in as much detail as possible, including their beliefs about the event and the consequences of holding such beliefs. Basically these are the ABC stages of the sequence. Below is an example, adapted from Davis *et al.* (1980).

A *Activating Event* A friend cancelled a date with me.
B *Beliefs* 1 Rational: She's under a lot of pressure at work right now. She hasn't much free time.
        2 Irrational: I'm worthless. Nobody wants to be with me. I'll be lonely tonight.
C *Consequences of holding these beliefs* I was depressed . . . was moder-ately anxious.
D *Disputing or challenging the irrational ideas*
1 Select the irrational idea. I'm worthless. Nobody wants to be with me. I'll be lonely.
2 Is there any rational support for the idea? No!
3 What evidence exists for the falseness of the idea? I have lots of friends of both sexes.

4 Does any evidence exist for the truth of the idea? No! I've talked myself into feeling depressed.

5 What is the worst thing that could happen to me? I'll spend one lonely night.

6 What good things might occur? I could feel more self-reliant and realise that I do have inner resources.

E *Alternative Thoughts* I'm OK. I'll make myself a meal, read and have a warm bath. I'm good at being alone.

Alternative Emotions OK. I feel a little disappointed, but it's not the end of the world and I can have a quiet, restful evening by myself.

After each person has listed his or her A to C responses on a piece of paper, participants work in pairs to discuss one another's case with an emphasis on D and E. The objective is on the listener – firstly, identifying the demands made by the speaker on themselves and others (expressed in 'ought', 'should', 'must' statements); and secondly, encouraging the speaker to dispute and contradict these and other irrational beliefs. Elements of co-counselling practice can be identified here. For example, the process of talking about the thoughts, feelings and actions of situations where stress is experienced is the 'literal descriptions' phase, while the role of the partner in asking the speaker to repeat key phrases involving emotional components is also associated with co-counselling. Similarly, the listener can encourage the speaker to associate present unpleasant thoughts and feelings with past happening, so as to understand their meanings better. This is important. People may need time to discharge old pain that keeps them stuck in distorted perceptions. Restructuring of these perceptions may not be possible without the phase of insight that follows emotional discharge.

Eventually, the whole group is brought together again, and anybody is invited to share their problem (not their partner's) with the group as a whole. This may well lead to an individual using the group as a vehicle for personal therapy. Although this is fine, particularly for members whose problem is that they always put themselves down for the good of the group, the leaders must recognise that such a development has to be consistent with the needs of the group as a whole. The contract is to participate in a workshop on coping with stress rather than to participate in a therapeutic encounter group.

This activity may well take the whole of Session Two (the afternoon), particularly if personal therapy is involved. It is likely to generate a lot of emotional energy, and at the end of it some form of tension-release exercise is desirable. If sufficient time remains, a number of choices are possible. One is to provide an opportunity for an individual who has made an offer to demonstrate that offer to the group. Our experience is that offers frequently lie within the area of body work: yoga, massage or breathing relaxation. If the group is willing (and suitably attired), such activities seem to provide a relaxing passage through which to bring the session to a conclusion. Indeed, were no offers to materialise, we would suggest that simple massage of head and shoulders (and perhaps of arms and legs) between couples is a highly suitable activity which reinvests attention into the body and sponsors peaceful and gentle emotions. It produces a quiet but warm ending to the first day, which is halfway through the workshop.

Other options

The process of working in pairs which is fostered in the cognitive restructuring work allows an opportunity to develop further the idea of co-counselling. Apart from offering a useful series of techniques for stress management, it focuses on the role of helper and of being an active listener, albeit within a particular theoretical framework. Moreover, like massage, it moves the agenda forward from cognition into mobilising body energy and discharging painful emotions. Another alternative focus to Session Two which we have found to work well is one which concentrates on transactional analysis. If this pathway is followed, we have found it useful to present to participants a discussion of the three life scripts of Rescuer, Persecutor and Victim. We then ask participants to complete a chart with Thinking, Feeling and Behaviour along the vertical axis, and Rescuer, Persecutor and Victim along the horizontal. The type of result this produces is shown in Figure 2.4. The contents of each box are descriptions of each life script in the three forms of expressions.

Participants can be asked to examine their own stresses, relating them

	Rescuer	*Persecutor*	*Victim*
Thinking	Positive	Superior, Dominant	Muddled
Feeling	Altruistic, Smug, Protective	Aggressive	Resentful, Self-pitying
Behaviour	Listening, Peace-maker	Physically and verbally abusive	Refuse to accept responsibility for self, Helpless

Figure 2.4 Life scripts and their thinking, feeling and behavioural expressions

to the extent to which they play one or more of these roles in particular situations and how they think feel and behave when in these roles.

Transactional analysis is probably best presented as a substitute for cognitive restructuring rather than as additional to it. Both necessitate a certain amount of theoretical explication and, taken together, the two probably provide a slightly heavy menu for one session; included in separate sessions they might over-balance a workshop of the kind outlined here. In diagrammatic form, therefore, the second session may look something like the following:

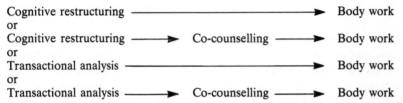

Cognitive restructuring ⟶ Body work
or
Cognitive restructuring ⟶ Co-counselling ⟶ Body work
or
Transactional analysis ⟶ Body work
or
Transactional analysis ⟶ Co-counselling ⟶ Body work

It goes without saying that no technique in a stress-reduction workshop should be used without sensitivity on the part of the leaders. This is not to be regarded as a rigid scheme but as an outline plan. It may well be that the nature of a group necessitates time being spent on rather different approaches to stress coping. Perhaps physical and body work and relaxation training need to be elevated in importance. This is the kind of question the leaders must continue to ask. There are also a number of progressive relaxation training techniques available, some of which employ *in vivo* application involving the principles of desensitisation (see Wolpe and Lazarus 1966). In some situations, with some people and with some groups this may prove to be more appropriate than, for example, transactional analysis.

SESSION THREE

After warm-up exercises and an opportunity for participants to say what it feels like to be back in the group again, we have found it useful to develop the third session by introducing the idea of lack of assertiveness, on the one hand, and, on the other, aggression as sources of stress. Assertiveness training is then presented as offering useful insights and even skills in coping with situations in a less passive, more assertive fashion but without aggression. Whereas the latter involves expression achieved at the expense of others, assertiveness involves emotional honesty and expression whilst at the same time respecting the position of others. Whereas aggression indicates self-righteousness and feelings of superiority, assertiveness is characterised by self-confidence accompanied by respect for the rights of others. The line between the two is often easier to draw in theory than in practice, but assertiveness can reduce internal conflicts and tensions and lead to more effective ways of coping with stress.

The idea of assertiveness implies that each person has a number of rights, including the expectation of respect from other people, to articulate his or her feelings and needs, to express his or her own opinions, and to decide whether or not to meet the expectations of others. In the words of the title of a well-known book on the subject, lack of assertiveness is characterised by the fact that 'when I say no, I feel guilty' (Smith 1975). It is not my purpose in this chapter to provide a detailed account of specific techniques (see Alberti and Emmons 1974, and Osborn and Harris 1975), but rather to indicate a few approaches which may be helpful in developing assertiveness as a coping skill. Assertiveness can be defined as concerned with the expression of personal rights and feelings, and is valuable because it encourages people to challenge the notion that their behaviour results inevitably from their personality traits. The idea that we need to learn ways of standing up for our rights without violating the rights of others inevitably produces positive reactions from participants, who seem to recognise instinctively the way in which lack of assertiveness produces stress. When asked to identify such situations, they mention areas like the difficulty in protesting to a shop about faulty consumer goods, challenging unjustified criticism from their superiors, or saying no to a request to take on unwanted additional work or for a date they do not really desire.

There are a number of ways of developing the use of the technique in coping with stress, but our experience has been that the best policy is to get into role play as quickly as possible. As a first step individuals can be asked to note down the salient characteristics of situations in which they experience stress. Once again, emphasis is put upon the identification of thinking, feeling and body states. The leaders then ask for volunteers willing to discuss their response with the group as a whole. After a situation has been described, the leaders encourage role play of the situation concerned. Any one situation may involve a number of role plays. For example, let us take the typical situation of the person who finds it difficult to return faulty goods to a shop because they feel vulnerable, open to attack, open to ridicule, frightened of rejection and so on. The role play may proceed something like this:

1 Subject plays customer. Another member plays shopkeeper or assistant. Group observes role play. Participants are asked how it feels to be in the part. Was the behaviour of the other person as expected? How did the behaviour of the subject influence the result of the interaction? Group members are then invited to comment on the interaction they have witnessed.

2 Roles are reversed. Subject plays shopkeeper/assistant. The customer

role is played by either the same person in the previous role play or
another participant. The same process is undergone.

3 Depending on the progress being made, variations on the theme can
be made. For example, the subject or the other person can be asked
by the leader to be aggressive, passive or assertive in order to offer
an experience of what it is like to be in such a transaction.

4 The process may well develop into the *Gestalt* technique of the 'hot
seat', in which the subject himself or herself engages in a debate
between internal parts of self; e.g., the part that says, 'It's OK to
complain', and the part that says, 'If I do I will look foolish.' The
hope is that this will facilitate the process of integration of these parts,
some of which may well be subconsciously disowned.

A number of such role plays can be developed, and gradually the leaders
can choose to introduce a number of skills which are helpful in increasing
assertiveness. Of these the best known is 'broken record', that is, simply
repeating one's demand in a clear, unequivocal way without being
diverted by an irrelevant or manipulative response. Another technique
which is useful in such an area is that of disarming anger by not reacting
aggressively to it.

The value of monodrama (by using the 'hot seat' method) has been
referred to above. We have found that as we have developed our work
in the area of assertiveness, individual participants have come to use this
method as a source of personal therapy, facilitated by the fact that the
method has developed in a naturalistic fashion from the role play. In
particular, painful feelings about bereavement and relationship with a
deceased person have proved amenable to this approach. Regret over
messages left unsaid can be released. It seems to offer a framework in
which old emotional 'tapes' can be replayed and emotional discharge can
take place.

If sufficient time exists before lunch, a brief guided fantasy may be
offered in which participants are encouraged to focus on visual images
of stress. They are then asked, however poor their degree of artistic
skills, to draw these images on large sheets of paper (one for each
person). This usually produces much interesting material for group discussions through interpretations of drawings. Individuals often report
insights of which previously they were only dimly aware. The activity is
useful in developing the point that images or models or ideas are often
difficult to communicate in words and that language is an obfuscator of
emotions as well as a medium of communication. At one workshop, a
participant had made small tears all round the edge of her paper. That,
she said, is how I feel when stressed: 'frayed round the edges'. At the
end of this activity, the third session can be drawn to a close, and lunch

taken. Diagrammatically, therefore, Session Three looks something like this:

Assertiveness therapy → $\begin{pmatrix} \text{if time} \\ \text{permits} \end{pmatrix}$ → Guided fantasy → Visual imagery
↓
Role play
↓
Monodrama (Hot-seat/*Gestalt*)

SESSION FOUR

As we move into the fourth and final session, the need for spontaneity on the part of the leaders becomes more and more important. They must be sensitive to unmet needs within the group and must structure the final session accordingly. The content of this session will depend upon the analysis made over lunch, but in practice often begins with some form of relaxation exercises, thus emphasising once again the body–mind–emotions link. This may be continued with a guided fantasy if this has not already taken place in the previous session. It can be followed by an open encounter session which allows individuals further opportunity for personal therapy, or by encounter games which encourage together-ness, increase spontaneity, make having fun acceptable and reproduce in symbolic form many of life's problems in areas like communication and decision making. Dynamic meditation (of which tapes are available on the open market) is another possibility, which involves some very active physical activity as a vehicle for bypassing cognitive processes. Alternatively, a lot of the methodology developed in the workshop can be drawn together through a more integrated practice of co-counselling, if this has not already been done sufficiently in Session Two. The point is that the leaders have many options. What they do at this stage is a function of their understanding of themselves and the group and of the skills they possess.

Following a similar pattern to that used above, we may, therefore, represent Session Four diagrammatically as follows:

Relaxation exercises → Dynamic meditation
Relaxation exercises → Open encounter session

As the workshop draws towards its end, we always offer some time for the group to get together as a whole to engage in a process of quiet reflection. This provides an opportunity for participants to complete any unfinished business and for the leaders to ask group members for feed-back about the workshop.

CONCLUSION

There is always a risk in a venture of the kind described in this chapter that through a process of *post-facto* logic, a series of activities that have little connection can be presented as a coherent and integrated process. We do not pretend that the model we have evolved is one we sat down and created from scratch. Indeed, to declare this would be to deny what we believe is the primary strength of the workshop, which is that it has evolved and developed as the direct result of the accumulation of experience upon which we have reflected and which we have analysed. This has enabled us to refine our theories in such a way as to reflect back upon practice. The result is an experience which makes sense in terms of theories of stress management and coping strategies, but which is flexible enough to take account of the needs of individual participants and of the nature of each group. I do not claim that the form we have created is the only model for this form of workshop or that it cannot be improved.

Finally, as I have emphasised that development and change is a primary feature of the workshops, it is appropriate to raise the question, how they are likely to develop in the future? The answer, simply, is that while we remain eclectic, we have increasingly come to favour the multimodal approach pioneered by Lazarus. The path forward seems likely to take us further in this direction.

NOTE

1 This chapter is a revised and expanded version of a paper entitled 'Coping with stress: a workshop framework', published in *The British Journal of Guidance and Counselling*, 12(2) (July 1984): 141–53. Material from that paper is published here with the kind permission of the editors of that journal.

REFERENCES

Alberti, R. E. and Emmons, M. L. (1974) *Your Perfect Right – a Guide to Assertive Behaviour*, New York: Impact Press.

Beck, A. T. (1971) 'Cognition, affect and psychopathology', *Archives of General Psychiatry*, 24: 495–500.

Bond, M. and Kilty, J. (1982) 'Practical methods of dealing with stress', Human Potential Research Project, University of Surrey (mimeo), Guildford.

Caplan, G. (1964) *Principles of Preventive Psychiatry*, London: Tavistock.

——(1968) *An Approach to Community Mental Health*, New York: Grune & Stratton

Davis, M., Eshelman, E. R. and McKay, M. (1980) *The Relaxation and Stress Reduction Workbook*, Richmond, CA: New Harbinger Publications.

Dryden, W. (1984) 'Issues in the eclectic practice of individual therapy', in W. Dryden (ed.) *Individual Therapy in Britain*, London: Harper & Row, p. 345.

Fewell, J. and Woolfe, R. (1991) *Groupwork Skills: an Introduction*, Edinburgh: Health Education Board for Scotland.

Holmes, T. H. and Rahe, R. H. (1967) 'The Social Readjustment Rating Scale', *Journal of Psychosomatic Research*, 11: 213–18.

Lazarus, A. (1981) *The Practice of Multi-Modal Therapy*, New York: McGraw-Hill.

Lazarus, R. (1978) 'The stress and coping paradigm', University of California (mimeo), Berkeley, CA.

——and Launier, R. (1981) 'Stress related transaction between person and environment', in L. A. Pervin and M. Lewis (eds) *Perspectives in Interaction Psychology*, New York: Plenum Press.

Murgatroyd, S. and Woolfe, R. (1982) *Coping with Crisis: Understanding and Helping People in Need*, London: Harper & Row.

Osborn, S. M. and Harris, G. G. (1975) *Assertive Training for Women*, Springfield, IL: Charles Thomas.

Pearlin, L. I. and Schooler, C. (1978) 'The structure of coping', *Journal of Health and Social Behaviour*, 19: 2–21.

Smith, M. J. (1975) *When I Say No, I Feel Guilty*, New York: Dial Press.

Wolpe, J. and Lazarus, A. A. (1966) *Behaviour Therapy Techniques*, New York: Pergamon.

Chapter 3

Stress at work: a workshop

Stephen Murgatroyd

Chapter 2 outlined a workshop programme examining stress and coping for members of the public. That programme, in which the author has actively participated for a number of years, makes two assumptions: (1) that the experience of stress upon which the workshop is focused is generalised rather than particular or individualised; and (2) that the coping strategies with which it is concerned relate to individual participants. In the workshop to be outlined here, the following assumptions are made: (a) that the stress upon which this workshop is focused is related specifically to the experience of work; (b) that the sources of stress are just as likely to reside in the way in which work is organised as 'in' the thoughts, feelings and behaviour of the person who is 'at' work; (c) that the coping strategies which the workshop seeks to examine are concerned both with the individual as worker and with the organisation of that individual's work; and (d) the workshop is therefore as much about organisational change and development as it is about stress management for individuals.

The workshops described here have been offered over the last nine years to a variety of professionals and other groups. These have included: headteachers, their deputies and other teachers attending management training programmes; police officers; probation service workers; nurses and hospital managers; health visitors; and the employees of medium to large companies undergoing change. Though most of this work has been undertaken for public service organisations, the workshops can be readily adapted to suit the specific organisation for which it is intended.

In all cases, the workshop has been preceded by a period of observation by the facilitator. This observation period is intended to produce 'real-life' examples of stress behaviour from within the organisation for which the workshop is intended, whilst at the same time enabling the leader to make concrete the examples which he or she wishes to use. In addition, this period of observation provides an opportunity for the individuals who are subsequently to attend the workshop to make known some 'stress points' to the leader. In some cases some stress evaluations have been undertaken using a standardised stress instrument (several are available – the leader should choose the one with which he or she is most comfortable).

The workshops have varied from between one and three days, and all have taken place during normal working time. The number of participants has varied from a group of twelve (in the case of the probation service workers) to a group of twenty-five (in the case of nurses and health authority managers). All have operated with one leader.

In this chapter, the basic assumptions of the workshop are examined and the workshop is described. Some specific examples are provided of the stress and coping materials which emerge, and a series of issues which the leader has invariably needed to address are discussed.

STRESS AT WORK: THE BACKGROUND

The experience of stress at work is commonplace. For example, in studies of teacher stress, up to one-third of the teachers in medium-sized mixed comprehensive schools have been found to be experiencing high levels of stress (Kyriacou 1980; Jenkins and Calhoun 1991), and this is true in both Western and other cultures (Wilson and Mutero 1989). Stress is not restricted to professional groups. A study of organisational newcomers in commercial and other organisations also reveals how ubiquitous stress can be (Nelson and Sutton 1990) and has led to the building of many theoretical and empirical models of the relationship between work conditions and stress experiences (see Levi 1990 for a brief overview).

The experiences of stress at work vary. Those that are mentioned often are listed below:

1 difficulty in thinking rationally and seeing a problem sharply from a number of viewpoints;
2 rigidity of views and extended prejudice;
3 out-of-place aggression, hostility and cynicism;
4 withdrawal from relationships;
5 the inability to relax, over-tiredness, impatience;
6 sexual harassment and unwanted advances.

A thoroughgoing review of these stress reactions is provided by Holt (1982), Chernis (1980), Cooper and Marshall (1980), Lazarus and Folkman (1984), and some particular aspects of the impact of stress on thinking and problem solving at work are provided by Ostell (1989). The substantive and comprehensive review provided in a collection of papers edited by Fisher and Reason (1988) is also well worth reviewing.

Holt (1982) provides a detailed and useful summary statement of the sources of stress at work which have been the subject of empirical study. These include:

Time variables: Non-standard work hours; Deadlines; Unreasonable time demands.

Social and organisational properties of the work place: The pacing of machines; Organisational irrationality and bureaucracy (red tape); Work overload due to poor planning/management; Responsibility load (too much or too little); Monotony of work tasks; Over-participation; Poor labour–management relations.

Job changes: Loss of jobs; Talk of redundancies; Demotion; Lack of promotion; Over-promotion; Fear of job-loss; Mergers and acquisitions and associated job change.

Role-related stress: Role uncertainty; Role conflict; Degree of control over work processes; Feedback and communication problems.

Other issues: Job complexity; New technology; Degree of connectedness to others at work; Gender inequality; Quantity–quality conflicts; Relationships with superiors; Appropriateness of pay.

Each of the topics mentioned above are associated with at least one and often more research papers. This list, and more extensive versions of such a list, provide a useful starting point for thinking about the issue of stress at work as a topic for group experiential learning. The list can be useful for initial observations and discussions in a particular organisation.

It is also useful to examine the kinds of variables which have been studied as 'moderating' the effect of work stress. These include: the stage of life a person has reached (Kellam 1974); the extent to which the person is a 'lark' or an 'owl' – more accurately, the capacity for wakefulness (Ostberg 1973); organisational attachment (Porter and Dubin 1975); Type A and Type B behaviours (Price 1982; Frasure-Smith and Prince 1987); Machiavellianism (Gemmil and Heisler 1972); group cohesiveness (Beehr 1976); social support within and beyond the workplace (Lieberman 1982); and organisational climate and structure (Argyris 1973; James and Jones 1974; Parker and DeCotiis 1983).

A growing concern, which will be voiced in most workshops, is with the gendered nature of organisational stress, with women experiencing both more and different stressors than their male counterparts (di Salvo *et al.* 1988). The issue here is not just one of sexual harassment (MacKinnon 1979) but also of different perceptual fields driven by gender differences in reacting to organisational events (Mills and Murgatroyd 1991). Linked to this is a growing interest in work–family connections, both from workers and their managers (Sekaran 1988).

In looking at such listings and issues, group leaders need to remind themselves of the complexity of work as a social and personal experience. Most workers have ambiguous feelings about both their own work and their place of work. Work stress is not easily divorced from stress in other areas of a person's life. Though it may be exacerbated or caused directly by some organisational feature, work may be inherently stressful because of the impact the need to labour has upon the way in which people think and feel (Leonard 1984); the capacity of people to reduce work stress may thus be limited by the importance which work has in the lives of workers.

This last point essentially concerns the relationship between the individual as a worker and the worker as an expression of an organisational 'system'. Experience of running and designing these workshops for specific organisations suggests that the group leader needs to have some understanding of what kind of organisational system they are working in.

ORGANISATIONAL 'FAMILY' SYSTEMS AND STRESS

In designing a workshop for a specific organisation (for example, a particular group of nursing staff working on one ward, a city's probation service or a specific school's staff), the group leader needs to have an understanding of that organisation as a system. A failure to achieve this will result (experience suggests) in the workshop focusing upon individuals as either the source or carriers of stress. One major purpose of the pre-group observation period is to examine the organisation as a system and to build a model of that system.

There are a great many models a leader can choose to work with. In selecting one (or some combination of models), the leader should remember that the reason for choosing a model is to provide a specific framework from within which workshop participants can better understand their own organisation. The model is a device to promote organisational development – a process described more fully by Beckhard (1959) and Mills and Murgatroyd (1991). In one sense it does not matter which model is chosen as long as it is well understood by the leader and has utility in providing participants with a conceptual framework and a common language which they can use to analyse their organisation and their place within it.

In preparing the workshops described here it might be useful to regard organisations as having similar properties to those of families seeking to overcome some specific distress through family therapy. In particular, the model of families as systems, derived from the work of Salvador Minuchin and others (Minuchin 1976; Minuchin and Fishman 1981), has been found to have special value.

According to this model, families and, in this context, organisations, can be understood as systems by reference to two dimensions. These are: (1) the extent to which those who are members of the family or organisation feel that they relate to one another; and (2) the capacity of the family or organisation to cope with challenge or change. This model, elaborated by Sprenkle and Olson (1978) and more recently by Pardeck (1989), envisages that these two dimensions can be represented as each having four points:

Relationships:

enmeshed . . . connected . . . separated . . . disengaged

Adaptability:

chaotic . . . flexible . . . standard . . . rigid

Elaborating these two dimensions, Mills and Murgatroyd (1991) describe them in the following terms. Firstly, in terms of relationships: (1) *enmeshed* – in which organisational members think, act and feel as one unit; (2) *connected* – in which the organisation is a unit which none the less derives strength from the individual contributions of its members; (3) *separated* – the organisation is essentially the sum of the individuals which comprise it; and (4) *disengaged* – in which the organisation is essentially a unit of independent persons with few personal or social ties. As is clear from these descriptions, this dimension concerns the extent to which people see their activities as arising out of their relationship with others. Secondly, in terms of adaptability: (1) *chaotic* – the organisation responds to the need to change or react to challenge in a disorganised and fruitless way; (2) *flexible* – the organisation responds with imagination and flexibility to challenge or change, reviewing decisions and adapting to circumstances in a pragmatic way; (3) *standard* – the organisation has a number of standard responses to challenges or change which it calls upon in some sequential way; and (4) *rigid* – the organisation has one response to challenge or change (such as denial) which it always calls upon, irrespective of the challenge. This dimension is essentially about the level of responsiveness to change shown by the organisation.

This model arises from the combination of these two dimensions in the form of Figure 3.1. As can be seen, the model presents a sixteen-category description of organisations, which is useful in 'diagnosing' stress. In particular, the categories represented by shaded areas in Figure 3.1 are thought to be most likely to promote what might be called 'systems stress'.

The ability of the group leaders to examine objectively the extent of 'systems stress' in the terms of this model is directly related to the amount of time they are able to observe the organisation and the kind of access they are given to those within the organisation with whom they are subsequently to work. In practice, it has been found helpful to briefly explain this model to several of those who are to participate in the

	Enmeshed	Connected	Separated	Disengaged
Rigid	██			██
Standard				
Flexible				
Chaotic	██			██

Figure 3.1 A model of organisations

workshop and to ask them to indicate which of the sixteen 'cells' in Figure 3.1 best represents their own view of the organisation. Leaders need to note that perceptions of the organisation differ with status, so that some in senior management tend to regard the organisation as 'flexible/connected' whilst those at a lower level within the organisation may regard it as 'disengaged/chaotic'. This is in itself an interesting starting place for the period of observation. The point to note is that the design of a workshop that is organisation-specific needs to take into account the perception of the organisation as a system, since these perceptions may of themselves give rise to stresses at work.

The model is elaborated here because it is the one that is found most useful. However, it is not the only model and may be too abstract for some groups. Leaders need to locate a model of an organisation which is appropriate to the group with whom they are working and which has value to the workshop they are offering.

SETTING UP THE WORKSHOP

There are a number of issues which need to be clarified before the workshop can take place. The first concerns the question, 'Who is the client?'

One view some organisations have taken when approaching the author to offer a stress workshop can be summarised in this way. Firstly, organisational stress exists here and is a problem for management – it impairs efficiency and creates an unnecessary barrier to change; secondly, management, in co-operation with staff, therefore wish to examine stress in the organisation; thirdly, the purpose of such an examination is to reduce stress so that the tasks determined by management can be better achieved; and fourthly, therefore, the client is management.

An alternative view is as follows: Firstly, organisational stress exists and presents one problem for management and another for those experiencing stress; secondly, a workshop in which work stress is explored honestly and genuinely is likely to involve the exploration of conflicts between different interests within the organisation as well as ways in which individuals contribute to their own stress by the way in which they view the organisation; and thirdly, therefore, the clients can be defined as the different interest groups which emerge during the course of the workshop.

It is important that the leader is clear about which of these two views he or she is working to, since they are likely to produce different 'outcomes' from a management point of view. The first, if adopted and successful, could increase the extent to which management objectives are fulfilled. The second, if pursued thoroughly, could lead to management being asked to rethink both what objectives they pursue and how they intend to pursue them, whilst at the same time exploring the way in which individuals cope with stress.

This issue is essentially about consultancy. Is the group leader working here exclusively for management or for that group of people who participate in the workshop? The view generally taken by the author in his practice is that the latter group is the client group.

A second question that arises in the setting up of such a group concerns the rules of self-disclosure. It is not difficult to imagine that a stress group within an organisation can be stressful to those who are not members of the group. Questions such as 'I wonder who they're crucifying now . . . ?' or statements such as 'I don't want them dumping their stress on me!' or concerns that 'Things said in confidence to a member of the stress group might be used in the group against me when I'm not there to defend myself' have all been heard in conversation about such groups within an organisation. The group leader needs to make sure that:

1 those within the group are clear that all that is said or done in the group is confidential;
2 talk about persons who are not members of the group should be restricted to statements of fact;
3 all members of the organisation should have a precise and clear statement about what the group is and what it is doing. These points are best conveyed in writing or through a general meeting of all staff.

This leads to a third point: who should be there? In one organisation the suggestion was made that only officers of a certain grade should be 'permitted' to attend such a workshop. It was pointed out both by several such officers and the group leader that this group was just one 'stressed' group within the organisation, and that other groups (most notably, secretarial and clerical staff and middle management) appeared to be experiencing a great deal of self-reported stress and should, therefore, be allowed to attend the workshop if they so wished. Senior management responded to this suggestion by drafting a memo to all staff essentially stating that it was 'not appropriate' for junior grade staff to experience stress, since their work was relatively less important than that of the officer grades in question. This draft memo (which was never sent out) was used as an example of the stress to which such 'junior' (*sic*) staff were subjected to by senior management, and led to all categories of staff being able to volunteer to attend the workshop.

The final point concerns the follow-up contract agreed by the group leader. Experience suggests that workshop participants need to know before the group commences what follow-up is possible from the group leader. In particular, they wish to know: (1) what individual support is available to them after the group ends; (2) what action the group leader (together with others from the group) might take if the group seeks to change some organisational processes; and (3) whether a subsequent meeting of the group facilitated by the group leader will be possible so that progress in stress reduction can be reviewed. Such contracts as are possible will vary from organisation to organisation. What is important is that the group is aware of the status of follow-up possibilities at the start of the workshop and that these follow-ups are explicitly contracted for.

A THREE-DAY WORKSHOP

Much of the remainder of this chapter describes the running of the three-day workshop on 'Stress at *THIS* Workplace'. The most extensive workshop is described so that those seeking to offer their own workshops may adapt and modify this design. Examples are given throughout of responses to the activities suggested, and the group leader's decision-making assumptions are examined where appropriate.

It has not been suggested that this design is the most satisfactory or the most extensive. Rather, this design is presented as a statement of the author's current workshop format which is being adapted and modified all the time. Nor is it being suggested that this design is 'original' or especially unusual. Rather, the design is being used to explore some of the training issues that arise during the course of such a workshop.

Day one

All workshops need to begin. Most workshops begin plainly and simply. The tone of the first part of a workshop is most frequently set by its first hour.

What makes running a workshop in a specific organisation difficult is that many participants in the group (and sometimes all) know one another well and have relationships both at work and beyond which make them very familiar with one another's habits, likes, dislikes and concerns. It is the leader who needs to be introduced to the group, rather than the group being introduced to one another by the leader. However, the leader has a task of exploring the difference between the extent to which participants *think* they know one another and the extent of their actual knowledge. Introductory 'games' (Brandes and Phillips 1978; Brandes 1984) which seek to encourage disclosure about feelings are especially helpful both in breaking the ice and in establishing the emotional climate of the group and its members.

Following a brief introduction to the themes of the workshop, usually done in the form of a brief lecture, the group is divided into smaller groups in order to perform a specific task in which specific managerial and production roles are played. Two such tasks have been especially useful: (1) the 'make a T-shirt out of a newspaper, staples, Sellotape and felt-tip pens task' in which members play the roles of designer, cutter, fitter, model and manager; or (2) the four-letter word task, in which groups of four people are given a dictionary and a hundred letters on a card (in 'Scrabble' order) and are then asked to make as many four-letter words as possible in two minutes – production targets are then stepped up at 500 per cent increments, and the group is observed to see how it develops and uses structure (full details are available in Woodcock 1979 at p. 153).

There are two points to these kinds of exercise (other examples are given in Woodcock 1979). Firstly, they create a team-related climate through activities which are essentially fun. Indeed, these activities are standard team-building 'games'. Secondly, these activities quickly permit the group as a whole to examine the stresses of role and production. The production task (T-shirt or four-letter words) matters little; the fact of a collaborative activity aimed at production is what matters.

Typical outcomes from these activities include these points:

- when roles are adhered to rigidly, then task performance is impaired and role conflicts are observed;
- the absence of roles or structure also inhibits task performance and, though conflict is not always apparent, frustration becomes a source of stress in the group;
- some roles are experienced as inherently stressful, but for different reasons; for example, in the T-shirt task the model is often stressed because of boredom whereas the designer is often stressed because of interference;
- stress is related to an understanding of the purpose of an activity: where a group can see no point to an activity they feel 'lost' or helpless, and in turn experience stress.

These points are brought out in plenary discussion of the experience of the team task. Such discussions are particularly helped if each of the task groups has been observed by a person who has been briefed about typical stress points to look out for.

This activity is then usefully followed by a number of structured documentation tasks: identifying the nature of stress as an experience, its sources at work and typical coping strategies. The same procedures as outlined in Chapter 2 on stress workshops have been found to be most useful, and the same charts are used. The only difference is that participants are asked specifically to look at the nature of work-related stress. One reason why the charts described by Woolfe are especially helpful is that they provide the individual with a way of documenting their experience of stress and coping under a specific series of headings: thinking, feeling, body and relationships with others. That is, the structured documentation tasks encourage participants to think of stress as an individual experience which he or she can document for themselves.

Experience suggests that the discussion of the materials produced during the small groups working on their documents raises these kinds of points:

– to what extent is the experience of stress to do with personality?
– to what extent are the physical effects of stress harmful?
– how many of the sources of stress at work can be affected by an individual acting within the organisation?
– to what extent is stress (or, more accurately, arousal) necessary to performance at work?

These issues, which often arise during plenary discussions of the materials generated in small groups, can be answered or examined in a variety of ways. In recent workshops we have used the Type A Behaviour Scale given in Meichenbaum (1983) to explore the first point about personality. Type A behaviour is, in a variety of American studies (but in only some British studies), linked to coronary heart disease. This provides a useful starting point for the discussion of the relationship between stress behaviour and personality. In addition, the Type A Behaviour Scale is also a reasonable description of the type of behaviour which many feel they have to engage in if they wish to be promoted within many organisations. This dual use has been effective in promoting active and lively discussion of all the points listed above and brings a degree of objectivity into the discussion. (If it is used, participants should be made aware that there is little British evidence linking Type A behaviour to heart disease.)

The question about the degree of arousal necessary to perform certain tasks is also useful; participants can be asked to list twenty activities they routinely undertake at work without any kind of 'stress' (in the sense of arousal) at all. They find this extremely difficult. In running these groups over a number of years the highest number of work activities offered for this task has been eleven (for example, writing letters on my own initiative; arranging lunches to thank people; sorting my mail in the mornings; distributing newsletters and useful information).

On completion of these tasks and the related discussion it is helpful to introduce the model of an organisation described earlier explaining the two dimensions (relationships and adaptability) and showing the sixteen-category model. This is not done in any elaborate or too academic way – a brief presentation of some 20–30 minutes is all that is needed. Participants are then asked to take the model home with them and perform two tasks: (1) locate the organisation for which they now work in one of the sixteen cells of the model; and (2) give six reasons why they think this 'box' is the right box for their organisation. They are asked not to discuss this with others attending the workshop either now or between the end of this session and the beginning of the next.

This is a long and busy day. Participants generally feel tired at the end of the day – they have, after all, done most of the work: the evidence of this is all around the room on flip-charts and in materials generated during the activities. The group leader needs to acknowledge this work and effort, and to indicate to them the value it has throughout the day and at the end of the day. In addition, the leader needs to take stock of two kinds of information: firstly, about the issues raised within the group; and secondly, about the relationships within the group. Listing key points that need to be picked up and used the next day is a useful exercise in ensuring that valuable points raised in the first day are not lost. In addition, the drawing of sociograms of the participants can be helpful in identifying the personal strengths and weaknesses of groups; it helps locate the inter-personal dynamics of the group.

Day two

Each day of the workshop needs to begin with some kind of team-building activity intended, firstly, to consolidate work completed, and secondly, to begin a new day in a spirit of mutual collaboration. A brainstorming activity in three small groups around the topic: 'ways management create stress, sometimes without thinking about it' is especially helpful. Although this in some senses repeats some of the work completed the day before, it is a useful reinforcer of previous observations and provides a direct link into the major work of the morning.

It is helpful to preface this brainstorming work with an ice-breaker activity. Full details of brainstorming can be found in Hanks *et al.* (1977).

The brainstorming produces varied responses in different organisations. Common amongst them are these:

- by assuming a greater level of communication within the organisation than is in fact the case;
- by responding *ad hoc* to situations which require planned reactions;
- by exploiting personal relationships within the organisation in order to ensure the completion of a task;
- by having inner and outer groups for decision making with only the inner groups being privy to the full rationale for decisions made;
- by setting targets for production (or work loads) which are impractical and which it is known that the managers could not themselves cope with; and finally,
- by discouraging initiative and reducing the incentives for making suggestions for change and development.

These points are not always made so clearly, but they are often evident in the points raised by groups of five or six who brainstorm around this topic. They can be brought out in a plenary discussion of the brainstormed lists. Whether or not these specific points are made, it is useful to classify the points made in terms of the two dimensions of the model – relationships and adaptability – since this provides a link to the 'homework' task and to the major activity to be undertaken in the remainder of the morning session.

And then to the major activity. Having identified the issues raised through the brainstorming and classified them in terms of the model, the group is then split into pairs to examine the results of their homework assignment: to position their own organisation on the grid. The pairs are asked to agree a contract, and three contracts are available to them. These are:

- Person X speaks and person Y listens; person X asks person Y just to listen and attend to what is said; then roles are reversed (the 'listen-to-me' contract).
- Person X speaks and person Y listens; person X asks person Y to question them for points of clarification or to improve understanding – person Y is not to challenge, confront, disagree or otherwise reflect upon the points raised by person X; then roles are reversed (the 'question-me' contract).
- Person X speaks and person Y listens; person X asks person Y to be devil's advocate and to challenge and push them to be clear and to think through what has been said, even if person Y agrees with all that person X says; then roles are reversed (the 'push-me' contract).

The pairs are asked to discuss their homework for a fixed time – either 20 or 30 minutes per person (40 or 60 minutes per pair). The contracts are chosen freely from these three. For many it is their first experience of setting a contract for dialogue, and they find this experience both interesting and illuminating. Indeed, many report that it is the first time they have felt actively listened to when offering their own thoughts for some time. These contracts provide a valuable learning point in themselves.

They are then asked to form groups of six to eight and share their experience of thinking about their organisation in this way. Through this 'pyramiding' of experiences some disagreements and issues begin to emerge about the organisation as an organisation, thereby highlighting different perceptions of the organisation and suggesting different organisational stress experiences. Groups are asked to record on flip-chart paper the issues which they would like to raise in the full group meeting that is to follow. Some groups raise one or two issues, others many. What matters most about this session is that groups explore genuinely and openly their understanding and perceptions of the organisation's own dynamics. Experience shows clearly that this model is readily understood by participants in the workshops, and is relevant and meaningful as a way of understanding what happens to them as organisational members. They can and do use it as a basis for structuring a great deal of experience.

All this is still being undertaken in small groups – the leader moving between them to help clarify tasks and to ensure recording. The major activity ends with all of the groups coming together and engaging in an encounter which seeks to share all that has been discussed, with the leader acting as the 'conscience' of the group as much as possible. The word 'encounter' has been deliberately chosen, since it accurately reflects what it is that happens at this point. Participants disclose their innermost feelings about their place as members of the organisation whilst at the same time they look at the organisation as an object.

This encounter is difficult for a number of reasons. The first is that the experiential grounding of participants in their organisation is more substantial than that of the leader. This leads to the organisation being examined at a variety of levels by participants, not all of which are readily available to the leader. This in turn puts some pressure on the leader to explore these levels without encouraging a flood of irrelevant anecdotes about the organisation. The second reason that this is a difficult session is that participants are generally not used to being so open about the organisation. Openness of this kind clearly carries dangers, especially since others present might subsequently pose 'threats' to the person who is disclosing. The leader needs to ensure both that the 'setting-up' contract is clear and that the contract is fresh in the minds of participants at the beginning of this encounter. The final reason that this is a difficult session is that it often involves painful disclosures. The leader has to work hard to ensure that this pain is not used to avoid key issues but is actually regarded as a necessary part of the learning process (Gray 1983).

A general discussion of these forms of encounter can be found in Rogers (1970).

This encounter session needs time: experience suggests that it will run throughout the afternoon. The leader should ensure that all the relevant material generated by the processes used to create the encounter (namely, homework, brainstorming, pyramiding, disclosure, contracting) are examined and acknowledged before the encounter is formally ended. This requires the leader to check out the thoughts and feelings of participants and to exercise skilled judgement.

Before moving on to develop the activities for the remainder of the workshop, the leader generally needs to inject some energy into the group. 'Mixed Veg', described more fully in Chapter 2 on stress workshops, is especially valuable. Whatever the 'game' chosen, it needs to involve the use of physical activity and humour.

Day three

At this point the workshop can take two directions. Either it can choose to examine the way in which this group might seek to affect the organisation so that it is a less stressful place to be; or it can choose to examine the extent to which these individuals can seek to change themselves so that they experience less stress within themselves when they are in the organisation. The discussion of this decision needs to be open and direct; it is not a decision that the leader takes on her or his own initiative, since it is critical to the nature and success of the workshop itself. The remainder of this chapter assumes that the decision is made to pursue the organisational option, since the personal option is examined in the chapter by Woolfe earlier in this volume.

When this decision has been made, the group needs to renew its contract. The success of the group depends upon its understanding of the contracts it has and upon the ability of the group to respect the rights and intentions of others. To some extent, the ability of the group to be an organisation in its own right provides the resources and incentives for the group to change or seek to affect the organisation.

The remainder of the workshop is concerned with: (1) promoting relationship change within the organisation, and (2) examining the ways in which the organisation can improve its responsiveness to change, challenge or external threat. In pursuing these two themes it is important to encourage individuals within the groups to accept responsibility for their own part in the organisation: the organisation is in part themselves.

RELATIONSHIPS

The focus of attention during the relationship development phase of the workshop is upon basic communication skills. Some of the language conventions used in *Gestalt* work, described more fully in Murgatroyd (1985), are used to teach participants that relationship quality is very much a function of the language used. In addition, some of the communication principles developed by Grinder and Bandler (1976) for dealing with three common communication problems (over-generalisation, systematic deletion and distortion) are also presented. It is also necessary to structure some practice exercises which show the way in which these communication problems arise and can be dealt with.

Problems about relationships within an organisation are more than problems of communication. By using communication as a starting point, though, it is often possible to show both how the relationship problem is communicated and what the person can do about it. Sometimes, the problems of communication relate to artificial boundaries created by the organisation around specific members. For example, there is a problem about communication between different status-level members within the organisation. It is important that the facilitator recognise that these difficulties cannot be overcome by reference to individual communication skills and understandings alone, but that some organisational change may also be needed. Typically, these changes involve separating out organisational function (to which status is related) and the quality of relationships between people within the organisation (which are not necessarily status-bound). This subtle point – that there is a difference between what people *do* and what people *are* – is often difficult for individuals to grasp, but is important if relationships are unduly affected by status concerns. Some of the work developed within rational-emotive therapy about relationships (see Dryden 1984) is especially valuable here.

Throughout this period of work (which can last a half day or more) it is important to utilise the communication skills being promoted within the group itself. Thus the facilitator needs to establish some basic communication rules for the group's work. These include: (1) discourage 'why' questions and encourage the conversion of such questions into statements about what happens or what is experienced and how this comes to happen or be experienced; (2) encourage talk in the first person and not in the third person – 'I' statements are preferable to 'it' statements since they encourage and enable a person more directly to own their thoughts and feelings; (3) stop individuals broadcasting their thoughts and feelings as if they were disc-jockeys on a local radio station – enable them to talk in specific and exact terms about their thoughts and feelings, and encourage them to talk directly to the person or group whom they feel should hear their message; (4) do not permit or encourage the use of 'can't' statements (such as 'I can't possibly say that to him') and instead require participants to say 'won't (such as 'I won't say that to him'), since this too encourages ownership of feelings, thoughts and actions; finally (5) discourage the use of questions and encourage the use of statements, since this also promotes ownership. These five language devices are intended to encourage individuals to become more direct in their statement of their own thoughts and feelings and to become more assertive within the organisation.

A second feature of this period of work is a concern with the purpose of communication and relationship within an organisation. For some reason, a great many individuals within an organisation think and feel that the organisation should be happy at all times, should be free from any organisational stress or individual distress and should not experience difficulty. That is, the organisation should possess a consensus-like emotional quality and be consistent in its qualities. The leader needs to examine the irrationality of these beliefs in terms of the set of irrational beliefs outlined by Ellis (1962). Of particular value is an exploration of these three irrational beliefs: (1) 'that it is important to be loved by all those who work in the organisation – if someone does not like you then you must act to make them like you'; (2) 'you must be thoroughly competent and achieving at all times if you are to be loved and respected within the organisation, a failure will lead others to reject you as a person'; and (3) 'it is terrible when things are not the way I would like them to be and I must work hard to secure changes that make things the way I would like them'. These three irrational beliefs, commonly understood by workshop participants, usually act as a trigger for the identification of other such beliefs. The leader needs to work with the group as a whole to show the irrational nature of these beliefs and to encourage a more rational statement of their underlying features.

By linking communication skills, assertiveness and rational thinking, the leader is able to develop an active programme of work for participants which seeks to develop their own skills for building relationships whilst at the same time locating changes that need to be made at an organisational level in order to facilitate relationship enhancement. This session normally ends with a group writing individual contracts about changes in their relationships with others which they intend to make and a group contract indicating organisational change which they would like to see implemented, so that relationship building can be assisted rather than hindered by their organisation.

The most substantial practical problem the leader needs to deal with during this phase of the workshop is the refusal to recognise that relationship difficulties stem from conjoint failures in communication. Individuals tend to attribute blame, and this in itself obstructs constructive communication. The leader needs to use any expression of blame or guilt as a vehicle for looking at the failure of communication linked to irrational beliefs.

ORGANISATIONAL CHANGE

When the group attends to the issue of enhancing the organisation's responsiveness to challenge, threat or change (usual in the final afternoon session), then the communication skills and rules which have been developed in the previous session provide valuable reminders of how open communication facilitates both connectedness and flexibility. The leader needs to begin this session with a reminder of the organisational model which forms a backdrop to the workshop (see Figure 3.1) and the interaction between the nature of communications and relationships and the capacity to deal with change. A brief reminder session is usually needed to achieve this.

At one time at these workshops, participants were asked to use historical experiences of change to understand what was wrong with the organisation's response. This practice has been supplanted by asking the group to examine the idea of quality circles. In part, this is because much of the material generated through historical reflection brought the group back to communication failure, and in part because it forced the groups to deal with these issues only with the tools already available to them. This task aims to provide a resource for the group to develop insights into organisational processes and to encourage systematic and careful evaluation of options. Quality circles permit this.

The idea behind a quality circle is simple: a group of like-status people meet regularly (every two weeks, for example) to discuss the quality of the organisation's work (its atmosphere, its 'products', its current challenges and so on), and to try to identify actions which the circle's members can complete which would contribute to improving the quality of the organisation. The circle members can be from any level within the organisation and can be concerned with just one feature of it (such as the quality of staff relationships) or several. The point is that a meeting takes place and issues are discussed openly and with conviction, with the intention that the expression of ideas and concerns will be carefully attended to by all other members and that some direct action outcomes will result. It is *not* intended that this circle should recommend action to others (namely, senior management) unless it can be matched by some action initiative from within the circle. Quality circles are described more fully in Mohr and Mohr (1983).

To aid the idea of a quality-circle meeting, the leader presents a simple device known as a STOP. This is an acronym for four headings which a quality circle will often use in brainstorming ideas and issues: *strengths* (what are the strengths of this organisation/suggestion/idea?), *threats* (in what way does this development threaten others?), *opportunities* (what opportunities would arise if we acted in the way suggested?) and *problems* (what practical problems will arise in our attempts to implement this strategy or idea or suggestion?). The idea is that a quality circle would take these headings and use a STOP as a basis for brainstorming around a specific issue within the organisation at this time.

What happens in the workshop is that the leader creates a quality circle by using the group to look at a specific issue and acting as a process consultant to the group. The task of the leader is (1) to highlight communication issues within the group; (2) to encourage the correct use of brainstorming; (3) to show how a STOP analysis facilitates active problem solving and connectedness; and (4) to provide a vehicle from which participants can generalise from this specific experience to the potential of a quality circle within their organisation.

To make this procedure more concrete, here are the results of a particular group of workers brainstorming the problems associated with the introduction of new technology (the source of much of the identified stress in the organisation):

Strengths
- speeds information exchange within the unit;
- ensures direct links between writers and printers;
- lower costs;
- shorter time between ideas and products;
- equalising roles within the same status level of the organisation;
- can be added to as technology develops;
- shared skills;
- recognition of the part played by others is more direct.

Threats
- individuals are swamped by the new technology;
- those who were highly regarded before find it difficult to master the new technology and find themselves held in lower esteem;
- threatens support workers who no longer need to support others;
- permits closer monitoring of staff than hitherto;
- requires staff constantly to update their technical skills irrespective of their interests in doing so.

Opportunities
- higher work rates;
- more control over 'products' than before;
- being able to collaborate with others without having to set up elaborate meetings (a specific feature of the technology).

Problems
- not well-understood;
- poor selling of the idea;
- difficult to get used to;
- can't teach an old dog new tricks.

This is usually a powerful activity. It can be powerful when the issue to be addressed is discerned by the leader before the workshop begins. This is best achieved by seeking to identify the most pressing issue within the organisation and by the leader seeking to anticipate what the STOP might look like when completed. The leader should also remember that his or her task is to act as a process consultant seeking to highlight the way in which the circle is communicating and relating to one another rather than seeking to add to the solution to the organisational problem the group is looking at. The leader's expertise is about *process*, not about this organisation at this time.

ENDING

This is a long and complex workshop which covers many issues and concerns. It is also usually highly emotional, and charged with anxiety about the link between participants and other organisational members. The leader needs to end by reinforcing several points. Amongst them are these: (1) the contract the group has about confidentiality; (2) the value of seeing organisational problems as linked directly to the quality of relationships; (3) the need for increased flexibility in organisational problem solving to be matched by better connectedness within the organisation; (4) the responsibility the individuals have for their own connectedness and the quality of their own relationships; and (5) the need for collectivity (through the quality circle), for promoting flexibility and change.

If the leader ended the session with a brief summarising presentation he or she would not do justice to the quality of individual learning which most often takes place when this workshop has been offered. These workshops normally end with two specific activities: (1) participants are asked to write a letter to themselves which will be posted back to them in six months' time – the idea being that this letter will be a self-contract committing them to some task; and (2) by trying to have some fun, usually through a game which shows the quality of relationships within the group (see Brandes 1984).

REFLECTION

This is an emotionally demanding group for anyone to run, as the description provided here shows. It is so demanding that there are times when the leader is inclined to lose focus. It might be helpful to carry a small card which simply reads 'I know too little about this organisation to seek to change it', which acts as a reminder that the leader is an organisational development worker concerned with the process of communication and stress reduction. He or she does not carry executive responsibilities within the organisation.

A second concern is that such a workshop can create expectations amongst participants that the organisation will be more responsive to their needs because (usually) the members of the group have become more responsive and sensitive to one another's needs as the workshop progresses. The leader needs to ensure that the group members are aware of how their experience within the group is unique to them and how they will need to work at their own communications and relationships with others if they want the work of the workshop to be translated in a useful way for others.

Finally, this particular stress workshop as a design is not necessarily the most effective use of the emotional energy available in the group. What is apparent is the utility of using a conceptual model of the organisation as a basis for linking concerns about relationships and change to stress. To some extent, all of these workshops validate this device as a learning vehicle for organisational members.

REFERENCES

Argyris, C. (1973) 'Personality and organizational theory revisited', *Administrative Science Quarterly*, 18: 141–67.

Beckhard, R. (1959) 'An organizational improvement program in a decentralized organization', in R. Zand and D. Buchanan (eds) *Organizational Development – Theory and Practice*, New York: Academic Press.

Beehr, T. A. (1976) 'Perceived situational moderators of the relationship between subjective role ambiguity and role strain', *Journal of Applied Psychology*, 61: 35–40.

Brandes, D. (1984) *Gamesters Handbook*, vol. 2, London: Hutchinson.

——and Phillips, H. (1978) *Gamesters Handbook*, London: Hutchinson.

Chernis, C. (1980) *Staff Burn-Out and Job Stress in the Human Services*, Beverly Hills, CA: Sage.

Cooper, C. L. and Marshall, J. (1980) *White Collar and Professional Stress*, New York: John Wiley & Sons.

di Salvo, V., Lubbers, C., Rossi, A. M. and Lewis, J. (1988) 'The impact of gender on work related stress', *Journal of Social Behaviour and Personality*, 3: 161–76.

Dryden, W. (1984) *Rational Emotive Therapy – Fundamentals and Innovations*, London: Croom Helm.

Ellis, A. (1962) *Reason and Emotion in Psychotherapy*, Seacaucus, NJ: Lyle Stuart.

Fisher, S. and Reason, J. (eds) (1988) *Handbook of Life Stress, Cognition and Health*, Chichester: John Wiley & Sons.

Frasure-Smith, N. and Prince, R. H. (1987) 'The Ischemic Heart Disease Life Stress Monitoring Program: possible therapeutic mechanisms', *Psychology and Health*, 1: 273–85.

Gemmil, R. and Heisler, W. J. (1972) 'Machiavellianism as a factor in managerial job strain, job satisfaction and upward mobility', *Academy of Management Journal*, 15: 51–62.

Gray, H. L. (1983) 'The pain of learning', *European Journal of Humanistic Psychology, Self and Society*, 10: 168–72.

Grinder, J. and Bandler, R. (1976) *The Structure of Magic* (2 vols), Palo Alto, CA: Science and Behavior Books.

Hanks, L., Belliston, L. and Edwards, D. (1977) *Design Yourself*, Los Altos, CA: William Kaufman.

Holt, R. R. (1982) *Occupational Stress – Theoretical and Clinical Aspects*, New York: Free Press.

James, L. R. and Jones, A. P. (1974) 'Organizational climate – a review of theory and research', *Psychological Bulletin*, 81: 1096–1112.

Jenkins, S. and Calhoun, J. F. (1991) 'Teacher stress – issues and intervention', *Psychology in the Schools*, 28: 60–70.

Kellam, S. G. (1974) 'Stressful life events and illness', in B. S. Dohrenwend and B. P. Dohrenwend (eds) *Stressful Life Events – Their Nature and Their Effects*, New York: John Wiley & Sons.

Kyriacou, C. (1980) 'Occupational stress amongst school teachers – a research report,' *Curriculum and Organizational Research in Education*, 4: 86–122.

Lazarus, R. S. and Folkman, S. (1984) *Stress, Appraisal and Coping*, New York: Springer-Verlag.

Leonard, P. (1984) *Personality and Ideology – Towards a Materialist Understanding of the Individual*, London: Macmillan.

Levi, L. (1990) 'Occupational stress – spice of life or kiss of death?', *American Psychologist*, 45: 1142–5.

Lieberman, M. A. (1982) 'The effects of social support on response to stress', in L. Goldeberger and S. Breznitz (eds) *Handbook of Stress – Theoretical and Clinical Aspects*, New York: Free Press.

MacKinnon, C. (1979) *Sexual Harassment of Working Women*, New Haven, CT: Yale University Press.

Meichenbaum, D. (1983) *Coping with Stress*, London: Century.

Mills, A. and Murgatroyd, S. (1991) *Organizational Rules – a Framework for Understanding Organizational Action*, Milton Keynes: Open University Press.

Minuchin, S. (1976) *Families and Family Therapy*, London: Tavistock.

——and Fishman, H. C. (1981) *Family Therapy Techniques*, Cambridge, MA: Harvard University Press.

Mohr, W. and Mohr, H. (1983) *Quality Circles – Changing the Image of People at Work*, New York: Addison-Wesley.

Murgatroyd, S. (1985) *Counselling and Helping*, London: Methuen/British Psychological Society.

Nelson, D. L. and Sutton, C. D. (1990) 'Chronic work stress and coping – a longitudinal study and suggested new directions', *Academy of Management Journal*, 33: 859–69.

Ostberg, O. (1973) 'Interindividual differences in circadian fatigue patterns of shift workers', *British Journal of Industrial Medicine*, 30: 341–51.

Ostell, A. (1989) 'The development of a diagnostic framework of problem solving and stress', *Counselling Psychology Quarterly*, 1: 189–209.

Pardeck, J. T. (1989) 'The Minuchin family stress model', *International Journal of Adolescence and Youth*, 1: 367–77.

Parker, D. and DeCotiis, T. A. (1983) 'Organizational determinants of job stress', *Organizational Behavior and Human Performance*, 32: 160–77.

Porter, L. W. and Dubin, R. (1975) *The Organization and the Person – Final Report of the Individual Occupational Linkages Project*, Washington, DC: Office of Naval Research, US Government.

Price, P. A. (1982) *Type A Behaviour Pattern – a Model for Research and Practice*, New York: Academic Press.

Rogers, C. R. (1970) *On Encounter Groups*, Harmondsworth: Penguin Books.

Sekaran, U. (1988) 'Organizational design for facilitating satisfying work–family linkages through a better understanding of couple dynamics', *Canadian Journal of Administrative Sciences*, 5: 14–21.

Sprenkle, D. and Olson, D. (1978) 'Circumplex model of marital systems – empirical studies of clinic and non-clinic couples', *Journal of Marriage and Family Counselling*, 4: 59–74.

Wilson, D. and Mutero, C. (1989) 'Personality concomitants of teacher stress in Zimbabwe', *Personality and Individual Differences*, 10: 1195–8.

Woodcock, M. (1979) *Team Development Manual*, Aldershot: Gower Press.

Chapter 4

Skills of communication and counselling

Tony Hobbs

THEIR RELEVANCE

A greater knowledge of the skills involved in inter-personal communication would be of benefit to very many people – not solely those involved in attempting to help others. An increased understanding of the skills which are basic to communication and counselling eases difficulties which many people experience in their relationships with others at work and at home. Such changes come about through developing a person's ability to receive more accurately messages from others and to respond in a manner which lets them know they have been understood and accurately express the return message. This helps people sense they are being properly listened to, directly encourages them to listen to themselves more carefully and to say more.

Two people in conversation have been described as each waiting for an opportunity to talk, to 'exercise their own egos', focusing on themselves and their own thoughts while listening with only half an ear to what the other person is saying, supposedly to them (Nelson-Jones 1975). However, the more counselling-orientated encounter is where the focus of the listener remains fully on the speaker. At appropriate moments the listener actively checks with the speaker the accuracy of their understanding of what they have heard.

It is not overstating the case to acknowledge that increased appreciation of these skills is of benefit in practically any situation where people meet to share important information. Personal, family and social relationships benefit from greater clarity of communication. Education, particularly where there is any form of participative activity, is more effective (Rogers 1983). Strained relationships at work can be eased considerably, and development of problems avoided by more effective communication; this can lead directly to greater productivity (Levinson 1956; Murphy 1988).

Their relevance in general health care

> Though grateful for cure or relief of their ailments, sick people and their relatives often claim that modern medical treatment, with its emphasis on high technology, is an unpleasantly dehumanising experience. . . . We believe that communication and counselling form the basis of both physical and psychological care for all patients and their families, and that these should be urgently incorporated into health care practices in a systematic and informed way.
>
> (Davis and Fallowfield 1991: xi)

The current deficiencies in health-care provision in the United Kingdom are not by any means solely the result of financial, staffing and practical-resource problems. Although psychological science has been directed to health-care needs for many years (Griffiths 1981; Davis and Fallowfield 1991), the present model of care remains biomedical and continues to omit systematic concern and provision for the psychosocial aspects of disease (Engel 1990).

An average dissatisfaction rate of 37 per cent (ranging from 11 to 65 per cent) with medical communication has been reported (Ley 1982). For psychiatric patients the dissatisfaction rate was 39 per cent, for hospital samples 38 per cent, and for general practice and community samples 26 per cent (Ley 1988). These reported rates will be an under-estimate, as in these kinds of survey people will tend to give the more socially desirable response.

The effects are serious. Stress on the health-care professional is increased (Gerrard *et al.* 1980). Accuracy of diagnosis, understanding of the patient's situation and compliance with treatment regime are all reduced (Davis and Fallowfield 1991). Indeed, non-compliance for taking prescribed medicine and following other medical advice runs at a frightening 50 per cent (Ley 1982). The course of the person's illness will be more distressing for the patient, family and friends, and the health professional. Pain will in some cases be unnecessarily high (Erskine and Pearce 1991), and in certain cases premature death will result (Carr 1981; Bennett and Hobbs 1991).

This reflects an intolerable level of avoidable distress, waste of scarce resources and undue source of stress on those who are already hard-pressed and working flat out to cope with high levels of demand in limited conditions. The training procedures described in this chapter provide many of the skills required by health-care professionals as an adjunct to their existing (or developing) expertise.

However, a note of caution must be emphasised: the training sessions described here deal with skills *basic* to counselling; they do not provide sufficient training for health-care professionals, be they in general medicine or psychiatry, to then view themselves as 'counselling-trained'. The author has, sadly, too frequently met well-intentioned but untrained (beyond the most basic level), self-styled counsellors, hindering rather than helping the personal development of someone in distress.

Their relevance to the practice of psychological therapies

Counsellors and other psychological therapists repeatedly witness the effects of miscommunication and lack of communication as being at the source of their clients' difficulties. An important and potent part of basic training as a therapist involves learning how to hear others and communicate with them, often with greater clarity than they have previously known. The role of the therapist is frequently to help clients gain a fuller understanding of themselves in their complex situation, to become aware of misperceptions, or 'internal miscommunication', and thereby become empowered to attempt to assume control over relevant aspects of their own life.

Individuals are almost always the only 'experts' on themselves. They are the only ones who know all that has happened to them, what it has felt like and, most important of all, what it has meant to them. They may insufficiently comprehend the personal relevance of what has happened to them or how they really do feel about it; much will be subconsciously stored and therefore indirectly active in their decision making.

A powerful threat to increased clarity of communication occurs when the strength of the therapists' beliefs in their chosen ideological model of therapy too greatly influences the manner in which they are then able to perceive their client's experience. In such a situation the therapist does not register all the information coming from the client, only that which confirms the preferred model of therapy. They quite simply overlook the skills most basic to effective communication and therapy.

The therapist's role is one of *collaboration* with the individual in achieving greater internal clarity and comprehension of what has happened to them – 'comprehension' here refers to an integration within the individual of intellectual understanding with appropriate emotional appreciation of the impact of relevant events. To be able to achieve this means appreciating that different people have their own ways of expressing themselves, they have their own 'personal language' (Mearns and Thorne 1988). They may describe life experiences which their therapist has also been through in his or her own life, and yet have had an extremely different experience of the event. They may even use the same words but with importantly different connotations or personal meaning. It is vital that the therapist relates to the client's perceptions of the world, and does not attempt to force or coerce the client into seeing it the therapist's way instead.

Therapists need to be highly skilful in careful, 'active' listening to the subtle inflections, nuances and personal meaning of the content of their client's expressions to them, and equally skilful in expressing themselves appropriately and intelligibly in return. The skills basic to communication described in this chapter form the foundation stone to development of later therapeutic competence, whatever the chosen model of psychological therapy to be practised.

Relevance at a political and international level

Considerable benefits of more effective communication have been demonstrated in politically sensitive areas, in situations where inter-personal misunderstandings are rife, sometimes dangerously so.

Almost fifteen years ago Carl Rogers described how providing experience in an encounter group in Northern Ireland enabled groups of Catholics and Protestants to come peacefully to appreciate each other's views, and how much they had misunderstood each other (Rogers 1978). Participation, with emphasis laid firmly on increasing the level of effective interpersonal communication, led directly to those few members of both religious groups actively recognising the manner in which their stereotyped prejudices affected not only their day-to-day lives but also the cultures in which they lived.

Rogers, in the final years of his life, devoted a considerable part of his working time to the more political applications of the person-centred approach (Rogers and Ryback 1984), and to running cross-cultural communication workshops designed to break down such barriers between representatives of different nations and cultures. This work took place in political 'hot-spots' such as South Africa, with senior political members from the strife-torn Central Americas, and in the Soviet Union (Hobbs 1986, 1990; Rogers 1986; Rogers and Sanford 1986; Sanford 1984).

RESEARCH EVIDENCE

The literature of psychotherapy has repeatedly supported the value of these basic skills. They are seen as essential to the effective practice of person-centred therapy and development as a therapist (Rennie 1990; Rogers 1942, 1951, 1961), and the humanist movement in psychotherapy has since largely adopted them as fundamental to its various approaches to therapy.

There exist a wide variety of approaches to therapy (Parloff 1976; Goldfried 1980). Influential reviews (Luborsky et al. 1975; Smith et al. 1980) together with frequently cited studies (Sloane et al. 1975) support the proposition that outcomes of these diverse therapies are similar. Such studies can be interpreted as lending support to the view that an important determinant in the outcome of therapy is the proficiency of the therapist in basic skills.

Furthermore, research in Britain has clearly shown that whilst therapists are often unaware of what their clients perceive as being helpful (Llewellyn and Hulme 1979; Llewellyn 1984), patients who perceived the therapist as communicating warmth and genuineness, two of the central counselling skills, improved more than those patients who rated the therapist as being less warm and genuine in their manner. The clients' perception of effective communication is a most potent factor. Earlier research had shown that this was the case, whatever the objectively measured outcome variables (Smail 1978).

THE SKILLS OF COMMUNICATION AND COUNSELLING

Counselling skills can be conceptualised as falling into three levels of degree of expertise: 'basic', 'intermediate' and 'advanced'. At the 'basic' level these skills are common with those fundamental to effective communication, and it is with these that this chapter is concerned.

The skills at this level are those of 'attentive' and 'active' listening (Egan 1982; Ivey 1971, 1983; Ivey et al. 1968; Ivey and Authier 1978):

1 attending behaviour and provision of minimal encouragements to talk;
2 use of 'open' and 'closed' questioning strategies;
3 selective listening skills: paraphrasing and summarising;
4 reflection of feelings.

It must be clearly recognised that in practice all these skills, at whichever level, are not 'techniques' to be applied in a mechanistic manner but are skills which are combined to form an effective way of relating to others. Just as smooth and safe driving depends on the driver having learnt to use the control pedals properly and concurrently, to steer the vehicle, use the gears, speed up, slow down, use the mirrors, stop, all at the same time as being fully aware of what other road users are doing, and be able to combine each of these individual skills until their integrated practice becomes second nature, so it is with these communication and basic counselling skills.

At the intermediate counselling level the skills are more to do with enhancing effective two-way communication with the client and developing personal exploration. They include the four therapeutic conditions which form the core of Rogerian or person-centred therapy, which underpins the international counselling movement and was originated by Carl Rogers (Rogers 1942, 1951, 1957). Rogers himself repeatedly emphasised the need to guard against the 'mechanistic application' of such skills (Hobbs 1986). Both these and the advanced counselling skills are only referred to briefly here; detailed coverage of them lies outside the remit of this book. Interested readers are referred to two excellent, succinct books on counselling training and practice (see Mearns and Thorne 1988; Mearns and Dryden 1990).

The intermediate level skills are:

1 therapeutic genuineness/congruence;
2 respect/unconditional positive regard;
3 empathic understanding;
4 concreteness/specificity.

In the person-centred approach to working with people therapeutically there exist two major phases. The first is where the therapist works to establish the safety of a therapeutic relationship between herself or himself and the client, drawing on skills particularly at the basic and intermediate levels. The second is where the therapist takes more of the initiative in the sessions and works towards helping the client both to make decisions and act. In a very real sense the therapeutic conditions at the intermediate and advanced levels are less skills that are taught, but more ones that develop in the individual therapists as a result of their own developing ability and comprehension of the philosophy of the therapeutic 'model' in operation. Murgatroyd, later in this book (see pages 180–1), expands this notion of developmental 'depth' in learning.

The 'advanced'-level skills are those termed to be 'action-orientated' therapeutic dimensions of person-centred therapy:

1 confrontation;
2 self-disclosure;
3 immediacy.

The focus of this chapter is on training in basic skills, possession of which is fundamental to effective development of a person's therapeutic abilities. Ability at this basic level does NOT make a person a counsellor or therapist. From the first moment of involvement with a client, the establishment of a therapeutic relationship will require the counsellor to be able to draw on a capacity to work at any of these three levels. This chapter does not provide a description of a complete counsellor training programme.

THE TRAINING SESSIONS

The micro-counselling skills teaching model

The training approach in these sessions is that of micro-counselling, as developed in the United States by Allen Ivey (Ivey 1971, 1983; Ivey and Authier 1978). This approach has been the focus of extensive research for over twenty years and is one of the few programmes to have been shown to be effective. The micro-counselling format focuses on the training of specific behavioural skills. From a research practitioner viewpoint, these behavioural skills are considerably easier to define and empirically demonstrate than are the comparatively less empirically observable variables of other approaches to counsellor training. It is also easier to assess their reliability. In over 150 research studies with trainees from various professional and non-professional backgrounds, there has been practical validation of the effectiveness of this format of basic skills training in achieving training objectives (Kasdorf and Gustafsen 1978).

The micro-counselling model itself provides a flexible structure for experiential learning to take place, and sessions are normally enjoyed by both participants and trainers – although they demand hard work which is often personally challenging in nature. Time spent on didactic teaching is minimised; participants are helped to become more consciously aware of the skills which they already possess and to develop and refine these skills further.

Micro-counselling teaching comprises five stages, and teaching of each of the four basic skills (attending, questioning, paraphrasing, reflecting) is approached separately but in the same manner. After exercises to 'warm up' the group, the first stage is for the participants to read a concise description of the specific skill to be focused upon. This is provided for them in the form of a handout by the trainer. Adequate time is needed for reading and reflection. Appropriate reading material is provided in this chapter, and may be copied and distributed for use in training sessions.

The second stage is to provide positive and negative demonstrations of the skill to be taught. Whether this is done by use of a pre-recorded video-tape or by live modelling by the trainer or a colleague (together, or with the help of one of the participants) is a matter of choice. Both methods have their strengths and weaknesses. A video-recording will enable the quality and clarity of the interaction to be controlled and so guarantee a clear demonstration of the skill in question. However, such recordings are considerably less personally involving than a live demonstration. The demonstrators cannot be asked questions about the events in the video (unless they are running the session) and video machinery may not be available for use in the training sessions. Live demonstrations guarantee a greater involvement for the observers, which is particularly of value in appreciating the nuances of emotional inflection in the person's voice and posture. They also act as a model for breaking the ice in observers' own subsequent role plays in the training sessions, as described below. However, it is not possible to guarantee the quality of the relevant skill being shown to the participants in a clear manner.

The third stage involves role-play practice in threes of the specific skill, each participant taking turns at role playing the counsellor, role playing the client and acting as careful observer of the interactions of the two role players. The fourth stage is one in which honest and constructive feedback is provided by participants and trainers on the content of the role plays. After a period for questions and discussion, the fifth and final stage begins. It involves repeating the third stage of role plays in threes, this time with modifications suggested in the feedback session being actively practised. This is then followed by a further feedback session.

In real-life usage, each of the relatively distinct basic skills taught by the use of this model will overlap considerably. It is useful to view these basic skills as a hierarchy; for example, reflection of feeling building on the foundation of attentive listening skills and the use of open questions.

The style of running these training sessions described in this chapter and based on this micro-counselling skills approach has evolved over time and has been modified by experience. The model has been found to be effective in teaching these basic skills to counsellor trainees, clinical psychologists, medical and nursing staff (including their trainers), physiotherapists, psychiatric out-patient groups, accident and emergency department personnel, members of the emergency services, schoolteachers and lecturers in higher education, social workers and varied groups in the industrial and commercial sectors.

Preparation

The following points will be useful in planning training.

Participants

The trainers need to make decisions about the number of participants. There are certain limiting factors, such as personal preference, the number of co-workers available, size of room or rooms available and the prior experience of the trainers. From experience, it would seem advisable not to have more than fifteen trainees. If there are more than nine persons (three groups of three) a co-worker is desirable. The sessions described here use triads as the basis for training. It is possible, if really necessary, to work in fours by having two persons acting as observers. It is undesirable to discard the role of observer because in this role important vicarious learning takes place. These training sessions provide very valuable opportunities to observe what works for oneself and for others, in addition to recognising and considering both own and others' 'mistakes' and their effects. It is far better for participants to 'get it wrong' in a setting where the effects can be examined and participants can learn immediately from constructive feedback.

Few participants have come across the micro-counselling teaching model prior to this training. It is therefore beneficial to prepare participants by informing them that they will be taking part in experiential training, in which they will be encouraged to assess their own skills and provide feedback on the skills of other members of the group. It is also useful to suggest to people that they might like to record themselves 'interviewing' a friend or other person for about fifteen minutes on whatever topic they might choose. This tape can later provide an interesting personal record for participants and act as a yardstick against which to measure their later development.

The physical setting

The physical setting affects the developing group atmosphere. As far as possible, the rooms in which the training is held should be warm and ventilated, comfortable, informal, private and free from external interruptions and noise. Ideally, a selection of rooms should be available. One of these should be large enough for whole-group discussions and demonstrations, while smaller rooms could be used by the triads for role plays. In order to encourage participants to relax, seating arrangements need to be as informal as possible, and some form of refreshment could be available prior to the beginning of the session.

A portable video system is helpful in providing immediate accurate feedback on performance. It is an effective way of enabling self-appraisal in the light of comments received from others. While people do become more anxious at the prospect of being videoed, they relax fairly quickly if it is used consistently. Audio-taping facilities are essential. Ideally, each role play should be audio-taped and used in the ensuing discussion to provide examples of statements and responses. Each triad needs its own audio-taping and playback machine.

Timetabling

The sessions can be run over a series of evenings, a series of half-day training sessions, over a couple of days or over a weekend. The availability of time between sessions for homework practice allows consolidation of the learning of each skill to take place. Restrictions on time are generally imposed by the constraints of the financing body or the participants may only be available at certain times, as may the trainers themselves. If participants are having to travel from afar, then two consecutive days might well be the only sensible approach to carrying out the training. Whatever the duration of the programme, each participant needs to make a clear commitment to attend all sessions: this is part of their contract.

In planning this training programme, a minimum of five sessions are required. Each of the first four sessions is related to a specific skill, while a fifth session is essential to combine the different skills into a coherent whole. Ideally, courses are run on five half-day training sessions, each of about three to three-and-a-half hours' duration. This allows ample time for people to warm up and relax, and to practise and discuss role plays before moving on to the next workshop.

Materials

The essential materials required are the sheets presenting the description of the different basic skills, audio-taping facilities plus audio-tapes, a portable video system if possible, demonstration video-tapes if required and a flip-chart, blackboard or overhead projector. Spare paper and pens can be useful for those who wish to make notes (the observers will need to do this). Ivey (1983) has developed feedback sheets for use by observers, which may also be used.

These groups, as they develop over time, will tend to reflect normal group processes (see Rogers 1970; Yalom 1975, 1983). Although it is inappropriate for a participant to use the workshop for 'free therapy', the fact that these sessions are concerned with experiential learning means that all the trainers will need to be acting in a facilitatory role. Participants learn by taking risks and by exposing their strengths and vulnerabilities, and the trainers must be sensitive to this. If any participant moves into personally distressing material, as does happen, it helps if one of the organising team is available after the session for that person.

Although the focus is on counselling/communication skills at the 'basic' level, there will be many occasions throughout the sessions where the trainers act as models of live counsellors in the course of facilitating the training. Aspects of this 'modelling' can usefully be acknowledged at appropriate times and provide examples of the more advanced skills of counselling. It is important for the trainers at the end of each session to discuss progress made and any issues arising, including those of group process.

SESSION ONE: ATTENTIVE LISTENING – COMMUNICATING ATTENTION AND PROVISION OF MINIMAL ENCOURAGEMENTS TO TALK

When the participants arrive they are likely to be feeling tense, uncertain about what the immediate future holds in store for them and whether they are going to like it. Unknown to them, this will be what the trainers are feeling too, but it is their role to help the newcomers feel welcomed and relax a little.

Setting 'rules' for group participation

After welcoming arriving participants, it is time for the trainers to establish a sense of safety for them in the training sessions. They need a period of time to 'arrive psychologically' and begin to feel confidence in their trainers, themselves and their fellow participants.

The trainers give a coherent preamble regarding the relevance to this training group of focusing on these skills, of their relevance in general (drawing on material presented above), and cover any organisational matters necessary.

They then clearly describe the following rules for each participant to agree to, in order that the training sessions be most effective, and seek a positive agreement from each participant before going further:

1 There will be no gossiping or discussion outside the training group about any personal material divulged by participants or about any person's performance during the sessions. All such information must be treated as confidential. This is to protect each individual as well as the whole group.
2 The training activities are not competitive. Each person must acknowledge that much learning arises from being open to examining 'what went wrong'.
3 All participants must acknowledge that they are each competent people/adults in their own right. Although personal involvement is without doubt a most valuable part of the group training experience, it is inappropriate to regard these training sessions as 'free personal therapy'. The trainers have a responsibility to offer effective training, but each participant remains responsible for herself or himself.

Any participant who does not agree to abide by these rules must leave prior to the commencement of training, and the whole group should be aware that this is the case. This may seem harsh, but what the trainers are doing at this time is absolutely vital to the successful running of these sessions. The rules exist solely to protect participants. Unless a sense of safety to reveal personal vulnerabilities is perceived by them, the quality of training will be impeded for all present.

Introductory activities

1 After a period of warm-up, group members join in the first formal exercise. It is designed to help them get to know one another and to recognise the relevance of listening skills. Participants are asked to work in pairs, choosing as a partner someone whom they do not know (or, if many of the group are already acquainted, someone whom they do not know well on a personal level). Their task is to introduce

themselves to their partner by speaking about themselves for 5 minutes. The partner's task in this period is simply to communicate their interest, and to listen and to speak only to clarify something they have not fully understood. After 5 minutes, the pair change roles, with the previous 'listeners' now introducing themselves to their partners. Trainers should also make themselves available for this exercise.

At the end of 10 minutes the pairs are asked to come together in the plenary group and sit in a circle so that all can see one another easily. Each person in turn is then asked to introduce to the whole group the person to whom they listened and to summarise briefly what they have learned of them. The task of the person being introduced is to listen to what is said about them and give feedback on its accuracy. In addition, they should comment on the inferences made by the talker on what was actually said. It is respectful to suggest that people check out with their partners before reporting back whether anything has been mentioned which they would prefer not to share with the whole group.

The trainers need to be attending carefully to each participant in this plenary session (as in others). Cues will be observable about levels of discomfort, interaction styles, and possible areas of unease which might well be overcome without help as the person relaxes, or might usefully be raised at a later point. Acceptance and acknowledgement of the reporter's attempt can be offered by the organiser.

2 It is often helpful to play a naming game. This may also aid in diffusing tension. Seated in a circle, person A introduces himself or herself, then person B (next to person A) introduces himself or herself and person A. So it continues with, for example, person F introducing themselves, then running back through the introduction of E, D, C, B and A. Once the end of this line is reached, the game is continued with each person introducing everybody until all have done so.

3 It is useful to clear the air of present but unvoiced concerns and expectations. Going around the group, trainers included, each person is invited to state their own expectations of and anxieties about the course. If there is someone who has been 'volunteered' against their wish, they may find it difficult to relax and join in freely, and this will impede other participants. It places limitations on what they are likely to gain and on what they can offer others. The person could be asked if they are willing to let themselves try the first session constructively and if it is not to their liking to consider the option of dropping out of the group. At a suitable later opportunity this issue needs to be taken up with their particular organisation.

An exercise that can be used, time permitting, is to ask each group member to spend a few minutes considering what the term 'counselling' (or 'therapy', 'interviewing' or 'communication', depending on the client group) means to them. Each person could be asked to write down their definition and then share this with the group. The organiser should highlight similarities and differences between these definitions.

Reading material

The material provided to each participant is the following:

Through carefully attending, the interviewer not only gains valuable information but also conveys respect to the client, communicates interest in what is being said, and so encourages that person to talk more openly and move to talk about areas of more central concern. If the interviewer talks too much he or she will have difficulty learning about the client. Carefully attending to the client means focusing not only on the cues coming from the client, but also on the cues which the interviewer gives out.

There are five main areas of which interviewers need to be aware in achieving effective attending behaviour:

1 *Body language*: If the interviewer is slouching in a chair, looks bored and stares blankly out of the window he or she will not encourage the client to keep talking to them about personally intimate matters. Both client and interviewer convey much through their posture, and if the interviewer looks attentive, clients are far more likely to speak about areas of personal interest (and thereby maintain the interviewer's attention). Many counsellors would say that clients know that their interviewers are interested if they sit leaning slightly forward, half-facing them, holding an interested expression on their face, and use encouraging gestures where appropriate. Such a position is awkward to hold over a long period when many clients are being seen. While such a position can be usefully borne in mind, it is important that the interviewer feels genuinely as relaxed as is relevant – that the client feels comfortable and has a natural posture. This enables the interviewer to concentrate more freely on the client.

At times where the client is experiencing particular difficulty in the meeting, it can help considerably for the interviewer unobtrusively (that is, *not* suddenly or distractingly) to move into a body posture which physically 'mirrors' that of the client.

Observation of client's body language reveals a considerable degree of important information. An open, relaxed posture suggests that is how they are feeling at that moment. Apparent uncomfortable shifting in the chair, combined with speech hesitations, stammering, breathing changes and so on, can suggest that a potentially distressing issue is being dealt with. Facial behaviour also reveals much non-verbal information, and particularly important to notice is discrepant non-verbal behaviour. An example of this is a person who, through tightly clenched teeth, growls menacingly 'I am *not* angry'.

2 *Eye contact*: Basically, if an interviewer wishes to express interest in someone, then he or she needs to look at them, initiate and maintain fluctuating degrees of eye contact with them. Clients will look at their interviewer from time to time to check out how they are being received. They need to see gentle, attentive interest, but not such an intensity of gaze that they look away out of discomfort. Interviewers can also usefully become aware of messages conveyed by client's eye contact. Does the client look away when particular issues are discussed? Similarly, interviewers also convey this information to clients through their own eye contact.

3 *Vocal qualities*: A considerable amount of information is conveyed not through what is said but how it is said. The rate of speech, pitch, loudness and timbre of the person's voice speaks volumes. Try saying 'I love you' in as many different ways as possible and it is easy to recognise that often it is not so much what is said that matters, but how it is said.

The interviewer will convey much through his or her tone of voice, in addition to learning much from attending carefully to the client's vocal qualities.

4 *Verbal tracking*: This is a most powerful skill. It is closely allied to the skills of paraphrasing, summarising and questioning, to be dealt with later. Verbal tracking is all to do with staying with the client's topic and verbal content, not introducing new variables or the interviewer's own inferences about what the client is meaning or leading to. Interviewers, by confining their comments and questions to the topics and content of the clients' speech, not only encourage the clients to talk further about the issue but also reinforce their dawning sense of self-direction, which leads to more spontaneity and frequently a greater sense of self-worth. Where the interviewer adopts the role of 'the responsible expert' (which has its valid place in some settings), external boundaries of what is acceptable to discuss are immediately placed on the client. The clients also rapidly learn that the interview will be directed for them and that, therefore, in effect the interviewer is assuming responsibility for resolution of the issues under examination. Left to speak for themselves, clients will direct the topic to the central issues of concern when they feel secure in the interview.

Attending interviewers will quickly realise that the client gives much information – so much so that when it is relevant to give a response the interviewer is often spoiled for choice. Which bit should be selected for further attention? Generally, the client will choose, but if ever the interviewer is stuck, all he or she needs do is first relax, then make a brief comment on what the client has just, or very recently, said. There is no need to attempt to direct the client by introducing a new topic. Verbal tracking is a powerful skill to use.

To summarise, the interviewer's aim is to maximise the client's time of talking (and cut down their own) by communicating their attentiveness primarily through use of body posture, eye contact, vocal qualities and tracking of verbal content.

5 *Provision of minimal encouragements to talk*: In line with this aim is the interviewer's use of minimal encouragements to talk. These convey to the client that the interviewer is attempting to understand and appreciate what the client is saying, and also to continue their expression. In effect they communicate, 'I'm with you, go on.'

Once the client has begun to talk in the interview, the interviewer need only say a minimal amount to facilitate continuation of expression. This word 'minimal' refers to both the amount said, or expressed non-verbally, through gestures by the interviewer and the degree of direction imposed by the interviewer on the client. For example, consider interviews you have had and think of the degree of direction imposed on them. Did it inhibit you? Many interviewers do not realise the powerful use of these minimal encouragements, and continue unknowingly strongly to influence the direction, content and value of the interview.

These minimal encouragements take the form of simple 'Mmmm's' or 'Uh-huh's', repetitions of one or two key words from what the client has just said (note the importance here of accurate verbal tracking and appreciation of vocal qualities), one word or simple questions ('Oh?', 'So?', 'And then?') designed to allow the client to open up this topic further ('How do you feel about that?', 'What does that mean to you?', 'Tell me more, give me an example').

Demonstration of the skill

After discussion of this material comes the observation of a demonstration of 'good' and 'bad' models of these particular skills. It is not, of course, possible to present only these skills in isolation, and so the group must be encouraged to focus particularly on the impact of the specific skills about which they have just been reading. There then follows the demonstration of the skill on video or *in vivo*, as discussed earlier, whichever method is being used.

Role play

The group now separate into sub-groups consisting of three persons. The trainer describes the three roles (interviewer, client and observer) to be assumed. The interviewer's role is to speak minimally and to attend to their own and the client's behaviour. The role of 'client' is something of a misnomer at this stage. The primary aim of the whole triad is to help the 'interviewer' reach a degree of competence in these skills by their behaviour, which should be supportive of the interviewer's attempts. This can be done by the client talking, for example, about an area of personal interest. The observer's role is to observe the interviewer's attempt and the impact of his or her actions on the client. The organiser oversees the whole process.

The main difficulty encountered by 'interviewers' at this stage is relinquishing the sense of responsibility held for the client. It is often difficult to relax and 'just' listen, there is a temptation to ask question after question. Interviewers who ask repeated questions should be urged by the trainer to relax and concentrate on attending to the client. Those who persist in asking questions should be banned from asking any question at all for the remainder of the role play, and their difficulty discussed afterwards.

At the end of each role play, feedback is given. All three participants share their thoughts and feelings. Feedback should focus on people's strengths and should be helpfully constructive, not negatively destructive. It should also be non-judgemental and focus on behavioural specifics. For example, 'You maintained eye contact much of the time, including during one period where your client appeared particularly uncomfortable with your gaze' is more easily received by an interviewer than 'You stared her into a state of fright!' If video- or audio-recording is used, this can be an excellent prompt for feedback discussions.

Roles are then changed within the triad, and the process continues until each member has assumed each role. Trainers need to be alert to participants' strengths and weaknesses in order to facilitate exploration and skill development during feedback sessions and later discussions.

After a short break for refreshment and relaxation, with people in the same triads the process is repeated. Prior to the beginning of the role play the interviewers need to remind themselves (and be reminded) of the issues just discussed on which they need to focus for their own development.

Ending the session

A plenary group discussion in which feedback, comments and ideas are explored brings the session to a close. Participants are asked to undertake 'homework' to be reported on at the beginning of the next session. The homework task is to take each element of the skills comprising attentive listening and see how its manipulation affects personal encounters outside the group. For example, in a conversation with someone, eye contact could be stopped for a while, attempts could be made to hold unflinching eye contact, or the effects of variable eye contact could be monitored and the effects of doing each of these noted.

SESSION TWO: THE USE OF 'OPEN' AND 'CLOSED' QUESTIONS

Before the training activities begin, participants are asked for feedback on the previous sessions and on their homework. When the homework task has not been carried out for any reason, comment should be made which conveys the message that this is a shame, as a valuable opportunity has been missed to expand and consolidate learning and development.

Reading material

The material provided for session two is the following:

In counselling-orientated interviews the client generally arrives with something in mind to talk about. Given an accepting atmosphere and some time and space, clients will often be able to unburden themselves. This is not the time for the interviewer to stage an unwitting takeover bid for responsibility for the nature and content of the session and the direction it is going to take. By bombarding the client with questions this is exactly what the interviewer does. By gentle use of appropriate open questions and use of the other basic listening skills, interviewers can facilitate clients in relating their generally painful and often untold stories.

An open question is one which points the client towards an area of focus, but does it in such a way as hardly to limit the client's freedom of choice of reply. It enables and encourages the client to be self-directing in selection of the important, personally relevant issues to be discussed. It is only too true that the client is the only real expert on his or her self in these matters; any attempt to take over that role by an outsider undermines the client. Asking an open question generally leads to information, rich in quality, on how the client perceives his or her own personal situation. This encourages further exploration and in turn provides a more accurate under-standing for the interviewer of the client's inner appreciation of the world, the client's internal frame of reference. Open questions invite clients to talk freely, and are asked in order to help clients understand themselves more.

Closed questions, on the other hand, severely restrict the range of possible answers the client has to choose from. In the extreme they leave a client the option of only a Yes/No answer. Whilst the use of closed questioning can be argued as valid in establishing factual data, their unwitting use or over-usage can seriously hamper the interviewer's attempts to establish a safe and accepting atmosphere in the session which is essential for clients to feel able to engage in personal exploration. Too often closed questions are asked really to provide information to satisfy the interviewer's curiosity, not to help the client. Furthermore, biased closed questioning frequently will provide the 'right' answers to support the interviewer's personal theoretical orientation, enabling classification and depersonalisation of the client to take place. Use of questions becomes seductive too. While thinking of the 'right' question to ask next; and while trying to find 'the ultimate question' – which will provide that elusive bit of the psychological jigsaw and allow the 'expert' to dispense correct advice – it is all too easy either to forget or to be unable to concentrate adequately on the client's response to the question the interviewer has just asked.

So open invitations to talk are extremely useful in a number of situations. At the beginning of the interview they allow the client to state what is important to spend time on: 'What would you like to talk about today?' or 'How are things for you?' or 'How have things been since we last met?' and so on. Open questions facilitate client exploration of the issue under consideration: 'How did you feel about that?', 'What does that mean for you?' They are most effective in eliciting examples of specific events so that the interviewer is better able to understand clearly what the client is describing: 'Could you give me a specific example?' (this is probably the most important question) or 'How do you mean "having a bad turn"?', 'What do you mean when you say there's a way out for you?' Effective open questioning builds upon the earlier attending skills, and is much based on the interviewer's accurate tracking of the client's verbal content and non-verbal messages.

Closed questions do have their use for gathering factual information where necessary: 'What sort of pills did you take?' or 'How long have you felt unable to catch a bus?', 'Can you go into the front garden without feeling anxious?' But beware of the reasons for using closed questions. Is their use for the interviewer's or client's benefit?

Role play

After these paragraphs have been read and discussed, the role play for this skill begins. Participants are asked to form triads once more, but are encouraged to select new partners so as to facilitate variety in feedback. The role plays progress as in the first session. There is sometimes a tendency amongst newcomers to this style of interviewing to ask many closed questions, and participants often find this session difficult. Participants need to be encouraged to support and help one another and to provide honest, constructive feedback to the interviewers. Trainers need to be alert to increasing frustration levels and reluctance by participants to relinquish well-established patterns of behaviour. The trainers can usefully facilitate expression of the more negative feelings if they occur. Sometimes some group members may blame their frustration on the skill under consideration, or the teaching technique used. This can reduce participants' motivation to perform the task in hand, and the organisers must decide if it is relevant to suggest calling a halt to the exercise and beginning a frank discussion of the difficulties arising. Occasionally, dissatisfaction is projected on to a particular member of the group and this person becomes scapegoated.

In the closing discussion participants are encouraged to examine their thoughts and feelings regarding the session. Many of these might well have been explored in earlier discussion. Time needs to be available for this work. If one triad has dealt with some of these matters, but the others have not, it is useful for one of the members of the triad to be asked to report back to the rest of the group what happened. This generally brings to the surface other people's similar experiences.

Once more, homework is set. This time it is to practise observing the effects of different questioning strategies outside the sessions.

SESSION THREE: PARAPHRASING AND SUMMARISING

The same structure is adopted as for each of the previous sessions. Observation on the previous sessions and on the homework is invited. It is important throughout the workshop that each participant feels that his or her contribution is regarded as valid and adequately heard. The trainers act as counselling role models for the participants in this respect. Participants are much more likely to be receptive to constructive criticism and open to attempting change of behaviour from such a position of confidence. Whilst it is important to recognise and deal with group process issues which might be brought up for discussion early on in the session, it remains necessary to work on the skill which is the focus for the session. The trainers may need to call a temporary halt to discussion of process issues in order to facilitate exploration and practice of the next building-brick in counselling skills acquisition.

Reading material

The material provided in this session includes the following:

Attentive listening – careful attending behaviour and provision of minimal encouragements to talk – communicates the interviewer's interest in the client and so encourages further exploration. The skills of active listening – careful use of questioning strategies, paraphrasing and summarising, reflection of feeling (to be examined in more detail in the next session) – communicate to the client that he or she is being understood and allows the clients to hear their own messages more clearly.

Both paraphrasing and summarising rely heavily for their effectiveness on the interviewer's accurate verbal tracking ability. They differ basically in the time span of the content covered.

Paraphrasing is the repetition to the client of the essence of what has just been said. It is not repeating in parrot fashion the client's own utterances, as can sometimes form useful minimal encouragements. Some of the client's own words can, of course, effectively be used in a paraphrasing response, though largely the interviewer uses his or her own words. However, it is both an opportunity for the interviewer to check out that the client's message is being accurately perceived and an opportunity for the client, recognising that the interviewer is receiving the message accurately, if this is indeed the case, to hear their own message more clearly. This leads on to further exploration and often to development of a fresh, insightful appreciation of the issue.

Paraphrasing responses can be made effectively relatively frequently in the interview, though not as often as minimal encouragements. They are often delivered in a slightly questioning manner. They are most certainly not vehicles for introduction of the interviewer's own views on the topic. They are opportunities to present the verbal content message to the client.

Some examples of paraphrasing are as follows:

Client: Everyday there's something new to choose from. There's football, tennis, swimming, even judo and fencing.

Interviewer: There are plenty of activities to choose from.

or

Client:　　So if I take the job I threaten our relationship. But if I don't I'm going to stay so depressed and then we just fight.

Interviewer:　Whichever way you turn you seem to lose, is that right?

When accurate paraphrasing is presented, the client will often respond with a version of 'Yes, that's right . . .' and move on to explore the area further.

When an interviewer summarises, the time span of clients' delivery of the material involved is generally greater, as is its quantity. Large chunks of information can be summarised, even whole interviews. Whereas paraphrasing statements tend to be fairly short sentences, summaries are longer. Again, the aim is to restate the client's own message, not the interviewer's theoretical interpretation of the client's situation. Again, its use is varied, as a perception check for the interviewer, as feedback to the client on the interviewer's accuracy and the client's own messages. Often the summary presents the client with views already expressed but in a more coherent and integrated manner. An underlying theme might have been returned to at various points in an interview (or even over several interviews), and the summary can sometimes pull facets of the client's perception of the issue together in a manner not previously recognised. Because comparatively large chunks of information are being dealt with, it is important to conclude the summary with an enquiry regarding accuracy (such as '. . . is that it?', or '. . . does that sum it up?' and so on).

Demonstration of the skill

Once more, after relevant questions, the group observes the video- or role-play demonstrations of both how effectively to paraphrase or summarise and how ineffectively to do it, before separating into triads.

Role play

By this stage it is likely that some participants will be seeking suggestions for topics for the client to discuss. While it is useful if an element of personal involvement in the role exists – as it makes the role play considerably more realistic when genuine emotions and views are involved – it can be unfair to both interviewer and client to use the opportunity for expression of deeply personally distressing material. The trainers can usefully be armed with several slips of paper, each outlining a particular circumstance in which clients find themselves and giving hints on how to develop the role. Such scenarios can be geared to the type of situation likely to be encountered by the participants, and should represent both more positive as well as problematic situations.

As this is the third session and half-way through the workshop, now is a useful time to invite participants to review their strengths and weaknesses, in addition to dealing with other issues of importance to participants.

SESSION FOUR: REFLECTION OF FEELINGS

Reading material

This is the following:

Effective practice of this skill builds upon all those preceding it in the course of the workshop, particularly those of accurately tracking the vocal qualities and non-verbal cues of the client. Within Western society there is considerable emphasis on the intellect and a relative denial of the importance of a person's feelings. The interviewer's noting and appropriate reflection of these can often act as a reintroduction for the client to a part of himself or herself whose importance has long been neglected.

In the end the interviewer aims to communicate to the client, 'I am accurately understanding and appreciating the world as you perceive it, I'm in tune with how you think and feel about things. Carry on further.' Reflection of feeling, combined to an extent with reflection of meaning, completes this aim. There is an art in accurately perceiving the client's feelings and in conveying them to the client. In some areas the client will be fully in touch with his or her own feelings, and the interviewer's reflection style needs to be aware of this (or risk responses such as, 'I know I'm angry, what the hell are you saying that for?'; at least an angry response such as this both confirms the accuracy of the interviewer's reflection and facilitates the client's expression of the emotion). Often, though, the client is dealing with issues where the accompanying feelings are ambivalent and therefore considerably more confused to both the client and the interviewer. At such times reflection needs to be gentle and almost questioning in its manner. For example, 'It leaves you feeling beaten and angry, is that right?'

The key to the effective picking up of emotional cues is to distinguish between verbal tracking, tracking of vocal quality and non-verbal behaviours. A person's body posture, level of eye contact and particularly their vocal qualities change with their emotional experience. Tracking the verbal content fastidiously leaves little opportunity to focus on the emotional cues flowing from the client. Relinquish focus on the verbal content and tune into the emotional tenor of the encounter. As with any skill, and certainly with all those which are the focus of these workshop sessions, the ability to use the skill develops in proportion to the amount of practice. In time it will be possible effectively to have one 'ear' on emotional tone, while the other continues to monitor the gist of the verbal content. Try relinquishing eye contact for certain short periods and focusing on the emotional tenor. Preface reflections to the client with the words 'You feel . . .'. It helps. Advanced reflection of feeling will sometimes, though of course not always, present a verbal content paraphrase in the appropriate emotional tone.

There is no need constantly to overdo reflection of feeling. Sometimes all that is necessary is a short reflection. As always, pace your responses to the client. Timing and degree of response are particularly important with this skill.

Role play

The usual format is adopted, with demonstration of the skill followed by role-play practice and a discussion period.

Trainers need to be particularly aware of the participants' own emotional tone in this session, as some participants may feel personally challenged. In this session those participants who role play invented and non-personally revealing scenarios will place their interviewees at a disadvantage. It can be worth reminding participants that the subject matter for role plays need not necessarily be an upsetting, miserable occurrence, but can be exhilarating and happy too.

The homework task is given: to be more aware of the impact of reflecting feelings.

SESSION FIVE: SKILLS INTEGRATION

Although a similar format is adopted in this session, there is no reading material *per se*. Instead, the time available is spent in longer role plays and an extended discussion period. Extended role plays are particularly relevant, as from now on the practice of these skills will demand smoothness of integration of the component parts. Exactly as in driving a car smoothly. The component skills are not in full conscious awareness but become more second nature as they are so well practised. The integrated real-life practice of these basic counselling skills relies not on the application of a set of techniques, but on a way of approaching an encounter with a client which is itself so well-practised that it becomes a genuine extension of that person's self. At that stage, the interviewer is more than ready to move on to learning more of the medium and advanced skills referred to earlier in this chapter.

There will be many issues which can be addressed in this final session – issues such as: 'Where do we go from here?', 'I feel I've just begun', 'What happens if we make a mistake?' – plus, of course, issues to do with termination of the group, which are likely to be more apparent for some than others. Further training sessions can be attended by those pursuing involvement in counselling-related activities. If courses are not available, then support and study groups could be set up to examine relevant issues and books. Newcomers to this field are helped by the trainers to open recognition that mistakes are made at times by all. Normally these will turn out to have no devastating effects, as the client recognises the interviewer as human and places faith in the general atmosphere of the relationship which they have created together. This can and does survive powerful knocks. Occasionally, however, with some clients mistakes can have serious consequences. At that time it can be important to seek an opportunity for both personal support and objective examination of the situation.

One further issue to be addressed in the final session of the workshop is that of confidentiality. Counsellors are highly privileged to share other people's most intimate thoughts and feelings. This reflects a degree of trust which should never be treated lightly or abused. For some clients being able to establish an effective therapeutic relationship might form the only viable way out of their difficulties, and if they are let down by one counsellor they might not seek another opportunity. It is necessary that participants appreciate fully the importance of respecting the confidentiality of the counselling relationship.

The trainers will still be working hard this session and can particularly usefully provide information on further aspects of counselling philosophy and approach, giving live examples from these sessions of where they have self-disclosed to the group, been empathic, confronted and so on. Participants can be invited to share how these experiences were for them and can derive considerable and important self-learning from such exploration.

REFERENCES

Bennett, P. and Hobbs, T. (1991) 'Counselling in heart disease', in H. Davis and L. Fallowfield (eds) *Counselling and Communication in Health Care*, Chichester: John Wiley & Sons.

Carr, A. T. (1981) 'Dying and bereavement', in D. Griffiths (ed.), *Psychology and Medicine*, London: British Psychological Society/Macmillan Press.

Davis, H. and Fallowfield, L. (eds) (1991) *Counselling and Communication in Health Care*, Chichester: John Wiley & Sons.

Egan, G. (1982) *The Skilled Helper*, Monterey, CA: Brooks-Cole.

Engel, G. (1990) 'The essence of the biopsychosocial model: from 17th to 20th century science', in H. Balner (ed.) *A New Medical Model: a Challenge for Biomedicine?*, Amsterdam: Swets & Zeitlinger.

Erskine, A. and Pearce, S. (1991) 'Pain in gynaecology', in H. Davis and L. Fallowfield (eds) *Counselling and Communication in Health Care*, Chichester: John Wiley & Sons.

Gerrard, B., Boniface, W. and Love, B. (1980) *Interpersonal Skills for Health Professionals*, Reston, VA: Reston Publishing Co.

Goldfried, M. R. (1980) 'Towards the delineation of therapeutic change principles', *American Psychologist*, 35: 991–9.

Griffiths, D. (1981) *Psychology and Medicine*, London: British Psychological Society/Macmillan Press.

Hobbs, T. (1986) 'Encountering Carl Rogers', *Changes: Journal of the Psychology and Psychotherapy Association*, 4: 182–7.

——(1990) 'The Rogers interview', *British Psychological Society – Counselling Psychology Review*, 4(4): 19–27.

Ivey, A. (1971) *Microcounselling: Innovations in Interview Training*, Springfield, IL: Thomas.

——(1983) *Interviewing and Counselling Intentional*, Monterey, CA: Brooks-Cole.

——and Authier, J. (eds) (1978) *Microcounselling: Innovations in Interviewing, Counselling, Psychotherapy and Psychoeducation*, Springfield, IL: Thomas.

——, Normington, C., Miller, C., Morrill, W. and Haase, R. (1968) 'Microcounselling and attending behaviour: an approach to pre-practicum counsellor training', *Journal of Counselling Psychology*, 15, Part II – separate monograph, 1–12.

Kasdorf, J. and Gustafsen, K. (1978) 'Research related to micro-training', in A. Ivey and J. Authier (eds) *Microcounselling: Innovations in Interviewing, Counselling, Psychotherapy and Psychoeducation*, Springfield, IL: Thomas.

Levinson, H. (1956) 'Employee counselling in industry: observations on three programs', *Bulletin of the Menninger Clinic*, 20: 76–84.

Ley, P. (1982) 'Satisfaction, compliance and communication', *British Journal of Clinical Psychology*, 21: 241–54.

——(1988) *Communicating with Patients: Improving Communication, Satisfaction and Compliance*, London: Croom Helm.

Llewellyn, S. P. (1984) 'The experience of patients and therapists in psychological therapy', unpublished Ph.D. thesis, University of Nottingham, Nottingham.

——and Hulme, W. I. (1979) 'The patient's view of therapy', *British Journal of Medical Psychology*, 52: 29–35.

Luborsky, L., Singer, B. and Luborsky, I. (1975) 'Comparative studies of psychotherapies', *Archives of General Psychiatry*, 32: 995–1008.

Mearns, D. and Dryden, W. (1990) *Experiences of Counselling in Action*, London: Sage.

——and Thorne, B. (1988) *Person-Centred Counselling in Action*, London: Sage.

Murphy, L. R. (1988) 'Workplace interventions for stress reduction and prevention', in C. L. Cooper and R. Payne (eds) *Causes, Coping and Consequences of Stress at Work*, Chichester: John Wiley & Sons.

Nelson-Jones, R. (1975) Personal communication.
——and Patterson, C. H. (1974) 'Some effects of counsellor training', *British Journal of Guidance and Counselling*, 2: 191–200.
Parloff, M. B. (1976) 'Shopping for the right therapy', *Saturday Review*, 21 Feb. 1976: 14–16.
Rennie, D. L. (1990) 'Toward a representation of the client's experience of the psychotherapy hour', in G. Lietaer, J. Rombauts and R. Van Balen (eds) *Client-centred and Experiential Psychotherapy in the Nineties*, Leuven: Leuven University Press.
Rogers, C. R. (1942) *Counselling and Psychotherapy*, Boston: Houghton Mifflin.
——(1951) *Client-centred Therapy*, London: Constable.
——(1957) 'The necessary and sufficient conditions of therapeutic personality change', *Journal of Consulting Psychology*, 21: 95–103.
——(1961) *On Becoming a Person*, London: Constable.
——(1970) *Carl Rogers on Encounter Groups*, Harmondsworth: Penguin.
——(1978) *Carl Rogers on Personal Power: Inner Strength and its Revolutionary Impact*, London: Constable.
——(1983) *Freedom to Learn for the 80s*, Columbus, Ohio: Charles E. Merrill.
——(1986) 'The dilemmas of a South African white', *Person-Centred Review*, 1: 15–35.
——and Ryback, D. (1984) 'One alternative to nuclear planetary suicide', *The Counselling Psychologist*, 12: 3–12.
——and Sanford, R. (1986) 'Reflections on our South African experience', unpublished manuscript.
Sanford, R. (1984) 'The beginning of a dialogue in South Africa', *The Counselling Psychologist*, 12 (3): 3–14.
Sloane, R., Staples, F., Cristol, A., Yorkston, N. and Whipple, K. (1975) *Psychotherapy Versus Behaviour Therapy*, Cambridge, MA: Harvard University Press.
Smail, D. J. (1978) *Psychotherapy: a Personal Approach*, London: Dent.
Smith, M. L., Glass, G. V. and Miller, T. I. (1980) *The Benefits of Psychotherapy*, Baltimore, MD: Johns Hopkins University Press.
Yalom, I. D. (1975) *The Theory and Practice of Group Psychotherapy*, New York: Basic Books.
——(1983) *Inpatient Group Psychotherapy*, New York: Basic Books.

Chapter 5

Training student health visitors in helping skills

Sylvia Rhys

The topic of this chapter is the dynamics of the process of planning, running and assessing a specific workshop; the theme running through it is the leader as learner. The belief underlying this theme is that the leader of a workshop, who is by the nature of that role facilitating the learning of others, must also be a willing learner in order to be effective as a leader. The workshop in question is a two-day one, run for a group of student health visitors.

Many interactions take place between people in the course of a workshop, and each participant interprets it through his or her own eyes. There are as many different accounts of such an event as there are people taking part. In this chapter the selections and interpretations are those of the leader, with particular emphasis on the leader as learner. It is hoped that this approach will perhaps stimulate some ideas which others who run workshops may be able to use to pursue their own learning. Leading a workshop is a challenging role because it is never possible to perfect it. There is always more to learn and room for improvement.

The chapter begins with some reflections on the processes of learning and teaching. I have been asked to make 'helping skills' the focus of attention in the workshop, and the chapter continues with accounts of how I planned the workshop, and of the workshop itself, and it concludes with some reflections upon it.

THEORETICAL BACKGROUND: ADULTS AS LEARNERS AND TEACHERS

Learning as defined in this chapter is not simply the cramming into our heads of more and more information, or the practising of many different ways of doing particular tasks. It is part of the long-term process of making sense of our lives. We each have our own theories and explanations which we use to try to understand ourselves and the world around us. As we learn, we are trying out new ways of coping with ourselves and our worlds.

New knowledge, new values, new feelings, new ways of going about tasks, however, may upset some of those theories and attitude filing systems which we already possess, and which give order and stability to our lives (More 1974; Mezirow 1981). More describes the process of changing theories and attitudes as one of intellectual and emotional interplay. This interplay may last only a few moments, for some learning is relatively easily assimilated and requires only a slight modification to the internal filing system. Indeed, many of us as we move through life adjust some of our theories almost without realising it. On the other hand, however, if the learning involves a shift in values central to our lives, then there may be internal conflict which lasts for days, weeks, months or even years, and a range of emotions, such as anxiety, anger and depression, may be experienced before the new learning is finally assimilated. In other words, we give up models or theories relating to one or more aspects of our lives and replace them by others. This process of giving up, particularly when it affects central values, can be compared to the mourning process, as described, for instance, by Parkes (1972). It takes time and effort to adjust to fundamental change.

While the majority of adults to a greater or lesser degree over the years engage in the process of constructing and reconstructing new models of themselves and the world around them, many also choose to take part in educational activities; that is, they take steps which are 'deliberate, planned and organised, undertaken with the conscious intention of bringing about change in knowledge, attitudes, or skills' (Open University 1984). From the work of Tough (1976) and subsequent studies, it seems that this process of planned adult education is more common than was once realised. Adults seek information and advice from other people, and from materials such as books, radio and TV programmes; they may go to lectures, join discussion groups, attend workshops and so on. They may choose to pursue learning independently, or to join a group. They may do it on a full-time or part-time or on a one-off basis.

Knowles (1970) has suggested that motivation for this is normally grounded in the roles which adults play in life, such as those of house-owners, parents or employees, and that it reflects acceptance of responsibility for improving our performance in such roles. The humanist school of psychologists – for example, Rogers (1969, 1983), Maslow (1970), Mezirow (1981) – believe that there is an innate drive in people towards an increased understanding of themselves and of the society in which they find themselves, and of the people who make up that society. Freire (1972) has suggested that education can have a liberating power, for learners see links between what they learn and their own actions, and this can lead to new forms of action with the potential for re-creating reality in some way. These perspectives lay emphasis on the ability of adults to take responsibility for their own learning, and to make constructive use of opportunities to advance that learning. It may be argued, of course, that people are not equal, for some have more opportunities and resources than others with which to move forward. This is, nevertheless, an approach which stands in contrast to the view of those such as Skinner (1971) who argue that human beings are moulded by their environments, and are not active agents in their own development.

If people do have responsibility for their own learning, then they have a degree of freedom to choose not only what to learn and how, but also how deeply to enter into it. It is essentially an individual process. Some people may decide, either with regard to some particular aspect of learning under certain circumstances, or as a more or less general rule, to modify understandings of reality only minimally. They prefer to avoid learning which might upset central values and create internal conflicts. This may be a reason why some adults on occasions, or habitually, prefer surface-level learning in which they focus on individual tasks for their own sake, assimilate knowledge in the form in which it is presented to them, and adopt a relatively passive approach to their learning generally. Others, however, prefer deep-level learning in which they are actively concerned with understanding not only the logic of arguments but also the assumptions and values on which they rest, and are prepared to question conclusions which might be drawn from them (Marton and Saljo 1984). Another way of conceptualising these differences in approaches to learning is in terms of stages which are characterised by qualitative changes in thinking. Perry (1970), for instance, distinguishes nine stages; the adult at stage one adopts a passive, accepting role to learning, believing that all questions have simple answers which are right or wrong, while an adult who has moved to stage nine has recognised the relativity of knowledge, and is willing to commit the self to a personal interpretation, expressing it through life-style.

The more sophisticated learner does not modify understandings of reality in a haphazard fashion, nor move by accident from one learning stage to the next. Such a person develops the skill of learning how to learn. This involves a search for methods which are best suited to that individual and to prevailing circumstances, and which help him or her to feel more confident about, and in control of, the personal learning process.

In general terms, this process may be conceived of as having four stages. At the first stage a person develops awareness of the thoughts, feelings and practical strategies being used in studying generally, or in a particular aspect of it. It is possible then, at the second stage, to evaluate those factors and reflect on them in the light of resources, opportunities and constraints which exist within the self and in the environment. This leads into the third stage, which involves looking for ways of building on what are perceived of as strengths and modifying what are regarded as weaknesses by adjusting or changing current methods of approach. In the fourth stage an individual tries out new methods, and adopts, modifies or rejects them as seems most appropriate (Woolfe *et al.* 1987). The learning process seen in this light is both an active and an experimental one.

The above is a description in general terms. The path of learning of each individual is essentially a process unique to that person. It can, however, be shared with others because we are able to communicate with one another. We can receive ideas and suggestions from others, which may be adopted in whole or in part, or rejected; and in turn we can offer to others the results of our own learning, and share difficulties and achievements. This has important implications for the process of facilitating learning in a workshop, to which attention will now be turned.

The process of facilitating learning

It has been stated that the assumption is being made that to be an effective leader a person must also be a willing learner. Thus the principles outlined in the previous section apply as much to the leader of a group as to the students in it. In addition, it has been noted that people can and do learn from one another; it is not necessary always to seek out someone who occupies an official role of teacher. It follows that if in adult education teachers can be learners as well as teachers, and students can be teachers as well as learners, the traditional role of teacher as expert who possesses all the knowledge is diminished, and the students, instead of occupying a traditionally passive role, become active participants. If there is freedom for inter-communication within a group, then the teaching/learning process takes on the character of a kind of conversation in which students' thinking and ideas are continuously utilised as a means of moving forward (Holmberg 1984).

This in turn affects the structure of a teaching/learning session. The leader is likely to have an outline plan relevant to a particular task if the workshop is a one-off, or of the entire course if it is part of a longer-term study process, which relates also to what he or she knows of the needs of the group. As intercommunication takes place, the plan may be followed, modified or even put on one side.

Exactly how the teaching/learning process develops, however, is influenced also by a range of other factors. Important among these are matters related to the size and composition of the group. Different students, as already noted, have different learning styles, and come with different needs, expectations and range of resources, which include both previous knowledge and also skills in understanding and learning to learn

(Svensson 1984). Nelson-Jones (1982) suggests that students' feelings of adequacy – that is, their sense of competence as learners – may over- or underestimate actual competence in terms of past achievements, and that altering the sense of competence may be a key to improvement. It may be that some adults whose previous experience of group learning has been confined to authoritarian situations find it somewhat difficult to take advantage initially of an opportunity for greater freedom for expression. They may be reluctant to expose what they regard as their weaknesses, and/or hesitant about making contributions from their own learning and experience for the benefit of others. It takes time to adjust to a new style, and all students do not necessarily welcome it.

The greater the range of student characteristics in a particular group, the less likely it is that the needs and expectations of all individuals can be met to the same degree. A leader whose approach is student-centred has to accept that a particular teaching experience cannot be all things to all people, and that some in the group will feel more satisfied than others.

The personal characteristics of the leader also influence how the teaching/learning process develops in a group. Assumptions and values on which different leaders base their approach to their task are not necessarily identical, and the premises outlined in this chapter may be expressed in practice in different ways. The reader will, for example, be aware of differences in style of leadership between authors in this book. Leaders differ in how they interpret their roles, and in the range of strategies and tactics which they employ. Important too is how interested and experienced they are as regards both the subject matter of the session and the facilitation of learning of others.

Environmental influences play a part. For example, if a group is large in relation to space available it may be difficult to arrange for small-group exercises. Time is often another limiting factor, and may be particularly constraining if the course is one with a syllabus which students are expected to cover to prepare themselves for formal assessment on a given date. In this case there may be tension between paying attention to short-term assessment goals and long-term personal developmental goals (Rhys and Lambert 1983).

The fact that so many different variables can exert an influence on group learning highlights the need for freedom in inter-communication referred to in the first paragraph of this section. It is important that all group members, both leader and students, should have confidence in, and mutual respect for, one another, so that a climate of warmth and safety may develop. This is a point emphasised by Rogers; for example, 'the facilitation of significant learning rests upon certain attitudinal qualities that exist in the personal *relationship* between the facilitator and the learner' (Rogers 1983). In this sort of climate it is safe to venture into the unknown, which is what learning involves. It is not sufficient for a leader to possess techniques; how that individual *is* as a person is an essential element in the situation.

From this brief consideration of the process of facilitating learning, it becomes evident that it is not possible to devise a universal, neat and tidy set of rules about how to run a workshop. Facilitating learning is as much an individual process as learning itself. Both carry risks and uncertainties as well as interest and rewards. For both leader and students a skill which is essential, to which reference was made on page 87, is that of reflection. Those who develop awareness of self and others can use reflection constructively to understand, analyse and assess present actions, thoughts, feelings and circumstances, and to make plans for coping with the path of learning in the future. In the words of Schon (1983), they become 'reflective practitioners', and, even though the way may not always be easy, they look forward to trying out and developing new constructs of reality.

The above has been an outline of principles and assumptions which lay behind the workshop run as part of their course for a group of student health visitors. The following is an account of necessary preparation for the workshop, and of the workshop itself.

PLANNING THE FIRST WORKSHOP ON HELPING SKILLS FOR STUDENT HEALTH VISITORS

Finding out about the students

Preparation began about two months or so before the date of the workshop. The leader had to make decisions on both the content and the form it would take. Because it was being run for a specific group of students she thought it necessary to increase her knowledge of their course, of the work of health visitors for which they were being trained, and to speak to other leaders who had run comparable workshops.

All the students were registered nurses, and had done midwifery or obstetric training. At the time of the workshop, the author was conducting a research project into staff stress in a hospital unit, and so had been talking to nurses and hearing from them about their training and their work in a hospital setting, as well as reading relevant literature. She had discussions with the tutor in charge of the Diploma Course in Health Visiting, looked at the syllabus for the Diploma, and found out more information from another researcher and from literature.

Health visitors in the United Kingdom work in the community and have regard for the medical, psychological and social needs of individuals and families. They have a wide range of duties and activities. For example, they give advice to expectant mothers; they visit all babies soon after birth and seek to ensure that their care is adequate and that the child is progressing normally, and they give help and support to mothers; in the school health service they are sometimes the principal link between the school, the family doctor and other agencies, and they may work as school nurses and health educators; they identify old people who require support and help, and give advice to them on health and maintain contact with the family doctor; they visit and help the chronic sick and handicapped and their families; they undertake health education in the community, such as in old people's clubs; and they carry out screening procedures, such as hearing tests for babies (Working Party 1969).

As the leader was running only one workshop with the student health visitors and was not otherwise involved in their course, it was arranged that she should have an hour's meeting with them about three weeks before it took place. At the meeting, the leader introduced herself, and then explained that in order to help her plan the workshop programme she would be grateful if the group would be willing to tell her something about themselves and the work they had been doing so far in the course. A short small-group exercise on the students' understanding of the term 'counselling' served as a catalyst for a lively group discussion.

Content of the workshop

The workshop needed a theme to hold it together. 'Helping skills' was the remit, and there were no constraints imposed by the tutor in charge of the course nor by the Diploma syllabus, beyond the need for the content to be relevant to the work of health visitors. The workshop was not part of the assessment process. As a result of her investigations described above, the leader came to the conclusion that a useful theme would be that of communication, with particular reference to those skills which can be brought to bear on the process of building up and maintaining a relationship with another person or persons in their own homes. Establishing such a relationship with clients is likely to be an essential part of the work of health visitors.

Communication is part and parcel of our everyday lives, yet is too often just taken for granted. A number of writers (for example, Argyle 1981) have pointed out that the importance of social skills is often underestimated. To be able to select the skills most appropriate for any given helping situation, a health visitor, like a teacher, has to be aware of and able to weigh up influences whose roots may lie in the self, in other people and in the environment. Students in a workshop have a chance to study in a sheltered environment their own ways of communicating and those of others. They can use workshop exercises as opportunities for reflection, self-assessment, experimenting and discovery.

There were a number of other reasons why the theme of communication seemed appropriate. All the student health visitors were trained nurses. Whereas communicating with others is an essential part of a nurse's job, training for it in the years prior to the workshop only rarely included the study of the process as a subject in its own right (Bridge and Clark 1981). A nurse's work is mainly task-initiated, and relatively greater emphasis is placed on 'doing' skills. As one researcher remarked, 'Nurses *do* things as their work. . . . If they are not doing something physical they are not working' (James 1984).

By the time of the workshop, however, recognition of the psychological and emotional needs of patients as well as of their physical difficulties was growing. Although nurses might appreciate that a particular patient might have a range of needs, their understanding was for the most part at a general level and they were not skilled in assessing the actual psychological requirements of a particular individual (Wattley and Muller 1984). Recommendations were being made that in all types of nurse training increased emphasis should be given to the development of elementary communication and human-relationship skills (for example, *Counselling in Nursing* 1978; *Project 2000* 1986). By the end of the 1980s more attention was being paid on training courses and in the literature to these skills (for example, Arnold and Boggs 1989; Burnard 1991).

It can be argued that it is particularly essential for health visitors to be versatile in communication skills. They are engaged in preventive and developmental rather than curative work, and they are likely to have on their case-loads at any one time a much greater variety of clients with a wider range of problems than does a nurse on a hospital ward. Clients are likely to include different age groups from different classes and perhaps from different cultures. Health visitors often communicate not only with their clients but also with relatives and friends of clients, whose ages and background and circumstances also differ widely. All these people themselves employ different styles of communication. Problems with which health visitors are likely to be presented can vary from how to care for a newly born child to the psychosocial problems of the elderly. How a health visitor communicates is likely to have an important bearing on the quality of help offered. Even straightforward information can be presented in a variety of ways, some of which may encourage a client to make use of it and others to reject it.

In addition, a health visitor is likely to be the only health visitor with whom any particular client has a relationship, unlike the hospital patient, who is cared for by a team of nurses. A health visitor may visit a home over a period of weeks, months or even years, and different ways of communicating may be called for at different stages in this relationship.

Another important factor which calls for versatility in communication skills in the health visitor is the setting in which the communication takes place. Health visitors are not dealing with a captive audience on foreign

territory: namely, the patient in a hospital bed. They are often communicating with people on their own territory, that is, in their home. They
themselves are guests in those homes and yet at the same time they are
professionals. The two roles may conflict. They cannot, in the way they
might for a patient in a hospital, lay down rules and regulations for their
hosts (McIntosh 1981).

Health visitors can use their communication skills to help one another
as well as their clients. They often work in greater isolation than do
hospital nurses. The work of home visiting, for example, they normally
do on their own, and time spent in communication with colleagues may
be limited. All nurses are traditionally expected to be self-reliant and to
cope unaided, whatever the circumstances (*Counselling in Nursing* 1978).
This may well be connected with the fact that the majority of them are
women, whose traditional role in society is to be supportive of others.
The giving of social support to others without receiving support oneself
(the support gap), it has been suggested, is a source of stress to women
today (Belle 1982). The problem of who cares for the carers is now
being given attention in some quarters, such as by the establishment of
CHAT, a counselling service for nurses, run by the Royal College of
Nursing.

Thus, it was decided that communication was to be the theme of the
workshop. Many different skills come under this heading, for example,
non-verbal skills, like body posture; verbal skills, such as different types
of questioning; cognitive skills – for instance, being able to follow the
reasoning behind a client's words; affective skills, such as conveying to
a client a feeling of warmth and respect. In two days it would be possible
to work on only a very few of these. From her investigations generally,
and in particular from what she learned from the pre-workshop meeting,
the leader concluded it was important to pay particular attention to non-
verbal communication, and to looking at individual skills in context as
integral parts of the overall process of communicating in the field.

Structure of the workshop

The decisions which the leader took on the structure of the workshop
were influenced not only by her thoughts on the content of the workshop
outlined above but also by a number of other factors. These included
the setting in which the workshop was to take place (a large seminar
room with furniture which could be moved around); her theories and
assumptions about adults as learners and teachers (outlined above); the
information that she learned from another leader who had run a similar
workshop; and her previous experience and her self-knowledge about
her capacity as a leader. She considered it important also that there
should be opportunities for the students to reflect, make self-assessments,

and to think about how they might carry on learning after the workshop was over.

The leader's overall strategy can be described as one of 'freedom within structure'. She decided that there would be a number of exercises, each followed by opportunity for discussion. She decided also to prepare more than there would be time for, and to select from them those exercises which seemed most appropriate on the day. She would provide guidelines for the exercises, but how each developed would depend on the actions and interactions of all participants. The students would be free to make suggestions about modifying the exercises, or adding new ones. While she had some ideas of the order in which the exercises might be used, she was prepared to rearrange that order if it seemed advisable.

The leader also gave attention to the need to include variety within the programme. This was partly because different students have different styles of learning, and she wanted to cater for as wide a range as possible. In addition, different tactics appeal to different people; some prefer thinking visually, others like active exercises, while yet others want discussion. Some 'fun' exercises were included; they can be useful not only to add variety but also to help break the ice and to increase the level of arousal of participants so that there is energy available to invest in gathering experience and information (Van der Molen 1985). Variety in both type of activity and in the pace at which activities were carried out would also help to maintain the interest and concentration of all concerned and to counteract any tendency to boredom.

The exercises which the leader prepared included some to be carried out on an individual basis, some in pairs, discussions in small groups and in one large group, writing, compiling charts, listening to tapes and role playing. She arranged for two friends to come in to help with a role-playing exercise during the second morning. This was the one piece of timetabling to which the group would have to adhere. Some of the exercises the leader was familiar with, others she would be trying out for the first time.

This pattern of freedom within structure meant that the leader maintained a dominant role in defining in outline what was valid knowledge for her students (see Woolfe and Murgatroyd 1979 for a discussion on this topic) and in the general way in which that knowledge would be explored. The details of the content and structure, however, would be filled in by the group during the course of the workshop. As explained, no detailed programme was prepared in advance. The programme which is outlined in the Appendix (see pages 106–8) took shape in the course of the workshop itself.

RUNNING THE FIRST WORKSHOP FOR STUDENT HEALTH VISITORS

Introduction

The workshop took place about half-way through the students' twelve-month Diploma course, and all the twelve students who took part had by then come to know one another quite well. Their ages ranged from the mid-20s to the mid-40s. Some came direct from hospital work to training for work in the community. Some had already had some experience in the community; for example, as school nurses. Some came direct from full-time paid jobs, others with families were returning to nursing after a break of a number of years. Eleven of the students attended on the first day and were joined by the twelfth, who had been ill, on the second day. In addition, one trainee nurse tutor took part throughout the workshop. Two friends of the leader, both of whom were counsellors, who took part in a role-playing exercise, were present for part of the morning on the second day.

The workshop took place in a medium-sized room. The furniture could be moved around, and there was space for a variety of activities, but pairs and sub-groups had to work in rather close proximity to one another. Coffee and tea breaks were taken in the room.

The Appendix (see pages 106–8) summarises the programme which developed out of the interactions of the participants with one another and with the leader. It is possible, in retrospect, to discern six principal stages of development. The following is a very brief summary, item by item, of a few aspects of the many happenings in the workshop over the two days. Making the selection was not easy. The aim is to offer an outline picture of the main events and to highlight a number of aspects which illustrate, from the leader's viewpoint, the processes both of facilitating learning in a workshop and also of learning from the workshop experience.

Day one

Stage 1: Getting down to work

The workshop began rather tentatively. After two terms the group members had come to know one another quite well, but had not worked together previously in a workshop and were not sure what to expect, and they had met the leader only once before for an hour.

The leader introduced the workshop by describing the sort of structure and the theme it would have and she explained briefly the teaching/learning principles which she had in mind. This led on to a consideration of the type of contract which would exist between members of the group during the two days – that is, everyone would be responsible for her own actions and would be able to choose how much to contribute to, and take away from, the workshop. The leader explained it was no part of her role to act as assessor; she was there to guide and to explore with the group the topic in hand, and there would be plenty of opportunity for discussion and comment. If anyone wanted to talk to her on an individual basis, they would be very welcome to do so at the end of each day, or during the day if it were urgent, or contact her after the workshop was over. The course tutor would receive a timetable of activities, but all inter-communications which took place during the workshop would remain confidential.

The students listened very carefully and seriously, and there was some brief discussion. They then joined, if a little hesitantly, in two group exercises. The first was a game which helped to lighten the climate by engendering some amusement. In the second exercise, which served to introduce the topic of non-verbal communication, each individual acted non-verbally an emotion for the others to guess. Some joined whole-heartedly, others a bit hesitantly, in a type of activity which was evidently new to them.

In the next exercise, on non-verbal communication, the students worked in pairs through some short exercises, following a set of written instructions. This type of activity appeared to give a boost to their self-confidence. They followed the instructions carefully and quickly, and in the discussion which followed were willing to contribute examples from their own experiences; the conversation was lively and full of anecdotes. The subject matter was extended by the group to the use of touch in different situations, with different types of people and with people from different cultures. During the chat over coffee several students remarked that they had not had an opportunity for 'such a good natter' for a long time!

Coffee-making itself (and tea-making in the afternoon) was organised very efficiently by the group, and after a not very long break members spontaneously tidied away cups and indicated that they were ready to restart. It was almost as if they wished to show how efficient they were when *they* were in charge. In this, and in other ways, they showed that they had devised methods for working together as a group. For example, during the course of the workshop, some of them would tease one particularly talkative person whenever it was felt that that person had gone far enough for the time being.

After the coffee break, the group itself initiated a follow-up to item 4 (see Appendix) with a discussion on the pros and cons of having to wear uniforms in the course of their official duties. Again, it gave an opportunity for sharing personal experiences. The group members appeared much more confident by now that they could cope with the workshop.

Stage 2: Increasing challenge of the learning process

After the topic of uniforms had been explored for a while, the leader detected a general feeling of readiness to move on, and, having checked this out with the group, introduced another exercise, this time one on listening, which was carried out in pairs. It proved something of a challenge to a number of the students, who found it very difficult to refrain completely from making comments while their partners were describing one of their cases. In the discussion afterwards, some students appeared confident that the process of communication with clients presented few problems, but some of the others began to admit to some difficulties which were worrying them, especially when they were visiting clients in their own homes.

After lunch, the warm-up exercise was being enjoyed enthusiastically by the group when it was interrupted by a member of staff working on the floor below, who complained about students larking about and was afraid that the ceiling would fall in! He was somewhat taken aback to find the leader also 'larking about', and rather bewildered to hear that having fun was part of the learning process! It was an interesting illustration of how learning is normally regarded as a serious and primarily passive activity.

After making a few amused comments on the interruption, members indicated that they were ready to get down to the more serious business of the afternoon. Item 10 (see Appendix), on questioning, was another exercise which presented the group with something of a challenge, this time as regards both the content and the nature of the exercise. The leader invited ideas about different ways of asking a client questions, and suggested that the students might like to give a brief role play to illustrate their ideas. That there may be different ways of asking questions was an idea new to many members of the group, and there was considerable reluctance to role play in front of other group members. The two people who did volunteer gave a useful illustration of a health visitor who peppered a client with questions, leaving the client with little space in which to explain difficulties in her own way.

It seemed important to pause and to think around this topic. The leader added some ideas about types of questions which had not yet been covered. She was interested to note that in the discussion which followed only limited attention was paid by group members to the difficulties there may be in gathering relevant information from clients, and to the need to have a range of methods to use as necessary. There was a tendency to keep moving away from uncertainties in the process of communication and to concentrate instead on practical difficulties, such as the logistics of coping with a queue of patients at a clinic when time is strictly limited. In other words, there was a tendency to concentrate on coping with difficulties arising in the environment, rather than on the strategies and tactics which the students themselves might develop to help others.

Item 11 began with an individual exercise in which members filled in charts with words which they considered described how they experienced particular feelings with different degrees of intensity. Group cohesion was by now becoming somewhat less marked. It seemed to be safer not always to swim with the current. The ensuing discussion both within and between the two groups into which the class split was vigorous, and it highlighted the fact that the same word used to describe a particular feeling may sometimes have different shades of meaning for different people. It follows that when talking with clients, it is important for health visitors to cross-check meanings, particularly of what seem to them to be crucial statements. Some students seemed somewhat dismissive of the significance of this, while others looked very thoughtful.

Division of opinion was again evident during the last exercises on the first day. There was time to listen to two short tape extracts, giving examples of contrasting styles of conducting initial interviews (item 13). (The parts of the counsellor in the two extracts were taken by trainee counsellors and the clients were role played.) Some students thought the counsellor on one tape too passive, and said they would have got up and walked out if they had been interviewed by someone who sat there and said virtually nothing. One or two were particularly indignant when the client exclaimed, 'I feel awful about this. I ought to be able to cope', because the counsellor did not respond by comforting the client. They wanted to apply their way of helping with physical difficulties to helping with emotional difficulties. Another student pointed out how important it was to give the client a chance to express herself. The leader took the opportunity to encourage this line of thought and suggested that there may be times when it is important to listen carefully and give opportunities to clients to formulate, reflect on and accept their own ideas and feelings.

Some of the strongest feelings were expressed by some students who said they recognised that they identified in some way with the client and/ or the situations. This served, *inter alia*, as an opportunity to discuss how important it is for a helper to be aware that strong personal feelings may be triggered off in a situation. If this happens, it is necessary, in order to concentrate on the client, to recognise those feelings, then to put them to one side for the time being, and reflect on them later, but not to try to ignore or repress them. The work for the day ended with some pondering on this topic.

Day Two

Stage 3: Resuming the task

Several of the group members began proceedings on the second day by commenting on the interruption the previous day by one of the staff, and offered suggestions for an alternative venue for future workshops. The leader thanked them for their comments and suggestions and made a note of them. It was interesting that no one suggested that the activity itself was inappropriate, and indeed everyone willingly joined together in another warm-up exercise, a less energetic one this time!

Empathy was one aspect of communication which the leader had thought might be useful to work on during the workshop; it had been mentioned several times during the previous day and was of importance to the topic on which the day had ended, but had not yet been the focus of attention. She now introduced a short exercise (item 16) on empathic responding. Students referred in the course of discussion to the work on non-verbal communication, and discussed for a time how what is said may have different meanings according to how it is said. There were some thoughtful comments on the importance of accepting clients and not making them feel inferior, and on how this might be achieved. There was not, unfortunately, enough time to give the topic of empathy as much attention as the leader thought it merited as an essential, but not always easily understood, aspect of the helping process. For logistic reasons, it was necessary to fit in before lunch the role play with which two friends were helping.

Stage 4: Role play (item 18)

The two visitors to the group role played clients in two different scenarios. In the first, they acted the part of parents of a young child who was refusing to go to nursery school. In the second, they were husband and wife finding problems coping with an elderly relative who was living with them. The two students who role played the health visitors experienced difficulties in coping with two pairs of very uncooperative clients with multiple problems, deliberately presented in this way to act as a challenge to the students.

The ensuing discussion plunged immediately into the practicalities of the two family situations. There were normative comments on the behaviour and attitudes of these clients in particular and of clients in general with similar presenting problems, and there was a plentiful supply of anecdotes and personal experiences. Most of the interaction was between the students themselves. They seemed to be looking to one another for support when discussing two situations with which they experienced difficulties.

The group needed the encouragement of one of the role players and the leader to concentrate on process rather than on content. In the course of the discussion, this role player challenged conventional, polite methods of communication. He pointed out that presenting problems are not always the basic problems and suggested that the two couples in the role play were playing games in which they looked for arbitrators rather than solutions, and that perhaps their games should be challenged. There are times when it may be important to give clients permission to be angry, and confrontation may be a constructive way of bringing conflicts into the open. Empathy is not about 'being nice', but rather it is about tuning into the world as it is.

As the group contemplated these ideas, some strong feelings began to surface. This way of communicating with clients seemed to run counter to the students' training as nurses, and there were reactions of doubt and disbelief and some anger. One person asked incredulously, 'Are you saying that you think we were being *too* polite?' It again appeared that there was reluctance on the part of the students to recognise the power which they themselves could wield in their roles as helpers. There was a tendency, as in the exercise, item 10, to concentrate on how to cope with factors external to themselves to the neglect of the influence which they themselves could exert on interactions with others. It was interesting, however, that by the end of the discussion a number of the students were beginning to look more closely at, and weigh up, what they saw as their own strengths and weaknesses as regards different ways of communicating.

Stages 5 and 6: Interlude and assessment, and evaluation

After this hard work, the group enjoyed lunch together at a local hostelry to celebrate the end of term. This, together with the afternoon warm-up exercise, were welcomed as light relief.

Some of the variety and intensity of feelings which had appeared in the morning reappeared when the students commenced the task of evaluating the workshop. They began by thinking about and evaluating their own helping skills and listing those which they already had, noting those which they thought they should improve, and those which they thought they should acquire (item 21). In the course of the group discussion which followed, they highlighted some problems which they saw as associated with the process of helping. The main ones were coping with anger, coping with crisis, deciding whether they would be able to see a case through, and taking risks. There was some lively discussion on whether and when to confront; it appeared that in this respect the deeply held beliefs of some of the students about always trying to be 'nice' to people were being challenged. Of those skills they thought they needed to develop, attentive listening came at the top of the list for a number of them. This was followed by empathy, confronting, coping with silences, guiding interactions, setting aside one's feelings, being aware of process as well as of content, and withdrawing from and then evaluating situations.

This exercise was followed up after tea by an individual exercise in which the students wrote down the steps they intended to take as a result of attending the workshop. The steps they listed included practising analysing conversations, being more prepared to listen, not being afraid of silences, being more alert for non-verbal cues, improving communication tactics and strategies, and weighing up more critically transactions between people.

In the final exercise the students again worked together as a group. They put forward ideas for future workshops for the next intake of students, which included suggestions on both content and structure. They seemed pleased to be able to round off the workshop by making these contributions and the leader was pleased to receive them.

REFLECTIONS ON THE WORKSHOP

Introduction

As the preceding account indicates, the leader was receiving different types of feedback while the workshop was running. At the end of each day she reflected on the events and looked at any jottings she had made. She wrote down her thoughts and feelings, and the following is a selection from them.

Some reflections on the workshop process and the students

The aim of the workshop was to provide opportunities for the student health visitors to learn more about skills in communication. The leader was particularly interested to know whether the students had found the workshop profitable to them as individuals, and how they regarded active learning in a workshop, an experience which was new to many of them.

After the somewhat tentative start the workshop as a whole had been lively and energetic. The students had put a lot of work and enthusiasm into it. Group members knew one another and worked well together as teachers and learners. This may have been one reason why they had felt it safe enough not only to seek information from one another but also from time to time to express frankly differences of opinion, and some strong feelings. It seemed that assurance of confidentiality also contributed to a climate of safety; at one point, two of the students checked out with the leader that particular remarks of theirs would not be passed on to anyone else, and the others waited for the reply before adding their comments to the topic under discussion.

There was evidence at various stages that some attitudes had been challenged, and some shifts had perhaps begun to take place in constructs of reality. For example, item 11, about different interpretations of the same word, aroused a considerable range of reactions; it would appear that a number of the students had not considered before just how flexible is language, and how important it may be to check out meanings. Similarly, the topic of being too polite to clients, discussed under item 18, aroused some incredulity; the wide range of strategies which health visitors may be able to employ constructively when communicating with clients was evidently a new idea to a number of the students.

There were strong indications from the discussions that many of the students did find different parts of the workshop of use to them, and that many, if not all, wanted to carry on thinking about their feelings, thoughts and practices in relation to their professional work. When asked to write down the steps they intended to take as a result of attending the workshop, there was little hesitation before they produced a variety of ideas.

Would the group recommend other students to attend this type of workshop (item 24)? Members were emphatic that two two-day workshops would be useful during the Diploma course, rather than just one, and in addition they wanted to have a study day about three weeks before the final examination. Taken as a whole, it would appear that no one considered the workshop a waste of time, although, as was to be expected, there were indications that some felt they had gained more than others.

Not all the students were accustomed to the looser structure and greater freedom of a workshop as compared to the conventional classroom situation. With this in mind, the leader reflected on how the students had tackled the exercises used at different stages in the workshop. It certainly seemed important to pay attention to grading the transition towards less structure and greater freedom. For example, she noted that the students on the first day had been hesitant about spontaneous role play, but had responded very readily to written instructions, with which they were more familiar, in the exercise on non-verbal communication (item 4). This had appeared to help to boost confidence, which, in its turn, was important in aiding the transition from surface learning to exploring thoughts and feelings which underpin visible actions. The leader decided that in future workshops with student health visitors she would consider whether to postpone exercises involving spontaneous role play to the second day, and perhaps, when they were introduced, to offer a little more guidance in the form of very brief written outlines of roles.

As regards the content of the workshop, once they began to explore the process of communication, many of the students were apparently somewhat taken aback to discover just how complex it is. This showed itself, for example, in their reactions to exercises on non-verbal communication, active listening, and cross-checking meanings of words and phrases, and in the course of discussions on being too polite, and the importance of not letting personal feelings intrude. As more emphasis is given to the process of communication during training, students will come to this type of workshop with more background knowledge. In this particular workshop, however, there was some confusion as this realisation dawned, but also a recognition by some, if not all, of the students that it was possible to explore the topic more deeply than they had done previously. This was accompanied by a recognition that there were opportunities for widening the range of strategies and tactics which would help them to cope with the more varied types of clients, problems and situations they would meet in a community as opposed to a hospital setting.

During the course of the workshop, several of the students said that one reason they wanted to move out of the hospital into the community was in order to gain greater autonomy in their work. Possibly, the fact that most of them appeared to regard the complexities of the communication process as an interesting challenge was in part associated with their desire for increased opportunity to act more independently, and have more freedom of choice in how they carried out their work. Had there been time during the workshop, this would have been an interesting topic to explore.

Some reflections on the workshop process and the leader

There are many facets to the role of leader of a workshop. During the two days it was necessary to play a variety of sub-roles – for example, speaker when introducing the workshop, games player, organiser of individual items, facilitator during discussions, and socialiser during breaks – and it was important to be able to switch rapidly between such roles. Whatever the role being played, the leader was alert for feedback to help her assess the progress of a particular activity, and of the workshop generally, and she used this information to guide her own actions, and to plan ahead.

Many different types of decisions had to be taken as the workshop progressed. It is always possible to reflect in retrospect how improvements could have been made if some remarks had been phrased differently, if more attention had been given to certain students, if a different exercise had been introduced at a certain juncture in the proceedings, and so on. Of course, it is not possible to know what would have been the consequences had such alterations been made. Also, it would have been interesting to have followed further with a group of enthusiastic people a topic which they found of interest and relevance to themselves. What is important is not to hypothesise about details, but to reflect on steps which were taken in their context, and to debate whether there are ways in which underlying principles might be better expressed on future occasions.

For example, the issue of freedom and structure was important in this workshop. The students were articulate, and enthusiastic about their work, and the leader thought it important that they should be able to discuss matters of particular significance to themselves. Sometimes, however, the leader had to decide whether or not to redirect the discussion when it went off at a tangent, and this appeared to be a way of avoiding aspects of communication which the students found difficult; for example, after the role play on the second morning when encouragement was needed to concentrate on process rather than on content. Another instance occurred at the end of the first day (item 13) when she encouraged the students to think further around two topics which were raised – that is, giving clients sufficient opportunity to express themselves – and how the difficulties experienced by a client may trigger off strong personal feelings in a helper. On the other hand, item 4, on wearing uniforms, was not on the leader's programme but was introduced by the students, and the leader encouraged discussion because the students were interested in the topic and because she judged it to be serving a useful purpose.

On the whole, the leader thought that probably a more or less appropriate balance had been maintained in this workshop between freedom and structure, taking into account students' needs as she understood them, her own interpretation of her role, self-knowledge and environmental factors, such as time available. She could not of course know whether the verdict of every one of the students would have been the same. Each individual would have her own personal interpretation of the reality of the workshop. If there had been a series of workshops, it might well have been important to have shared attitudes towards and opinions about processes within the group.

As regards practical improvements which might be made, besides thinking about role play (which has already been mentioned), the leader thought that it would perhaps have been helpful for at least some of the students if she had summarised rather more often at the end of an exercise the main points (as she saw them) which had been raised, and their relationship to underlying themes, such as the importance in communication not only of content but also of the quality of relationships. Threads can be lost and the whole exercise seem somewhat confusing to a student who may be coping not only with new knowledge but also with new learning processes. Even this, however, has to be done with care, for what are the most significant points to a leader may not be for each of the other participants.

If there is to be freedom for inter-communication, then a leader has to be able to tolerate the uncertainties which accompany this approach, as well as the uncertainties associated with the process of learning. She is not exercising constant control if she opts to be a teacher/learner and the students are learners/teachers. It is a situation which demands flexibility. If in doubt about how to move forward, then it can sometimes be helpful to discuss this with the group, giving reasons for it. Such a process of self-disclosure would not be possible in a situation of teacher as expert and student as passive learner. The leader in this workshop tried to share as much information as possible so that the students felt continuously involved. She aimed also to listen actively to what the students had to say, and to maintain a friendly, trusting climate. It was particularly important in this workshop on communication to seek to provide a positive example of a communicator!

Concluding comments

It is in many ways easier for a leader to make detailed plans in advance and to play the role of expert in the workshop than to follow the principle of freedom within structure. If the latter course is adopted, then, as noted above, coping with uncertainties becomes an integral part of a leader's role. It is necessary to make preparations for a workshop, but in the knowledge that flexibility is required on the day, because it cannot be known with certainty in advance how appropriate particular information and exercises will be. Students come to learn. Learning involves change and carries risks, and is associated with feelings as well as with thoughts and actions. A leader cannot know beforehand how participants are going to cope with it. This applies to individuals and to the group as a whole, for each group has its own path of development.

Assessment as to how students are coping can be made as the workshop progresses, and it is possible to obtain feedback at the end of it, as happened in the one described. When a workshop is a one-off event, however, follow-up in the longer term may not be possible. What can be done is to offer opportunities for learning on the day in a climate which is as far as possible conducive to the process, and to trust participants to use the opportunities in ways which they find appropriate for themselves as individuals, and then to go away and build on the learning, if they so choose.

As far as personal learning is concerned, a leader can choose whether to use the experience of preparing for and running a workshop as a learning experience, or when it is over to put it on one side and out of mind. To make the most of a workshop requires continuous concentration and thought while it is in progress, and time afterwards for reflection.

Running a workshop is, on the one hand, associated with difficulties, uncertainties and much hard work. On the other hand, however, running a workshop can also be both challenging and full of interest, and an experience through which the leader as well as other group members can widen and deepen understandings of, and find new ways of coping with, themselves, other people and social processes in the society of which they are a part. And this learning is an ongoing process, for there is always more to discover as we each move along the path of our life.

APPENDIX

Stage	Topic	Type of exercise	Details
Day One			
(1) *Getting down to work*	1 General introduction	Brief talk by leader	General introduction to the workshop
	2 Warm-up exercise	Group exercise	Getting to know one another; give Christian name and adjective with same initial letter; throw cushion to indicate next speaker
	3 Non-verbal communication: feelings	Group exercise	In circle, each person acts emotion and others guess what it is
	4 Non-verbal communication: body language	(a) Exercise in pairs (b) Group discussion	Each pair given list of exercises on body and seating positions
	5 Coffee	General chat	
	6 Non-verbal communication: uniforms	Group discussion	
(2) *Increasing challenge of the learning process*	7 Listening and summarising	(a) Exercise in pairs (b) Group discussion	One person describes case for 5 minutes; partner listens, then summarises and comments on verbal and non-verbal communication; checks for accuracy. Reverse roles

Stage	Topic	Type of exercise	Details
	8 Lunch	Individual arrangements	
	9 Warm-up exercise	Group exercise	'Mixed Veg' (for description, see Chapter 2, page 25)
	10 Questioning	(a) Group exercise	Role play by two group members
		(b) Group discussion	
	11 Talking about feelings	(a) Individual exercise	Completion of charts describing degrees of intensity of certain feelings
		(b) Discussion in two groups	Aim: reach consensus on how to complete charts
		(c) Group discussion	Comparison of results
	12 Tea	General chat	
	13 Initial interviews	(a) Listening to recorded extracts from two tapes	Extracts from two interviews with different patterns of client/counsellor interactions
		(b) Group discussion	
Day Two			
(3) *Resuming the task*	14 Venues for workshop	Group discussion	Discussion arising from interruption to item 9
	15 Warm-up exercise	Group exercise	'The Knot'[1]
	16 Empathic responding	(a) Individual exercise	Rating of counsellors' responses to statements by clients
		(b) Group discussion	
	17 Coffee	General chat	
(4) *Role play*	18 The health visitor and her clients: Initial visits	(a) Two role-playing exercises	Two visitors to the workshop played the role of clients in two different situations; two students played the role of health visitor
		(b) Group discussion	
(5) *Interlude*	19 Lunch	General chat	
	20 Warm-up exercise	Group exercise	'The Knot'[1]

Continued on next page

Stage	Topic	Type of exercise	Details
(6) *Assessment and evaluation*	21 Learning in the workshop: assessment	(a) Individual exercise (b) Group discussion	Self-evaluation of communication skills
	22 Tea	General chat	
	23 Building on the workshop experience	Individual exercises	Each student wrote a letter to herself beginning: 'As a result of this workshop, I will . . .'
	24 Future workshops	Group discussion	Suggestions for workshops for the next group of student health visitors

Note:
1 'The Knot': All participants join hands in a line; first person weaves in and out of the line and round in circles, then joins hands with the last person so that the line has now become a complicated knot; the task of the group is to untie themselves from the knot without anyone letting go of the hand of the person on each side, and then finish up facing inwards holding hands in a circle.

NOTE

1 A number of the ideas for practical exercises used in the workshops described in this chapter were adapted from suggestions in Nelson-Jones (1983).

REFERENCES

Argyle, M. (ed.) (1981) *Social Skills and Health*, London: Methuen.

Arnold, E. and Boggs, K. (1989) *Interpersonal Relationships: Professional Communication Skills for Nurses*, Philadelphia: Saunders.

Belle, D. (1982) 'The stress of caring: women as providers of social support', in Leo Goldberger and Schlomo Breznitz (eds) *Handbook of Stress: Theoretical and Clinical Aspects*, New York: Free Press.

Bridge, W. and Clark, J. M. (eds) (1981) *Communication in Nursing Care*, London: H.M. & M. Publishers.

Burnard, P. (1991) 'Acquiring minimal counselling skills', *Nursing Standard*, 5 (46), 37–9.

Counselling in Nursing (1978) Report of a Working Party held under the auspices of the RCN Institute of Advanced Nursing Education, London: Royal College of Nursing.

Freire, P. (1972) *Pedagogy of the Oppressed*, Harmondsworth: Penguin.

Handal, G. and Lauvas, P. (1987) *Promoting Reflective Teaching: Supervision in Action*, Milton Keynes: SRHE and Open University Educational Enterprises Ltd.

Holmberg, B. (1984) *Adult Education: Students' Independence and Autonomy as Foundations and as Educational Outcomes*, Ziff Papiere 49, Fernuniversität, Germany.

Hopson, B. (1982) 'Counselling and helping', in J. Hall (ed.) *Psychology for*

Nurses and Health Visitors, London: British Psychological Society and Mac-millan.

James, N. (1984) 'A postscript to nursing', in C. Bell and H. Roberts (eds) *Social Researching: Politics, Problems and Practice*, London: Routledge & Kegan Paul.

Jaques, D. (1984) *Learning in Groups*, London: Croom Helm.

Knowles, M. S. (1970) *The Modern Practice of Adult Education*, New York: Association Press.

McIntosh, J. (1981) 'Communicating with patients in their own homes', in W. Bridge and J. M. Clark (eds) *Communication in Nursing Care*, London: H.M. & M. Publishers.

Marton, F. and Saljo, R. (1984) 'Approaches to learning', in F. Marton, D. Hounsell and N. Entwistle (eds) *The Experience of Learning*, Edinburgh: Scottish Academic Press.

Maslow, A. H. (1970) *Motivation and Personality*, 2nd edn, New York: Harper & Row.

Mezirow, J. (1981) 'A critical theory of adult learning and education', *Adult Education*, 32 (1): 3–24.

More, W. S. (1974) *Emotions and Adult Learning*, Farnborough: Gower Publishing Co.

Murgatroyd, S. (1985) *Counselling and Helping*, London and New York: British Psychological Society/Methuen.

Nelson-Jones, R. (1982) *The Theory and Practice of Counselling Psychology*, London: Holt, Rinehart & Winston.

——(1983) *Practical Counselling Skills*, London: Holt, Rinehart & Winston.

Open University Course E355, Block A (1984) *Educating Adults*, Milton Keynes: Open University Press.

Parkes, C. M. (1972) *Bereavement: Studies of Grief in Adult Life*, Harmondsworth: Penguin.

Perry, W. G. (1970) *Forms of Intellectual and Ethical Development in the College Years: a Scheme*, New York: Holt, Rinehart & Winston.

Project 2000: a New Preparation for Practice (1986), UK Central Council for Nursing and Midwifery.

Rhys, S. (1988) 'Study skills and personal development', *Open Learning*, 3(2): 40–2.

——and Lambert, C. (1983) 'Tutorial styles and tutor assumptions', *Teaching at a Distance*, 23: 63–9.

Rogers, C. R. (1969) *Freedom to Learn*, Columbus, Ohio: Merrill.

——(1983) *Freedom to Learn for the 80s*, Columbus, Ohio: Merrill.

Schon, D. (1983) *The Reflective Practitioner: How Professionals Think in Action*, London: Temple Smith.

Skinner, B. F. (1971) *Beyond Freedom and Dignity*, Harmondsworth: Penguin.

Svensson, L. (1984) 'Skill in learning', in F. Marton, D. Hounsell and N. Entwistle (eds) *The Experience of Learning*, Edinburgh: Scottish Academic Press.

A Systematic Approach to Nursing Care: an Introduction (1984), Open University Course P553, Milton Keynes: Open University Press.

Tough, A. (1976) 'Self-planned learning and major personal change', in R. M. Smith (ed.) *Adult Learning: Issues and Innovation*, Northern Illinois University: ERIC Clearing House in Career Education.

Van der Molen, P. P. (1985) 'Learning self-actualisation and psychotherapy', in

M. J. Apter, D. Fontana and S. Murgatroyd (eds) *Reversal Theory: Applications and Developments*, Cardiff: University College, Cardiff, Press.

Wattley, L. A. and Muller, D. J. (1984) *Investigating Psychology: a Practical Approach for Nursing*, London: Harper & Row.

Woolfe, R. and Murgatroyd, S. (1979) 'The Open University and the negotiation of knowledge', *Higher Education Review*, 11(2): 9–16.

——, Murgatroyd, S. and Rhys, S. (1987) *Guidance and Counselling in Adult and Continuing Education*, Milton Keynes: Open University Press.

'Working Party on Management Structure in the Local Authority Nursing Service' (Mayston); report published in 1969, and referred to in 'A discussion document' produced by the Health Visitor Advisory Group of the Royal College of Nursing Society of Primary Health Care Nursing (1984), London: Royal College of Nursing.

Chapter 6

An introduction to working with sexuality

Richard Pates

INTRODUCTION

Sex is one of the strongest of human drives, something that is universal and natural and not a subject usually taught in a formal way. We arrive at our own sexuality through different sorts of learning, through conditioning and experience. So, are workshops on this subject necessary? Sex, despite its universality and inevitability, despite its essential role in procreation, is still the subject of strong embarrassment and ignorance, especially with regard to others. The emphasis of this chapter, therefore, is on communication with others regarding sex and sexuality.

The content of the chapter is the result of experience of having run workshops over a number of years. These have been for different groups, for differing durations, with the discoveries of one workshop being put into the next, so that a model has been developed. This is essentially a personal view, gleaned from experience, and is a part of an ongoing process.

The important feature of the workshops is that they are experiential and are never 'lectures' solely for the purpose of providing facts. They are a way of looking at sexuality, the issues raised, attitudes and ideas arising.

Why workshops?

The decision to run workshops as a learning experience is based on two complementary reasons. Firstly, from a personal point of view it is felt to be a more comfortable method of learning; the degree of personal involvement required removes the distancing effect of didactic teaching. Because of the emotional nature of the subject, a closer, inter-personal style of working is needed. Secondly, this is borne out by others' experience of teaching on sexuality. Dow and Sclare (1982) found that medical undergraduates showed a preference for a small-group discussion to supplement lectures and multidisciplinary panel discussions for learning about psychosexual problems. Bell *et al.* (1979) found that when they were training clinical psychologists, the use of role play and other group activities were important aspects of training in human sexuality.

Should sexuality be taught?

The question of whether sexuality should be a subject that is taught or not has attracted controversy in the past and to some extent still does. This is especially true when dealing with aspects of sex education in schools: should it be taught or left to parents? It is now policy in Britain that the school governors have the right of veto over sex education in schools. Schools are obliged to have a policy on sex education, and sex education is touched on in parts of the National Curriculum.

The question of responsibility and the passage of personal values is highly relevant here and has been hotly debated elsewhere; for example, Steinbacher (1984) and Parrott (1984) provide an interesting discussion about the merits and demerits of this question, especially from a religious perspective. Philliber and Tatum (1982) discovered that a sex education course which increased sexual knowledge neither encouraged nor discouraged sexual activity amongst the subjects involved, nor did it remove the role of instruction from the home. In the area of learning difficulties, one still comes across the parental and professional views which suggest that knowledge leads to action and therefore is undesirable, the assumption being that lack of knowledge leaves these persons safe in ignorance (Craft and Craft 1981, 1982).

This controversy cannot be dealt with in an unbiased way in this chapter for the very nature of the chapter and book presupposes that this teaching method is worthwhile and that the subject of human sexuality is one subject amenable to this type of experience. However, it is also true that when requests are made for workshops, the groups or individuals making that request feel that a need exists and therefore that the request is meeting a demand. It would be inappropriate to use this format when participants objected to the subject matter, and it would, of course, not be functionally feasible to run such a workshop without willing participation. It is also important to be able to run the workshops on one's own terms; the offer to run the workshop should clearly include responsibility for style and content resting with the person running the workshop. This should be explicitly negotiated at the first contact so that both parties are clear about the contract.

What should these workshops include?

The aims of running workshops on sexuality will be expanded later. This chapter explores the reasons for doing this work and the anticipated changes that this will produce for the participants. One question that needs to be raised early is this: can the content realise the aims of the workshop? Dow and Sclare (1982) maintain that the three principal, inter-dependent areas that are essential to any training in sexuality are attitudes, skills and information. Attitudes and skills are dealt with in terms of the nature of the workshop and the exercises subsequently described, but the question of information impinges upon the area of sex education for sexual knowledge. This was not initially seen to be the role of a workshop on sexuality because sex education is a large area in itself, but the educative part of this subject cannot be separated from the passage of factual information, especially where myths need to be explored and beliefs examined.

Beliefs change over the years with increased knowledge and shifts in society's perceptions of morality. For example, Marie Stopes, writing in 1919, warned against the use of the condom, as she believed that male semen had a highly stimulating effect and affected the woman's whole orgasm.

On questioning people from 16 to 60 in workshops, concerning the level of sex education that they had had and from where it came, a wide diversity of answers have been received. Typically, however, it is evident that much of the responsibility for the acquisition of sexual knowledge has been outside the home, or inadequately dealt with within the home, and that the teaching in schools has often been woefully lacking. This situation is changing, but it is still apparent that there are wide differences in levels of sexual knowledge attained by the school leaver and the methods of that transmission of knowledge.

Is sex education not sufficient?

It can be argued that were sex education adequately accomplished in early life, then the training of people subsequently would be unnecessary, but it is inevitable that information gained at adolescence will be inade-quate for later needs if one's role in life is involved with other people's sexuality. The amount of knowledge that can be acquired early in life may be adequate for coping with adolescence and early adult sexuality from a 'user's view point', but when dealing later with, for example, cancer sufferers, spinally injured patients, those with learning difficulties, and so on, more specialised knowledge may be required as well as the ability to cope with possible attitude changes. It is important, therefore, to include an educative component where this is necessary, but this is not usually the prime aim of the workshop.

Why are workshops requested?

Reasons for being asked to run a workshop on sexuality are many and diffuse, as are the ages, experiences and roles of the intended participants. There are aspects of running workshops on sexuality that will have much in common with workshops on other subjects, but there are also other aspects that differ fundamentally. For these reasons, it is not possible to provide a 'blueprint' for running workshops on sexuality.

It is important to remember that we are all sexual beings, whether or not we are in relationships, whether or not we have or have had sexual experiences and whether or not we have the full physical and mental abilities to sustain or understand sexual feelings and responses. We may be equipped to understand sex, but may need help in doing so. Sexuality, therefore, should be a part of a person's range of experience as much as any other experience may be and, as such, parallels other areas of skills training on the one hand and counselling training on the other.

What level of knowledge can be assumed?

Despite the fact of sexuality being universal and inevitable, it is also cloaked with embarrassment, ignorance and mythology. The possible extent of this should be realised before attempting to run a workshop. Having once been told during a workshop that a nun teaching in a convent sanctioned oral sex in 'proper relationships' because she assumed that this referred to kissing, having argued with bewildered peers at age 12 about the function of a condom, and having realised whilst working with 16-year-olds that some parents still totally deny the sexuality of their offspring, it becomes apparent that little can be assumed about the status quo of sexual attitudes and knowledge prior to a workshop. One of the roles of the workshop will be to explode myths and reduce and cope with embarrassment, but the existence of these needs to be acknowledged at the outset. Running a workshop on sexuality can be viewed as a voyeuristic experience by outsiders and by participants before the start, and your participants may have difficulty in being with you from the beginning. This should not be underestimated, and participants may anticipate that their sexuality will be exposed to their colleagues during the workshop. Ways of coping with this will be explored later, but it is important to realise that this is one of the basic and fundamental issues which will be around at the very start of the workshop.

The need for caution and sensitivity

While taking a facilitative or exploratory role (which some will see as provocative) in organising these workshops, it is necessary to be responsive to the needs and feelings of others regarding sexuality. You, as organiser, facilitator, have your own views, which may or may not be acceptable to others, as have your participants, and it needs to be made clear at the beginning that attitudes and personal codes of morality of yourself and participants are neither right nor wrong and that whatever your position you can always find someone else with a more extreme view than yourself or who would totally disagree with you. Dow and Sclare (1982) maintain that 'one can scarcely underestimate the importance of personal values and attitudes in our acceptance, assessment and management of sexually related issues. No man or woman however naive, approaches sexual issues neutrally, each brings to the subject his or her own experiences, responses and values.' Differences should be the basis for discussion rather than criticism. Before stating that which you perceive as being objective fact regarding sexuality, remember that your sexuality is going to be a strong influence on the workshop and therefore needs to be thought about carefully whenever controversy arises or you are making a point. It is difficult to be honestly objective about sexuality without impinging your own sexual subjectivity upon it.

The concerns that participants will have about what will be happening in the workshop will vary greatly. They may be imagined as being wild, exposing and controversial, asking one to do things that are totally out of character (for example, Albery 1984) or may be perceived as a fairly passive passage of information or knowledge, such as in a study day (for instance, Sebba 1981). It is important when organising a workshop to make it clear to the parties requesting the workshop that they will involve people sharing thoughts and feelings but that they will not be asked to do bizarre things which are outside their realm of experience. A fear of the unknown may be useful to a degree to heighten the state of attention of the participants, but one should also be sensitive to the vulnerability of others. A valuable motto for these workshops could be: 'Don't do unto others what you would not have done unto yourself.'

THE AIMS OF THE WORKSHOPS

The aims of the workshops vary slightly according to the group of people with whom you are dealing, but basically are three:

1 *To increase the awareness of participants' own sexuality.* It is extremely hard to talk to others in an honest and helpful way if feelings about one's own sexuality are confused or repressed. By use of large-group, small-group and dyadic discussion, role play and so on, it is hoped that barriers can be lowered and an honest perception of one's own sexuality can be established. This may seem unnecessary, but experi-

ence has shown that people are often unwilling to acknowledge their own sexuality in relation to others.

2 *To increase the awareness of others' sexuality.* Hard as it may be for people to talk about their own sexuality, it is often as hard to talk about or to acknowledge the sexuality of others. This is particularly so if the other party happens to be disadvantaged by mental or physical infirmity or by age. To accept that those with a learning difficulty, the physically disabled, the chronically sick, the young, the old and even one's own parents are all sexual beings and are capable of feelings and responses is not something that has always been generally held to be so in the past, and even today is not a universally held belief. The 'swinging 60s' and the 'permissive 70s' were, if we are to believe many contemporary sources, the sexual liberation of the young, trendy and healthy but not the rest of society. However, even for non-disadvantaged groups the acceptance of their sexuality is not automatic.

3 *To be able to discuss sexuality with others.* This is relevant when a workshop is being run for the benefit of a particular group. This may not seem essentially different from the previous aim, but while it is one thing to accept the sexuality of others, it is quite another to be able and willing to talk to them about it. It may seem that this view is orientated towards groups with specified difficulties, but it is hard to imagine any group of people to whom this does not apply, whether they are a group labelled by their particular disability or a couple experiencing difficulties in a relationship or a friend who needs to work through some personal problems.

The aims may seem loose and arbitrary, but I believe them to be the foundations of successful work in this field and without which it is difficult to imagine the ability to function effectively in dealing with others' sexuality.

Different needs of different groups

When a request is received to run a workshop on sexuality, it is usual for the person making the request to have some particular aim in mind. It may be for a group of people who potentially will benefit from the workshop, a group who feel the need for education in the area, an identifiable client group for whom advice is needed, or a group for whom knowledge is available but where counselling techniques are needed. Whatever the group and whatever the eventual aim of the workshop, many of the aspects of organisation and content will be common to workshops for all these groups.

There is sometimes an assumption that those people in the care of professionals represent only the diagnosis with which they have been labelled and that the corollaries of these are mainly practical issues. With more thought it becomes clear that the area of sexuality is relevant to many conditions. Atwell (1984) describes how rarely cancer sufferers are counselled about sexuality even though patients may have had disfiguring operations such as breast removal or operations such as colostomies that will produce body changes and patterns of behaviour, may have impotence as a result of treatment or have great emotional difficulties due to the impact of illness. Yet, according to Atwell, many health professionals do not discuss sexuality or sexual functioning with their patients because of personal value conflicts or because of feelings of inadequacy about this subject.

Zwerner (1982) reported a study on the provision of sexuality counselling services for women who had suffered spinal cord injury which showed that less than half of the subjects questioned had received any counselling post-injury, but 85 per cent had felt that some individual or group counselling would have been useful for their sexual adjustment. Kitzinger (1982) emphasises the need for sexuality counselling during pregnancy and in the post-partum period. Often during this period of a woman's life there are fears about damage to the unborn baby or religious taboos about sexual activity. This is a time of great importance for the couple, and the changes that occur as a result of pregnancy and childbirth should be recognised.

Other groups may be in need of counselling or education – for example, those suffering from heart problems, those with learning difficulties, the physically disabled, adolescents in care, or the elderly – and frequently the person who is asked about a problem or for advice is not necessarily the person in charge. It is more likely to be the person with whom the individual has most contact and with whom trust has been established. It is, therefore, important to recognise the needs of others in your care or trust who might approach you with a problem or a worry, and the need to be able to cope with that request and not merely be embarrassed or pass the responsibility to another individual.

The differential needs for different groups should be addressed in the planning stage of the workshop. One aspect of planning that is frequently underestimated by those requesting workshops is the time needed to cover a realistic programme, so that when relating sexuality to a particular topic or group, it is necessary to spend part of the workshop on general matters of sexuality and warming up the group, and to use the latter part of the workshop for the more specific work. By this stage, the participants may realise they need more time (half a day or one day is rarely sufficient to reach a stage of feeling that enough has been achieved). Invariably, follow-up sessions are requested.

The following are examples of workshops run for specific client groups:

Training workshops as a prerequisite for running sex education courses for those with learning difficulties

Having covered in the early part of the workshop the issues of individual sexuality and the warming-up process of the group, one then looks at how those affected by learning difficulties acquired their knowledge of sexuality and the differences they have, compared to other members of society who may have wider access to sexual knowledge. Other components of the day's workshop would be to look at attitudes regarding the sexuality of this group of people and the prejudices that exist among them, and to explore some of the myths that are likely still to be extant in the community. Other sessions will cover the sort of materials that one would use in such a sex education course.

These need to be very carefully selected, because it may be that the people one is trying to train have an insufficient grasp of abstract thinking, which would render many diagrammatic illustrations incomprehensible. It is, therefore, necessary that both the materials and the teaching methods for this group are looked at very carefully in the workshop. Another issue that is particularly relevant to this client group are the legal and moral issues related to the caring for a group who are sometimes deemed by law not to be capable of making their own decisions. Role play will be used in the workshop as well, to try to enact some situations where specific help is required either as a result of complaints or problems of confrontation, and this becomes a very valuable tool with staff working with people with learning difficulties.

Workshop for awareness training – staff working with rehabilitation patients

The staff working with patients who are recovering from potentially crippling conditions – such as spinal injury, coronary disease, chronic respiratory problems and so on – often require advice and counselling regarding future capabilities, handicaps and difficulties, and it has been noticed that the patients will approach staff with whom they are working closely and whom they can trust. This may not be an identified person who has training or knowledge regarding sexuality and prognosis of future sexual activity. It is necessary to enable the staff to cope with the situations in which they find themselves. Again, the first aim of the workshop will be fulfilled in the early sessions; the second and third aims will need to be approached so that the participants feel that they can cope when requests are made of them. The feelings of inadequacy they may have in dealing with problems is explored, as is the counselling function and sexual knowledge related to this client group. Even if they are not able to respond clinically to questions, the training given in this workshop would enable them to provide some sort of guidance to the appropriate source for the patient.

In this workshop the existing knowledge of the participants is examined with regard to what they understand about certain conditions and the difficulties that people might have in coping after, for example, spinal injury, and alternatives are explored for sexual fulfilment. One important aspect is being able to pinpoint alternatives for people who previously have regarded sexual intercourse as being the only means of sexual fulfilment. Role play is again used with this workshop and is a very useful way of exploring the difficult issues of being approached by patients about sexual matters, or going to other people for advice about the handling of these matters; how, for instance, a nurse or physiotherapist might handle the first shy questionings about sexual functioning following an accident, or an incident of sexual harassment on a ward where perhaps there is a high level of unexpended sexual energy!

In addition, an area which needs to be explored where the participants are staff involved in close bodily contact, such as physiotherapists or occupational therapists, part of the workshop is used to examine the difficulty of performing what to the rest of us is a very intimate function, namely, having physical contact with a stranger and a breaking down of the taboos that this involves. Although it is part and parcel of the work for these therapists, for the recipient it may be a very stimulating experience in a clinical environment, and the perception of the recipient needs to be examined.

Workshops with people working with adolescents, or with adolescents themselves

With this group the initial parts of the workshop are similar in looking at an individual's sexuality and the 'warming-up' process. However, this part of the work is carried out in a more substantial way, because it is often at this level that there is greater need.

An emphasis here might need to be on training in social skills in order to help socially unskilled individuals initiate relationships, the provision of specific information about factual matters such as contraception, and of an arena for discussion of contemporary morality and social mores (this may be more necessary than with other groups), reflecting a need not to overestimate your group's understanding and level of knowledge. Street-wise kids can still carry a lot of ignorance around with them. There is a need for great sensitivity and awareness of sexual orientation. Some young people might be confused about their own sexuality or may be in the process of discovering their sexual orientation. It is also important to include some educative work on safer sex practices and for all people, including the young, to be made aware of the risks of unsafe sex.

With this group of people it is also very important not to use one's own experience as a way of showing distance and, therefore, belittling the potential lack of experience of the participants, who may be feeling that they are a little at sea in an adult world. It is also interesting to note how attitudes do change, and one needs to keep abreast of the changes that occur and explore with the group what their kind of thinking is and what the attitudes of their peers are regarding sexuality and other inter-personal issues. For example, I have found that girls' attitudes to the importance of virginity are different when the views of present-day 16- to 18-year-olds are compared to those who were in late adolescence twenty to thirty years ago. This type of group may have greater inhibitions at the outset, but, once those initial fears are calmed, provide a very stimulating group.

These three illustrations show the need to think about the client group and integrate parts of a programme which may need to be designed specifically for this group. It may also be important to vary the depth and pace of the workshop with respect to the experience and background of the participants. If groups of individuals are well acquainted with one another and are vastly experienced in their client group, they may take to things more quickly and easily than a group who are generally strangers and new to their chosen field of work.

PRACTICAL ASPECTS OF THE WORKSHOP

The success of the workshop will depend partly on careful planning. Not only is the programme an important factor, but the practical aspects of organisation that are carried out beforehand are also crucial.

Space and materials

Because of the potentially threatening nature of the subject, efforts should be made to ensure that the participants' room is as comfortable as possible and all necessary services are provided. Rooms should be adequately heated, of a sufficient size to allow for breaking up into small groups, or with the provision of extra rooms for this purpose, carpeted if possible, as at some stage the participants may be required to sit or lie on the floor and be free from the distraction of other activities in the vicinity. Rooms should also be private and not overlooked by other people.

Materials need to be provided such as large flip-charts, felt pens, overhead projectors, pencils, papers and feedback material. These may seem obvious, but their omission does provide a source of some difficulty!

Meal breaks

Provision of tea and coffee for morning breaks (and the facility for people to smoke during these breaks if they so wish) is important so that the participants do not have to break up and go elsewhere for refreshment. If the workshop is for a whole day, then lunch should be provided and brought to the site, or participants could be asked to bring lunch with them or asked to provide some food for a communal lunch. It is important to have lunch provided on site by whichever means, so that your group stays together through lunch and maintains the cohesion that has been established during the morning and is not distracted by other matters such as shopping or work at lunchtime! This may seem trivial, but means that re-starting the afternoon session is easier if the cohesion of the morning is still present.

Duration

It will probably be found that it is not worthwhile to run a workshop on the basis of less than one day's duration, for it takes some time at the beginning to get the group relaxed and into the subject, and a three-hour period is not really long enough to cover an adequate amount of material. If a half-day session is in the afternoon, people come from work thinking of work and if it is in the morning, they will have appointments to go to and they will lose concentration by the end of the session. A full day is probably the minimum time necessary for a successful workshop. Participants should be asked to keep the whole day free and not expect to work after the workshop.

Group size

When a decision has been made on the practical aspects of space and equipment, the number in the group needs to be determined and the programme provided. It is important that the group is of a size that is comfortable both from the organisers' point of view and that of the participants. A group of ten to twelve is probably the optimum number, a number that is large enough to break into small groups and dyads, which can be re-formed into new groupings several times, and small enough for participants to feel identifiable as a group and for a cohesion to be established. It is also difficult with larger groups to remember names of people just introduced, and to ensure that all participants are heard and seen, not just pushed into the background by more forceful members. An upper limit of sixteen group members has been found to work, but this is more difficult than a smaller group.

Programme

The programme should be clearly defined well before the day so that the day hangs together coherently and there is adequate spare material if any part of the day falls flat or finishes before its allotted time. In practice this rarely happens, but one needs to be sure that material is available. This also means the day should be sufficiently flexible to allow for developments that occur during the sessions. To this end it is advantageous not to issue a programme in advance other than to discuss with the agency requesting the workshop what the general topics will be. It is not realistic to have the content dictated to a workshop facilitator, for it is the facilitator who is providing the expertise. By having the programme clearly in mind and also only broadly outlined in the minds of the participants, it will give flexibility and will not create too much anxiety for the participants before the day of the workshop. Even the choice of title is important, to be sufficiently flexible and non-threatening and acceptable to those funding the day! It should also reflect the relationship and emotional aspect of sexuality, and not just the physical aspects of this subject.

THE WORKSHOP

The following is a plan or schedule for the workshop based on several that have taken place. It follows a general outline and would be adapted as necessary to particular client groups. In planning the workshop, cognisance should be taken of the needs of the group for whom the workshop is intended. Although the workshop follows a general model, inevitably individual and group needs should be recognised. It is not intended to be a sexual instruction course or to be a training course for those involved in sex therapy. Intended participants are those whose daily work involves contact with others when sexuality may be an issue, or in the case, for example, of adolescents, of a self-awareness process. The format has proved successful in so far as the feedback received after the workshop has indicated that the purposes of the workshop have been achieved.

The day starts with an introduction by the facilitators of themselves, explaining who they are, what they do and their interest in the subject of sexuality. The length of time taken with introductions should be sufficient to allow participants to settle and feel at home in their surroundings. This is an important stage to be achieved in a comfortable manner, for at this point the facilitators will feel a degree of anxiety, thinking about the way the day will unfold and the possible pitfalls that may occur during the day. The participants will also feel anxious because of the uncertainty about what the day will produce and the sharing of intimacy with strangers. Although the purpose of the day will be to explore, confront and provoke discussions – and for this a degree of psychological arousal will be beneficial – it is necessary to reassure the participants who feel most threatened at this point about the non-threatening nature of the facilitators! Because of the difficult nature of the subject, participants are also told at this stage that they may have access to the facilitators after the workshop, in the event of the need to discuss items or difficulties that have arisen from the workshop. This is done via a work telephone number.

Following the introduction of themselves, one of the facilitators will talk briefly about the need for the interchange of the day to be kept confidential within the group. They will offer the hope that what will be learnt will be of use to the participants, but given the honesty that people are being asked to offer, the corollary is that this degree of mutual confidentiality should be maintained after the group has dispersed. Participants are also told that they will be encouraged to discuss, argue and challenge anyone, including the facilitators, but their respect for others' views is requested. Given the widely differing backgrounds and experience of participants, this needs to be reinforced. Facilitators especially need to be non-judgemental.

The participants are then asked to introduce themselves and to say a little about themselves as a way of introduction. This is done with one proviso: that everyone present will use forenames during this day and that any individual's rank will be disregarded for the day. This is important where one is working with a group of staff some of whom supervise or are employees of the others. This is the one strict rule that is laid down by the facilitators, to ensure that rank does not inhibit the processes of the day. The introductions are done by each person introducing the person next to them and then themselves in a cumulative fashion, so that the last person has to introduce the whole group, having had most names already rehearsed. This is a useful exercise for remembering names but also to introduce a level of humour where some recall of names becomes difficult and thus acts as another ice-breaker.

By this stage (which will have taken about 10 to 15 minutes) the participants still have little idea of what the day will have to offer and how threatening it will be, other than its title and statements about confidentiality. The participants are asked to divide into couples and discuss with each other their anxieties and expectations about the day. They are asked to state what they think will be covered in the day, what they would like to have covered and what they are worried about. The couples are then asked to report back to the group about the thoughts expressed by their partners. This exercise serves several important purposes. Firstly, it introduces the informal, discursive style of the day and makes people participate immediately. Secondly, it allows people to express their fears and vulnerabilities openly so that these can be acknowledged. Thirdly, it allows them to see that their fears, far from being idiosyncratic, are shared by the majority of the group and therefore illustrate a natural anxiety. Fourthly, it provides feedback for the facilitators about the state of thinking and anxiety of the participants. And finally, it gives an indication as to what the participants are expecting in terms of content.

The concerns that are usually expressed are about the need for self-disclosure of sexual activity or opinions, and the content is usually anticipated as being an acquisition of greater knowledge regarding sexuality. The facilitators can then use this material to respond to the participants' expectations and to voice their own expectations and anxieties about the day. The emphasis of the response is that no individual will be put in a position of self-disclosure unless that is comfortable; that no one will be coerced into doing anything they do not wish to do; and that the day will be essentially participative rather than a series of lectures on sexuality. The content is explained as being a series of exercises examining various areas of sexuality where attitudes and ideas are as important as knowledge and that the amount of knowledge obtained from the day may be limited, but that it is more important to be able to use the knowledge acquired than just knowing facts.

The facilitators also respond with their expectations. These might be:

1 that participants will enjoy the day;
2 that they will feel more confident in talking about sexuality;
3 that they will question the facilitators and one another, now and after the workshop;
4 that they may feel confident about tackling the problems that arise.

Before proceeding to the next stage of the workshop one of the facilitators issues what has come to be called a 'vulnerability caveat'. This is a statement from one of the facilitators reminding all the participants that we are all sexual beings, that it is a potentially difficult subject for all and we need to explore ourselves before teaching others. The continuum of sexual liberality is explained; that is, that viewpoints regarding sexuality are not bipolar but a continuum; where a person places themselves on that continuum is a personal decision. Inevitably some will be more conservative or more liberal than others about some issues, and personal values should not be pushed as being correct: listen and respect.

The next exercise involves a change in pace, and is crucial to the aims of the workshop in lowering inhibitions and talking about sex. This is an exercise on the language of sex. It is one that causes much embarrassment and difficulties in starting, but once achieved, makes the rest of the day an easier experience. Sex is talked of in language that reflects an impersonal and clinical feeling about sexuality, that achieves distance and therefore feels safe by dissociation. We can talk more easily about sexual intercourse or genitalia than we can use common language and by doing so we talk at a different level than we would if talking to spouse, lovers or other intimates. If as an individual you are approached by another with a request for help on a matter of sexuality, or if that need is perceived, it may be inappropriate to talk in a different code of language to that person. Therefore, it is important to be able to use the same language as the person with whom one is working, although, of course, it is not an issue that should be forced unnaturally.

The main aims of the exercise are as stated; lowering inhibitions about discussion of sex and using vernacular language tends to do this quickly and also to introduce the idea of the need to understand other people's phraseology about sexuality. This also acts as an ice-breaker and gets participants talking to one another.

The participants are divided into small groups of three or four people, and each group is given a large piece of paper, A1 size, and a felt pen. The paper is divided into four columns and the columns are headed 'Male genitalia', 'Female genitalia', 'Sexual intercourse' and 'Masturbation'. The groups are then given 15 minutes to write down as many words they can think of for each column. When this is completed, the groups then place the sheets of paper in the centre of the floor or on the walls and the groups then circulate to look at one another's work. Experience has shown that more than twenty-five words may be produced for the first three columns and slightly fewer for the fourth. It is interesting to note that with each new group, new words or phrases unknown to the group facilitators are produced! Feedback follows, and discussion, which is useful in terms of people's feelings about certain words and the way that the language of sex is often used in a derogatory way, especially towards women. This is one exercise that has been found to break down inhibitions and enables the rest of the day to be more relaxed.

It is useful at this point to discuss what sexuality means, as this is a workshop on sexuality and we have not yet defined it. It is up to the participants to provide a definition which will produce a broad, wide-ranging discussion which may include the emotional, the biological, the physical or the biochemical bases of sexuality. It is unlikely that consensus will be reached, but the issue needs to be discussed and chaired by the facilitators.

Bancroft (1989) says that the characteristic of human sexuality which sets it most clearly apart from that of most other animals is its relative separation from reproduction. He adds that for him human sexuality is an enigma or riddle, despite twenty-five years of studying human sexual behaviour.

The next exercise consists of an examination of viewpoints on sexuality. This is prefaced by a discussion about how we acquire a knowledge of sexuality and how potentially biasing the effects of jokes, stories, books, films, TV, siblings, friends, pornography and so on can be in describing sexuality to someone with little knowledge or experience. Too often it appears that sexuality is portrayed in an unrealistic and often sexist light and without any emotional relevance. Two passages are read to the participants; the passages remain unidentified at the beginning; at the end of each passage, participants are asked to write down their first thoughts about the passages, the relevance of this to their own experience, and they are also asked to guess whether the authors are male or female. The passages can be selected from many different sources that illustrate some area of explicit sexuality. Two that have been used very successfully are *The French Lieutenant's Woman*, pages 303–4 (Fowles 1969), the section describing the seduction of Sarah Woodruff, and a section of a short story by Anais Nin, 'The Veiled Woman', from the *Delta of Venus*, pages 88–90 (Nin 1977), which describes the erotic seduction of a man by a mysterious woman. The use of these extracts illustrates a diverse portrayal of sexuality, the difference in perspective when seen from a male or female point of view and the statements of sexuality stripped of romanticism. The styles of writing are oddly balanced in that the majority of participants identify the first extract as being written by a woman and the second by a man, whereas the reverse is true. This is a useful point to make about expectations of sexuality.

Another way of using this exercise, although it requires a good deal of preparation, is to use video clips. By having a range of situations on video-tape showing portrayals of sexual encounters, from the coy and clothed where sex is merely suggested, via non-explicit but erotic engagements and more explicit erotic encounters through to explicit couplings. The range and number of these can be varied, but facilitators need to be aware of the possible offensiveness of showing explicit material to some groups, even if it is done to illustrate media portrayal of sex. The need is for a variety of different portrayals of sexual behaviour rather than the desire to shock.

The discussion that follows this can be led according to the comments produced but will make people think about sexuality, and the facilitating commentary can be used regarding whether the portrayal is realistic and whether this builds up false views on sexuality. The fact that fiction often ignores the practical aspects of sex can be introduced here.

By the end of this first session and a welcome coffee break, we have covered initial thoughts, broken down some taboos on language, discovered viewpoints on sexuality and had people talking freely about sexuality.

The second session involves the preparation of a 'continuum of acceptability' generated by the whole group. A series of strips of card 50 centimetres by 5 centimetres are prepared. On each strip is written clearly in large letters one of the range of sexual behaviours, activities or orientations. For example, marriage, pre-marital sex, masturbation, pornography, oral sex, anal sex, homosexuality, bestiality, extra-marital relationships, prostitution and so on. Each participant, including the facilitators, is given one card at random. A space is created on the floor about 3 metres long, and at one end the word 'acceptable' is placed on the card and at the other end the word 'unacceptable'. Participants are then asked to read out the word on their card, define what they think it means and then place it where they wish between the two ends of the continuum. After all the cards have been placed, each participant has the opportunity to move one card and to explain why they wanted it moved.

The result is a continuum of acceptable or unacceptable practices which will generate much discussion. It will also clearly illustrate the range of opinions in the group and the fact that we all hold strong beliefs about something related to sexuality. It is important that the facilitators are firm in controlling the exercise, allowing each person their opinion and ensuring that the continuum stands as constructed.

Before a break for lunch the group should be asked whether there are any issues that need resolving before the afternoon session. After the lunch break, before starting on the afternoon session, an energiser game is used to reactivate participants, after their lunch. This is a game requiring energetic activity for about 10 minutes.

The afternoon is divided into two sessions, the first being a role-play session and the second a whole-group discussion. The content of the role-play session will vary greatly with the type of group at the workshop. If, for example, the group is a single professional group, then at this stage the work will be orientated towards their field of work.

When working with people who work with others who have learning difficulties, scenes are devised which are typical of confrontation situations and participants are required to role play these in groups of three or four people. Different roles are given to people by means of descriptions of the roles being played and their perception of the situation. Each individual is given a slightly different script which replicates the sort of position found in this area. Situations such as discussions about the rights of individuals to masturbate or inappropriate handling of sexual parts by others are the sort of scenes that are role played.

With adolescents, the role play would be more appropriately linked with assertiveness training and courting ritual. By using cross-gender roles here it can help to facilitate understanding of the other's gender role in these sort of situations. For example, a girl would be asked to try to ask a boy out, which may be much against their cultural norms.

The role playing of telling parents about a teenage pregnancy or requesting advice at a Family Planning Clinic are also typical.

With other professional groups the role plays would be devised to cover areas mentioned before the workshop as being of relevance. These are usually situations that are understood to be difficult, and often follow a counselling mode for discussion of sexual problems. Usually only one or two scenes can be role played in the time and are done in groups of three or four with all group members involved or with observers feeding back information to the group.

With all the role plays great care is needed to establish the scene properly before the start. Ensure that people are in role and take it seriously. This is only achieved by explaining the point of the exercise before the start and the necessity for approaching it seriously. It is necessary to discuss the problem with the group whilst still in role so as to understand the impact of the role and feelings it generated, and also to give adequate debriefing at the end to ensure that participants are out of role.

Another method of using situations similar to role playing is to use a carousel exercise. Dixon and Gordon (1987) describe using this exercise in sexuality workshops. The group is divided into two sub-groups, A and B. The chairs for group A are placed in a ring facing outwards, with the chairs for group B each facing one of the chairs in the inner circle. We thus have two concentric circles of chairs, the inner ring facing the outer ring. Each participant is asked to think of a question or situation that they find difficult. This may be related to advice about sexual practices, how to tell a parent of one's sexual orientation, tell a partner that one has acquired a sexually transmitted disease. Group A in the inner circle first asks their question to the person from group B opposite them. Five minutes is allowed and then 2 minutes for the respondent to give feedback. The outer circle then moves around clockwise one chair and faces a new question from the new face opposite them. After four questions the groups change places, and it is time for group B to ask the questions, and the process is repeated.

The aim of the exercise is to air difficult questions, to be faced with some difficult situations and see different responses to these situations. This is done in a safe and controlled environment.

For the final session, which will be the last hour of the day, all the participants and facilitators come together in a group to discuss anything that has come up in the day in a large forum, argue controversial matters, discuss what relevance this has to their professional groups, what is needed in the future and what has been inadequate about the day. At the finish, the participants are asked to complete a feedback form, and the group is closed promptly at the end of the allotted time.

This is a description of a one-day workshop. If this were continued over two days, then the afternoon sessions would be greatly expanded to include more relevant work for that group, especially in the area of role play and discussion of professional matters to do with sexuality in a group format.

Variations can be made to this format, with the use of different exercises or the inclusion of other aspects. But the general format tends to be used as an outline for any group.

OTHER ISSUES RELATED TO THE WORKSHOP

Facilitation

Experience has shown that it is preferable for the workshop to be led by two people rather than one. It has been found that when running workshops with one facilitator it imposes a lot of stress on that person who has to be aware of all of the dynamics of the group and also to cover all the aspects throughout the day. However, it is difficult to share the facilitation of the group with another person unless that person is sufficiently familiar with one's style of working. Effective running of a workshop with a co-facilitator requires those two people to be able to understand each other's viewpoint and to be able to back the other up where that is necessary. The ideal combination for a workshop on sexuality is to have one male and one female facilitator, especially when these two are comfortable with each other's style and are well known to each other. This allows for a complementary viewpoint to be present with regard to issues of gender, or where it may be felt by participants that because of the nature of the topic a person of one sex or the other is more appropriate to deal with a certain matter. When two people work together and their style is familiar to each other, then they can act as an important source of support for each other throughout the day and afterwards, providing feedback about each other's performance during the day. A single-handed group facilitator does not have this level of support or feedback regarding his or her performance.

As previously stated, it is of course important to try to remain objective throughout the workshop, although it may be advantageous at times to adopt a role or position in order to facilitate discussion or provide a controversial viewpoint. This is something that must be gauged from the mood of the workshop and the level of functioning of the participants. The ability of the facilitators to function effectively is soon gauged by the feedback obtained from the participants as the day progresses. As in all workshops or groups, there are times when much energy needs to be involved in facilitating development of the process, and group facilitators must, therefore, be aware of the climate of the group as it progresses. Facilitators must also be sensitive to issues that may be present as undercurrents of discomfort of workshop members which may not have been voiced or acknowledged. Although an outline is provided for the workshop, it is important to establish that where issues become important, or a lot of discussion is taking place, the programme may need to be changed in order to accommodate what is important to the participants. On the other hand, it is of course important to avoid being side-tracked unnecessarily with other issues.

In a workshop on sexuality it is likely that the subject of child sexual abuse will be raised. This subject is raised increasingly, and it may well be that one of the participants was abused as a child. Clearly, this needs to be handled sensitively, and the group needs opportunity to air its feelings. However, it is important that this does not take over the rest of the day, as can easily happen. If a participant is distressed, then they should be allowed space to talk privately and facilitators need to be aware of possible referral routes for specialist help if necessary.

It is important to realise that in running a workshop on sexuality, one's own sexuality may be questioned and direct personal questions asked. Although this is unlikely to happen, one must be prepared for this eventuality, and if the subject matter is one that provokes discomfort then facilitation of the group should not be attempted.

Another issue that needs to be addressed is the subject of HIV. This is, and must be, a major area of concern regarding sexuality. For those working in the sexuality, drugs or HIV field, it needs to be addressed separately and at greater length, but it should be part of this day in the sense of being acknowledged and some notion of safe sex discussed. This in itself means that the facilitators need to be aware of risk behaviours and familiar with safer sex techniques and have the ability to discuss the issues.

Controversies

The subject of sexuality is one which inevitably is controversial. It is likely that nearly every area of sexuality has become controversial at some time, and one has to remember that at the beginning of this century, matters such as masturbation were very controversial. Masturbation was thought by some to produce insanity and to be a very deviant form of sexual activity (Godfrey 1901). That controversy is probably generally resolved, in that masturbation is no longer felt to lead to insanity, but in some areas it is still a controversial matter. In working with people with learning difficulties the rights of an individual to masturbate or the teaching of masturbation where someone is unskilled at doing so is a very controversial matter. This is an example of something that was seen to be controversial in the early part of this century and, although it is resolved for part of the population, it is still controversial for other parts of the population.

In a workshop it is inevitable that controversial items will emerge and need to be discussed. The sort of things that will come up are sex roles and sexism, where norms and beliefs may vary throughout the country, but one may often find that acknowledgement is different from mere acceptance. Taking on a sex role in role play may be helpful in exploring this area.

Homosexuality is another area which is sometimes controversial. It will be appropriate to raise this subject at some time during a workshop because of the large number of controversial statements and viewpoints that are current. The chapter may seem to have focused on heterosexuality, yet the content of the workshops is relevant to any sexual orientation. Indeed, the specific issue of sexual orientation may well be raised and the facilitators will need to be aware and prepared for this.

In relation to feminism and the exploitation of women the area of pornography will often be raised, and this again is a controversial area. It can be viewed from the position that any pornography is degrading to women and therefore should not be available; or, from another viewpoint, it is an extension of eroticism, erotic art and its use can be seen as therapeutic in sexual therapy and also in some sex education. The issue can be discussed in the form of a two-chair debate. In this exercise two chairs are placed in the centre of the circle and each chair is allocated a point of view. For example, one chair might say, 'Pornography is degrading to women and should be banned', and the other might say, 'Pornography is a legitimate expression of sexuality and is an inevitable part of a free society.' Participants are invited to sit in the chairs and to debate their chair's point of view. Any other participant can replace the occupant of the chair by tapping on their shoulder, rather like tag wrestling. The chair's occupant must give way. The idea is to involve as many of the participants as possible and to air as many views as possible. Participants may occupy both seats at different times of a debate, as the views are those of the chair rather than the individual. Debates like this are good for airing controversial issues which allow for anything to be said, and participants may choose the protection of the chair to make their point.

Another item of controversy is the whole area of sex education and the delineation of responsibility for sex education. This has already been discussed earlier in the chapter, but is one item which does crop up consistently. With all of the afore-mentioned areas of controversy, it is important that opportunity is available to discuss these and that they can be fully aired in a non-judgemental way by the facilitator. It is inevitable that within the group of participants there will be differing views, and all these should be heard. But remember that with many of these items the basic beliefs and ethical and moral values of individuals can be threatened, and therefore sensitive handling of these is essential. It is extremely unlikely that any of these issues will be resolved within a workshop, but their discussion is an important part of the process.

Evaluation

It is important that any workshop that is undertaken should be evaluated at some stage. However, this produces problems of definition in that the efficacy of a given workshop may be not apparent at the time. It is important to try to obtain feedback at the end of the workshop in written form or rating scales given to the participants, and this can provide a fairly instant feedback or the success of various components of the workshop and of the general level of success. It is inevitable that different groups will present different sorts of feedback, and for some groups this will be harder to obtain than from others.

However, one of the important aspects of evaluation is whether the workshop has made any significant changes over time and whether participants' time was well spent in the workshop. This information may not be easy to obtain unless one has contact with the participants after the workshop and unless one has any measure of evaluation for the workshop. One way of doing this is to see what has been done in the area: for example, whether a sex education programme has been set up following a workshop or whether people are talking more about what they have done and whether in the long term participants feel that they have a greater ability to talk about sexuality and whether this is relevant to their current working situation.

It is equally important for the workshop facilitators to evaluate for themselves what they have achieved within that workshop, to look at possible areas of change, of development and success. Facilitators need to be able to get together after a workshop to discuss these matters to ensure that what is learned from the day will be used on subsequent occasions. It is probably inevitable that each workshop run will produce some change in format, in exercises adopted, changed or dropped, or in style of presentation. Changes that have occurred include dropping exercises that prove too threatening, altering format to introduce an exercise at an earlier stage and, most importantly, checking with participants whether they are present through choice or whether they have been 'sent' to the workshop without being given the choice. This check was introduced after one workshop where some of the participants did not know why they were at the workshop or the nature of the content!

Finally, facilitators may wish to use background reading material. Useful among the Family Planning Association's publications are *Working with Uncertainty* (Dixon and Gordon 1987) and *Sharing* (Heather

1987). There is a particularly good book, *Aids to Loving Relationships* (Cassidy 1990), which is an Australian publication. Bancroft's (1989) *Human Sexuality and its Problems* is an invaluable resource book on sexuality.

The ideas expressed in this chapter are by no means definitive and, as stated, are the result of experience. The model has been shown to be successful but is continually evolving and will do so as long as workshops are needed.

REFERENCES

Albery, N. (1984) 'Dice therapy', *Self and Society*, 12(3): 132–40.

Atwell, B. M. (1984) 'Sex and the cancer patient: an unspoken concern', *Patient Education and Counselling*, 5(3): 123–6.

Bancroft, J. (1989) *Human Sexuality and its Problems*, Edinburgh: Churchill Livingstone.

Bell, S., Dickerson, M. and Stuckey, N. (1979) 'Human sexuality in the training of clinical psychologists', *Bulletin of the British Psychological Society*, 32: 68–70.

Cassidy, A. (1990) *Aids to Loving Relationships*, Canberra: Australian Government Publishing Services.

Craft, A. and Craft, M. (1981) 'Sexuality and mental handicap: a review', *British Journal of Psychiatry*, 139: 494–505.

——(1982) *Sex and the Mentally Handicapped: a Guide for Parents and Carers*, London: Routledge & Kegan Paul.

Dixon, H. and Gordon, P. (1987) *Working with Uncertainty*, London: Family Planning Association Education Unit.

Dow, M. G. T. and Sclare, A. P. (1982) 'Teaching medical undergraduates about psychosexual problems', *British Journal of Sexual Medicine*, 8(80): 24–9.

Fowles, J. (1969) *The French Lieutenant's Woman*, London: Jonathan Cape.

Godfrey, J.A. (1901) *The Science of Sex*, London: The University Press.

Heather, A. (1987) *Sharing*, London: Family Planning Association Education Unit.

Kitzinger, S. (1982) 'Sexuality in pregnancy', *British Journal of Sexual Medicine*, 9(82): 44–6.

Nin, A. (1977) *The Delta of Venus*, London: W. H. Allen & Co.

Parrott, A. (1984) 'Sex education should occur outside the family in schools, youth centres and agencies', in H. Feldman and A. Parrot (eds) *Human Sexuality, Contemporary Controversies*, London: Sage Publications.

Philliber, S.G. and Tatum, M.L. (1982) 'Sex education and the double standard in high school', *Adolescence*, 17(66): 273–83.

Sebba, J. (1981) 'Sexual development in mentally handicapped people: a critical look at staff attitudes', *APEX*, 9(1): 22–3.

Steinbacher, J. (1984) 'Sex education is the right and responsibility only of the family', in H. Feldman and A. Parrott (eds) *Human Sexuality, Contemporary Controversies*, London: Sage Publications.

Stopes, C. M. (1919) *Wise Parenthood*, London: G.P. Putnam & Sons.

Zwerner, J. (1982) 'Yes we have troubles but nobody is listening: sexual issues of women with spinal cord injury', *Sexuality and Disability*, 5(3): 151–71.

Chapter 7

Coping with death

Workshops for those helping with the dying and bereaved

Mike Shooter

Anyone setting out to offer a workshop experience for those helping with the dying and bereaved has two questions to ask: why choose such a well-trodden field as death education, and why in a workshop?

It is arguable that the answers to both questions are the same. It is not the words of counsellors that help most, but the outlet they offer for their clients' grief; and so it is with the counsellors themselves. They do not require yet more words of advice, but an opportunity to express the emotional pains of helping that might otherwise prevent their knowledge being put into action. An experiential workshop offers that opportunity.

CONTEXT: ACHIEVEMENTS AND NEEDS

Nearly twenty years ago, the Senior Editor of the American Medical Association claimed that 'dying is being worked to death' (Vaisrub 1974). He felt himself submerged in a tide of essays, editorials, books and journals on the subject of death and dying, overflowing from the medical into lay literature and the mass media. The tide has continued to run. Books are giving way to video-discs on theoretical and clinical perspectives (American Journal of Nursing Corp. 1991). There are complete training packs for would-be counsellors in specific contexts, such as schools (Ebeling 1988–90) and primary health care (AARP A/V Programs 1991). There are even self-awareness computer programs (University of Delaware 1989) and videos (Stuart 1991) for the bereaved themselves. There are specialist magazines for bereavement counsellors (*Thanatos, Omega, Death Studies*) and an *Encyclopaedia of Death* (Kastenbaum and Kastenbaum 1989). To scan the medical and sociological shelves in any bookshop or video store is to be aware that for the aspiring author there is more life in death than any other subject!

The growth of knowledge: the 'normal' framework

Clearly, knowledge of the phenomena of death and mourning are essential. For clients and helpers alike, one of the greatest fears is of unleashing a boundless chaos of emotions against which the only defence is to keep all feeling firmly battened down. Experience accumulated in practice and communicated to others lays down landmarks in the chaos by which 'normal' may be distinguished from 'abnormal' and the paths of interventions plotted.

There are dangers, of course: knowledge itself can easily become a straitjacket. Good counselling needs intuitive freedom to take account of appropriate group and individual variations. Death comes 'wreathed in culture' (Porter 1982); because people have different personalities with different ways of doing things, there can be no one way of helping the dying (Stedeford 1979). The stages of grieving so clearly set out in pioneer work from Freud (1917) to Kubler-Ross (1969) now seem too ordered and rational. They are giving way to more flexible, cyclical models of mourning (Shooter and Hobbs: in preparation) that allow for the normal, irrational whirlpool of grieving phenomena within an overall sense of tasks that must be accomplished, if in no set order (Worden 1989). We continue to learn from families facing up to a prolonged illness where a switchback of relapse and remission makes all models seem simplistic. Mourning can indeed be very complicated (Rando 1991).

However, empirical knowledge, hard-won from face-to-face work with clients, has helped push back some general attitudes and extend counselling to new areas of 'bereavement'. The child's conception of death has been re-examined and a path opened occasionally, through a thicket of misguided protection, for children once more to share in the process of mourning (Wass and Corr 1984; Wells 1988). The views of parents and paediatricians (Vienello 1988) contrast with the views of children themselves facing up to their own death (Lansdowne 1989). Death reframed as a family affair (Pincus 1974) has attracted the attention of family therapists (Detmer and Lamberti 1991). 'Even fathers grieve too' (Bryant 1989), and their reactions to infant death in general (Cordell 1990) and perinatal death in particular (Page-Lieberman 1990) have been validated. The need for grieving recognised relatively recently in such areas as stillbirth (Lewis 1979) has led to wholesale change in obstetric practice. Where their feelings were once swept under a carpet of encouragement to 'get on with life', parents are now allowed to hold their dead baby, to retain photographs, wrist-bands and other mementoes around which to focus their grief, to give their baby a proper, individual burial and to include their other children in the ritual.

The concept of mourning has spread to the analogous catastrophes of divorce, handicap and mutilating illness and to the ordinary life transitions of growing up and retirement (Brammer 1990; Riker and Myers 1989). A clearer understanding of how to help people in crisis has at least been rescued from the devastation of a string of mass disasters (Hodgkinson and Stewart 1991). Isolated but eloquent workers have begun to speak for the 'hidden' griefs of miscarriage (Oakley *et al.* 1984; Ilse and Burns 1985) and abortion (Michels 1988). The once unmentionable bereavements of suicide (Wertheimer 1991) and murder (Redmond 1989) have found a voice. It has taken medicine 400 years to hear Shakespeare's plea to 'give sorrow words' (*Macbeth*, IV. iii. 209), but the lesson is a good one none the less.

Practical skills: development of counselling

Upon this knowledge have been built the basic skills of counselling – the art of establishing a trusting relationship, of working through grief with the client and of withdrawing without compounding the loss. And upon such skills are created systems of help offered by professional services and 'expert' support, or voluntary and self-help groups like Cruse and The Compassionate Friends, Sids and Sands groups (the Foundation for Study of Infant Deaths, and the Stillbirth and Neonatal Death Society), offering mutual support in their distress or their own past experiences to help others going afresh through the same agonies.

The experiential growth in the annual conference of such umbrella organisations as the National Association of Bereavement Services is testimony to the popular recognition of their role. In the United States, the Association for Death Education and Counselling is taking responsibility for the training of bereavement counsellors and for setting testable standards of proficiency.

Earlier questions about the effectiveness of such counselling (Raphael 1977; Parkes 1980) have been difficult to answer scientifically, but some objective studies have been made of general professional services (Scruby 1989) and the role of volunteers (Di Mola 1990). Brave claims are made by individual counsellors for their impact on the hospital system (Weisman 1990)!

The gap between words and practice

And yet, despite all this accumulated knowledge about death, dying and how to help, there still seems to be a huge gap between words and practice. All the knowledge acquired and the counselling skills developed, all the encouragement towards open expression and the sharing of grief, struggles to counteract the increasing 'sanitisation' of death in the modern age.

There have been theoretical challenges to the social barrier that divides

off 'a place for living, a place for dying' (Trent 1988); some workers
have scrutinised attitudes towards hospital-based terminal care (McKee
1988); the whole hospice movement could be seen as an attempt to
reintegrate death into the community. But in practice, more and more
people die in hospital, not in their own homes.

Ironically, it has been medicine's obsession with the preservation of
life that has transferred the setting of death from the family bedroom to
the hospital ward – or, more often, to a screened-off cubicle as far from
the sight of others as possible. The morgue in the hospital basement has
taken the place of the front-room parlour as a resting-place for the body.
Children are seldom present at the death, often prevented from visiting
before death, and they rarely get the chance to say 'goodbye' after death.
As the very sight of death is removed from the home, so it has ceased
to be part of a child's or anyone else's familiar education. With this and
a widespread breakdown of religion and a belief in the afterlife, death
has become increasingly feared and decreasingly talked about.

In 1980, the London Medical Group called its conference 'Death: the
Last Taboo'. Over a decade later, the National Association of Bereavement Services talked of the 'unmentionable losses', with an opening
address on 'Conspiracies of Silence' (Shooter 1991). Educators, despair-
ing of the United States as a 'death-denying society' (Crase and Crase
1974), were still demanding a 'national initiative in death-related
phenomena' after fifteen years (Crase 1989) – and the taboo takes root
in children, in the schools. Grief is beginning to force its way, grudgingly,
on to the classroom curriculum (Gatcliff 1988). Packs are becoming
available for teachers to use with children (Ward 1989) and workshops
for teachers, administrators and parents (Metzgar 1991). Some assessment has been attempted of the general impact of what little death
education exists in schools (Schonfeld 1990), some using a dramatic
criterion like the prevention of suicide (Leenaars and Wenckstern 1990).
In more enlightened schools, intervention programmes have been organised for adolescent groups (Humphrey 1991), although few adolescents
see teachers as a source of grief support (Schachter 1991); bureaucratic
obstacles are thrown in the way of even the most determined counsellors
(Cullinan 1991). Much of the work is done in a haphazard, crisis-orien-
tated fashion with little official encouragement and the individual teacher
is still left to struggle through the death of a pupil and its effects on his
classmates by his own compassion and insight (Evans 1982).

Medicine both reflects and reinforces the general taboo. Death education had made little inroad into the US medical school curriculum in
1975–80 (Dickinson 1981). Despite all the effort in between, a survey of
over 100 medical schools ten years later (Mermann et al. 1991) found
that 11 per cent had no teaching about dying or death at all, 30 per cent
confined it to one or two formal lectures in the first few years, and

another 18 per cent offered an 'elective'. Participation got little further than a class presentation of a 'case'. The model course offered as antidote included many patient interviews and small-group discussion of 'the personal effects of serious illness, coping techniques used in daily living, the characteristics of the caring physician and skills needed', but does not seem to have challenged self-awareness in an experiential way. More pessimistically still, a random survey across the whole of the caring professions 'revealed no evidence of a consensus on the need for death education . . . , no evidence of systematic development of course content or approach, and no evidence of any attempt to integrate training and facilitate collaborative team care' (Dupont and Francoeur 1988). In the United Kingdom, a strong warning that 'only minor attitudinal changes in coping with dying persons can be expected when the lecture is the major teaching tool' (Field 1984) has been heeded by some, more enlightened courses (Black 1989). Little has been done to assuage the regrets at 'a woeful lack' of training for general practitioners at postgraduate level (Keane et al. 1983).

We may applaud, perhaps, isolated attempts to tackle key areas like the breaking of the news of death to survivors (Tolle 1989), or of life-threatening illness in children (Woolley 1989), and at least a recognition that the physician might have some general responsibility towards bereaved families (Schmidt 1990). But for the typical hospital houseman, his emergence from behind the screens on the first night of casualty duty will be the first time in his medical career he has had to tell a waiting relative of their loved one's death. Consultants will continue to pass the buck to their juniors, hiding their own tears behind the assertion that these things can only be learned by experience.

Many nursing schools offer courses in caring for the dying and are willing to analyse their effect (Hurtig 1990) on nursing attitudes. Practically, the results are obvious in the invitation to relatives, even children, to share in the process of terminal care on some wards and a general attempt to 'dignify death' in intensive-care units (Wilson 1990). But progress is precarious, and in more than one major teaching hospital over the last few years the seminars that did exist were threatened by financial cutbacks on the grounds that they were the most expendable part of the postgraduate course! Most social workers and health visitors work alone with their dying and bereaved clients, with little guidance and less opportunity for emotional support.

Inter-agency confusion: the lack of communication

Since a number of caring agencies are likely to be involved with the dying and bereaved at any one time, knowledge is essential in another way too: the knowledge of what each of these agencies is saying and doing so that they may work as a co-ordinated network to help their clients, not increase their distress by pulling, emotionally and practically, in opposite directions. Again that knowledge goes largely unheeded.

Within hospitals, the individual professions may examine attitudes to 'heroic' life-saving measures in the terminally ill (Marin 1989) and concoct a 'prescription for peaceful death' (Williston Park Group 1989). Whole conferences have looked at ethical considerations in emergency department management of dying patients (Strange 1989). Yet the literature is still full of battles between nursing and medical staff (Watts 1990) that lead at best to passive paralysis and at worst to an active fight over the prostrate patient in bed.

Out in the community, the autonomous interests of different agencies in different bits of terminal care can sometimes seem like a battle for 'ownership' of the dying patient that plays out tensions within the family and leaves the individual with little sense of their identity. Inter-agency communications are stretched to the limit and beyond – with appalling consequences. A woman talks of being visited at home for the 'first postnatal check' because no one had bothered to inform the health visitor that the baby had been miscarried (Oakley et al. 1984). It is no one's responsibility directly to tell a child's teacher of a death in the family; and yet close parent–school co-operation is essential if the teacher is to be sensitive to the grief that can so dramatically alter the behaviour of the child and his classmates.

Clients as the sufferers: the loneliness of death

Not surprisingly, the ultimate sufferers are the clients themselves. The lucky minority die in an open, warm, home atmosphere supported by family and outreach services like the more community-orientated hospices and the Macmillan Nurses. The prevailing image for the modern age remains one of 'The invisible death' (Aries 1981), in which dying has been hidden under medical routine; of the loneliness of the terminal ward where the dying are corralled off from the living in 'A Silent Conspiracy' (Knight and Field 1981).

It has been repeatedly shown that adults are well aware that they are dying (Hinton 1980), need an outlet to share their knowledge, and are condemned to an emotional quarantine if the professionals around them are afraid to admit it. Those workers who have had the courage to speak directly to children struggling with chronic renal diseases, the protracted and ultimately fatal muscular dystrophies (Witte 1985) or over whom hangs the Sword of Damocles of cancer (Koocher 1981), know that they too are keenly perceptive of their fate. The older ones are aware of all sorts of cues around them: what happens to their peers, the nature of their treatment, the emotions of adults (however much they may be trying to keep a 'stiff upper lip'), and the way they are handled. Discipline slackens from a simple relaxation of limits to a terrifying abdication of all control on the grounds that it is caring to give children whatever they want for what little time they have left. The younger ones seem to have an 'awareness' of the imminence of death even at a pre-conceptual level when they would find it difficult to put it into words. The children speak of a craving to be recognised in themselves and the seriousness of their illness, of wanting someone to be with them until the end, of real practical worries about life in the family after their death rather than a terror of death itself, and of a need to share all that with loving parents and staff. 'To let a child talk about his death is to let him talk about his life' (Raimbault 1981). Again and again a child prevented from doing so 'shuts himself up in the loneliness' of feelings he is unable to confide.

In a technological and litigious world, where relatives (and perhaps administrators too) measure success in terms of saving life rather than enabling a better death, nurses and doctors wrestle alone on the ward with impossible decisions about last-ditch resuscitation (Letter Series 1990) and their general responsibility towards the 'hopelessly ill' (Wanzer 1989). In the 2 a.m. emergency there is no time for reflections on the relative sins of 'acts or omissions' (Glover 1990). Even the hospice movement, magnificent as its conception may have been in its family approach (Saunders 1972), can become yet another way of tucking death away into a corner of society where none of us need be aware it is there, trapping staff as well as their clients in the stress of a continual confrontation with death (Gray-Toft and Anderson 1986–87).

A generation after Vaisrub's editorial, the Ombudsman's attention was still being drawn in the United Kingdom to the failure of the caring professions to handle appropriately the dying and bereaved (Annual Reports 1980–84). Perhaps, in one way, Vaisrub was right: 'It is too easy to write about death'; it is much more difficult for those words to take effect.

Why, then, has there been such a gap between our knowledge of the dying process and how best to help, on the one hand, and the implementation of that knowledge in everyday practice, on the other? How might a workshop be best designed to fill it?

AIMS AND THEIR RATIONALE: WHY THE NEEDS REMAIN

Recognition of the helpers' feelings

The workshops have been founded on the assertions that helping in any way with the dying and bereaved is emotionally 'painful' and that the behaviour of helpers, no matter what their intentions, is subject to the same defences against that pain as those they are trying to help. Existential dimensions there may be to the professionals' dilemma (Barnard 1988) but this is selling it short; the terminally ill patient presents a challenge to the family physician (Durand 1990) that confronts him as an individual person, partner or parent behind the white coat and stethoscope.

Fear of being overwhelmed

The dying patient demands an intensity of communication that can feel overwhelming to relative and helper alike. It 'can invoke the fear of being drawn into the dying process itself' (Hagglund 1981). The dying loved one is held, emotionally and physically, by those who love them within an envelope of professional caring that contains them all (Gilley 1988). In the 'intimacy' of the experience it is easy for the worker to take over as partner or parent in a very real sense. There can sometimes seem no half-way house between being absorbed into a mother–infant symbiosis of total dependency or avoiding contact altogether.

Our own death anxieties

'The dying patient, the physician and the fear of death' (Seravalli 1988) are inextricably bound together. Helping the bereaved inevitably arouses the fears of our own mortality that we all carry within us. A decade ago, the need to repress those fears was so great that over half the general practitioners questioned denied that they existed or made counselling difficult (Keane *et al.* 1983)! A conference on how physicians might 'deal with their own impending death' (Clark 1990) seems progress indeed.

Memories may be invoked of actual bereavements in the life of the helper; a therapist may be bereaved during the course of therapy itself; clients and the system may even have to cope with the death of the doctor (Kowlerschke 1989). Therapists may be faced with walking a tightrope between helping their own grief through the client and denying the client any share of their own loss at all. How successfully they walk that tightrope towards an appropriate use of their own experiences that can increase awareness of client needs will determine whether the helpers merely re-enact pathological responses in the client's family or offer a model for healthy resolution (Givelber and Simon 1981).

The sense of failure

For those trained in preventing illness, healing the sick and prolonging life, the death of a client can mean a loss of self-esteem and its replacement by a sense of failure founded on the fallacy that the only true hope that can be given is that of cure rather than help with the dying process and its aftermath. For some helpers the crisis may be a growth point in their personal and professional lives. There may have been a transformation in the self-understanding of surgeons 'whose treatment efforts were not successful' (Gerber 1990). Some physicians may agonise over 'hope and hopelessness' (Davis 1990), and wonder whether they should 'always offer hope' after all (Rifkin 1989), or at least reframe 'hope' in new terms.

But once the client is consigned to the inevitable, it is not surprising to find the physician hurrying away from the scene to deal with other patients who are not dying but recovering and with whom he or she can regain lost composure and a sense of accomplishment (Silver 1980). Where death is caused by major disease it is difficult enough, but the helpers' 'guilt' may be made part of a corporate responsibility of medicine or assuaged by a sense of the natural order. The 'failure' to carry a client through a healthy process like pregnancy and childbirth makes still birth and miscarriage almost as unbearable for worker as client.

The death of a relationship

No matter how much the helper struggles to retain a professional objectivity, a relationship is built up with the dying and their relatives that cannot be broken without its being a bereavement in itself. A patient admitted repeatedly to hospital or visited at home over a long period is to a helper no longer the woman in such-and-such a room, but the friend to whom she has listened, with whom she has planned care, faced the pain of illness and hope for the future (Sonstegard 1976). 'The transition from care-giving to bereavement' faces the counsellor too (Bass 1990); the death of a client is a death for the helper and helped alike.

HOW FEELINGS INTERFERE WITH PRACTICE

Mutual defences

Distress, therefore, may be as severe amongst care-givers as patients; care-givers may go through exactly the same grief cycle with all its tasks and attendant emotions of anger, guilt and misery as the bereaved – and against them they may marshal the same defences. 'There is no reaction amongst patients that cannot also occur in care-givers' (Weisman 1981).

Some of these defences may be necessary to professional survival, but the danger is that the care-givers' struggle with his own feelings becomes not simply a reflection but a reinforcement of that of the clients. Defences of care-giver and cared-for become intertwined.

Suppression of information

Thus it is clearly established that sharing knowledge of prognosis between the dying and their relatives draws them closer together in their grieving, but that this conflicts with a natural desire in the survivors to protect themselves and the dying from the emotional pain of it. The model for good sharing that they need comes from the professionals involved in their care. 'A unit where people are quite prepared to speak honestly and openly with the dying' encourages more of their patients to talk with their wives or husbands (Hinton 1981). Changing attitudes to talking about death percolates down through physicians, students and patients (Jeret 1989). But repressing pain by repressing information is all too common and in the process interferes with honest, inter-personal relationships within the family.

We are still agonising over 'the attitudes of medical personnel towards informing the terminal patient' (Pacheco 1989); still exhorting helpers to listen in turn to the words of dying patients that are 'communications not hallucinations' (Dugan 1989); still worrying that 'fostering hope in terminally ill people' (Herth 1990) does not become a denial of the reality of death; still working towards an honest, two-way sharing without which there can be no 'last goodbyes' (Justin 1989). The medics' need to protect themselves, albeit couched in a need to protect their patients, can destroy 'the mutual confidence between husband and wife' that might otherwise flourish and deepen, even in the hour of death (Silver 1980).

Tailoring what is said

Many carers claim to 'tailor' what they say to the dying and bereaved, according to the strengths and weaknesses of the people concerned. Disputes have remained unresolved between those who claim that 'what one tells a patient requires individualisation and medical art' (Silver 1980) and those who point out that surgeons in the out-patient clinic say roughly the same thing to everybody, and that is very little (Maguire 1976). Despite the warning of early editorials that such tailoring often results in 'little more than an inconsistent ad hoc practice growing from the early example of tutors followed by the accretion of troubled memories, avoided embarrassments, deferred decision and the encouragement of those who have died well' (*British Medical Journal* 1974), workers treating cancer patients still run the risk of entering into the 'uncertainty, collusion and denial' of the clients with whom they are trying to communicate (Maguire 1988).

Such may be the vulnerability of the carers and their need to defend themselves against their own distress that the suspicion grows that dying people actually tailor what *they* discuss to the character of the carer rather than the other way round! The end result may be a loneliness of grieving, with staff, patient and relatives isolated in their wish to protect themselves and the others from the pain they would so much more constructively share. The author has known doctors, nurses, the social workers and the health visitors, all aware of a particular client's diagnosis and unable to discuss it, while the dying client, his spouse and his children retired separately to the same attic bedroom at different times to cry alone lest they damage the others: carers and cared-for divided by knowledge rather than united by it in their grief.

How the workshop might help

How could we help? How might we begin to dismantle those understandable but inappropriately erected defences that 'cause more suffering than any other problem except unrelieved pain' (Stedeford 1981)? Stedeford believes that it is the easiest problem to treat because the answer lies within ourselves as carers rather than those we are trying to help – but that, of course, is the very nub of the problem. In order to come to terms with their own feelings, carers need as much emotional support as they give to those in their charge. Since the then National Organiser of Cruse appealed for workers to 'accept our need of help no matter what our profession or status within it' (Nuttall 1977), 'caring for the carers' has become a battle-cry throughout hospital, clinic and community. But such are the depths of the defences involved in trainers and helpers that any forum that does exist is still lecture-based. Most workers with the dying do so without emotional support. Few services recognise that the 'plight of the caregivers' (Weisman 1981) is as valid as the distress they are trying to resolve.

The workshops are aimed to do just that by providing an opportunity for carers from all walks of life to share their feelings within safe boundaries. By doing so, they do not set out to decrease the death anxieties of those involved. Too many studies have set out to evaluate the impact of bereavement training in just such terms and with inevitably equivocal results (McClam 1980). This seems as misguided a view of the needs of the carers as those who, in turn, criticise the concept of the grief cycle for not decreasing the pain of death for the dying and bereaved. What the workshops *are* designed to do is to provide an outlet for those feelings and, therefore, to stop the need to repress them otherwise interfering in the quality of care. Only by facing up to our feelings as carers can we encourage those we are trying to help to do likewise. As with the dying and bereaved themselves, what the carers need and what the workshops set out to provide is not more words but listening – listening to painful feelings and offering a chance to share them with others in mutual support.

The following is an account of the experiences of the author in running such workshops over the past ten years. It will be seen that they have changed a lot over that time in response to the feedback from consumers in a variety of contexts. The changes have been charted, as they occurred, as an example of the flexibility that is essential for all experiential learning. The watchword throughout is that training workshops need to respond to their worker-clients with exactly the same sensitivity with which the workers respond, in turn, to those they are trying to help. It is the model of learning that the workshops set out to provide.

FORMAT: PRINCIPLES

The workshop leaders

The Coping with Crisis Research and Training Group, under whose aegis the workshops were originally run, was drawn from a wide variety of professionals with a common commitment to working with people in life crises, including bereavement. One of the expressed aims behind the formation of the group was the sharing of problems between people of overlapping fields of work but whose angle of approach was different enough to provoke new ideas; nowhere does that seem more vital than in bereavement. Death education is still dominated by physicians (especially psychiatrists) and theologians (Dickinson 1981). It would be begging the question, to say the least, to expect two professions about whose attitudes much concern has been expressed, to instil a more insightful approach! The composition of the training group reflected the social network of different agencies helping with the dying and bereaved in co-operation, rather than one stereotyped view.

In practice, after that initial launch, the author has run over 200 workshops alone, and has had to rely on the individual flavour of each new workshop and the sounding-boards he has used outside to remain fresh, unblinkered and open to surprises!

The participants

For the same reasons, the initial aim was to open each workshop to all those working with the dying and bereaved in any way instead of offering separate workshops to different groups of workers in turn. Discussion is enhanced in a multidisciplinary setting. It was hoped, in addition to personal growth, to foster links between people appreciating for the first time the particular problems confronting those in other professions rather than carping at each other from rival ivory towers. The workshops were, therefore, advertised by a comprehensive mailing list and by posters and leaflets in hospitals, health centres, child guidance clinics, schools, social services headquarters, university and local government offices. Acceptance was so arranged as to ensure a good mix rather than on a first-come-first-served basis. The workshops would be about sharing in all senses of the word.

The author still strives for a mixed bag of participants wherever possible, but has had more often to give in to the demand from single agencies to offer workshops for their staff.

The importance of boundaries: size, timing and setting

In any group activity designed to encourage its participants to expose painful, hitherto well-defended feelings, 'boundaries' are clearly important, and considerable thought has been given to the size of the group, the length of the workshops and the building in which they have been run. The exercises involved (see below) require an ideal of around twelve people. This has meant running the workshops more often than had been envisaged, to satisfy the demand, but the rewards of retaining an intimate small-group atmosphere have been great. The author has occasionally given in to pressure and doubled the number, but this then becomes a large group with all its attendant problems. The potentially greater cross-current of experiences and opinion has been stemmed by the need to divide into smaller sub-groups within the workshop in order to retain any sense of 'safety'. Most workshops so far have been for one day only with two three-hour, morning and afternoon sessions and a break for lunch that itself has usually been a communal activity, but in which the participants have been allowed to 'escape' if they feel the need for privacy. Empirically, this structure seems to give the time and continuity to facilitate emotional expression without the threat of things 'going on forever'. In other words, the aim has been to promote a good experience of sharing within safe boundaries that the participants may then carry over into their lives outside the workshop. There is no promise to resolve all the feelings provoked within the day itself, nor would that seem appropriate. The workshops require a building that has a large enough space for whole-group discussion and a number of separate rooms for small-group activities, where appropriate. It must be easily accessible, free from interruption and non-hospital, non-educational, non-religious, 'neutral' territory. To say that it should be warm and comfortable sounds prosaic, but anyone who has tried to run workshops in cold, barren barns will appreciate the links between physical and emotional 'climate'! Perhaps the author has been lucky with the resources at his disposal, but it is not really difficult to do better than the rushed, sporadic, too large and formalised seminars run in lecture halls and anatomy dissection rooms that have passed for 'workshops' elsewhere (Marks and Bertman 1980)!

Experiential nature: for participants and group leaders

Within these boundaries the emphasis has been on as experiential a programme as possible. Only by challenging people at an emotional level can significant changes be expected (Durlak 1978). That being so, it has been important to make sure that all those applying for the workshop have a clear idea of what they might be expected to contribute. Each workshop has been accompanied by a carefully worded leaflet distributed with the publicity.

One of the clearest messages to those who come to the workshops is that it is impossible to help with the dying and bereaved successfully by remaining professionally detached and aloof; the helpers must share in the pain. And the same is true of helping the helpers; it is important for the organisers of the workshop to set the model by participating in the experiences of the day.

If the workshops are being run by a leadership group, this can be made easier by different members of the group being responsible for different sessions of the day, freeing the rest. One member of the group, in rotation, could attend each workshop solely as a 'consumer'. In practice, the author has more often worked alone and must strike a balance between those exercises he can fully enter into and those from which he needs to keep himself free to act as a practical and emotional safety net around the participants.

FORMAT: STRUCTURES

Structure and flexibility: responding to the moment

How can one 'plan' for spontaneous experience? Clearly, the workshop needs to have some sort of loose structure for members to hold on to in exactly the same way that helping the dying and bereaved needs a sense of the normal landmarks of grieving. Within that, it needs the flexibility to respond to the immediate needs of individuals and the groups as a whole as they arise. This means interspersing the exercises with discussion periods. Talking about and listening to the feelings around is as important as the exercises provoking and carrying them, just as the sharing of the feelings of grief are as important as the rituals of funeral and burial that are a vehicle for them. It may mean amplifying an exercise by another, if necessary (for example, sculpting relationships emerging from a role play) or spending double the amount of time on one bit of the day at the expense of a 'favourite' exercise the organiser had planned for alter! It may mean altering the whole course of the day to suit the circumstances. It will always mean responding not only to group 'temperature' but also watching carefully throughout for the reactions of each individual. No two people will react in the same way. We start with different backgrounds and different vulnerabilities; one individual will sail through an exercise that another will find devastating. People will get upset during the course of the day; we are dealing with upsetting feelings. But the organiser needs to be sensitive enough to individual casualties to help them begin to work through that upset and to emerge from the day with enough strengths to carry on working with those feelings when everyone has gone home and they do not have the sustaining intimacy of the group around them.

General structure

The structure of the workshops has changed significantly over the ten years the author has been running them. The original 'plan' divided the time roughly equally between a three-hour morning session devoted to invoking the feelings involved in a variety of bereavement situations and a three-hour afternoon session looking at the problems they present to us as professionals working simultaneously with those feelings inside ourselves and the clients we try to help. The afternoon session was greatly changed in later workshops and the whole day eventually modified to reflect the opening, middle and end sequences of a relationship and the particular issues arising in each phase (see below).

Both original sessions were prefaced by 'warm-up' exercises: in the morning to break the ice of unfamiliarity in a group that may contain one or two people who have met before, but who are otherwise strangers to each other; in the afternoon to get people moving again both physically and emotionally after the necessary 'let-down' of lunch.

EARLY FORMAT

Morning session: role playing of common bereavement situations

The value of role play in 'death education' has been well documented (Barton 1975). Inevitably it meets with some resistance in a group of widely different familiarity with active techniques, and the danger is to try and cope with that by a long period of explanation and reassurance. In the author's experience this does little more than give people longer to get nervous! There is no better way of coping with resistance than by getting on with it as soon as possible.

Preparation for the role plays

The large group divides into two, three or four sub-groups according to numbers (each role play requires five or six participants), which are led to separate rooms with one or two organisers per sub-group, if available. If one leader is working alone, he or she needs either to keep the whole group together or to split it only into as many sub-groups as can be effectively observed in rotation! The participants are randomly handed a 'script' each for one of the roles, which gives them a brief description of themselves and their attitudes, the other family or community members, the general situation facing them all and an immediate 'flash-point'. This is not meant to be followed to the letter as a film-script, but as a framework which the role player will spontaneously begin to fill in from the fabric of personal experience in his own family and those he has tried to help. In the process, the role play becomes a powerful vehicle for feelings thus made accessible for working through in the rest of the day.

By the law of numbers, some female roles will have to be played by men and vice versa; adults will have to play children and single people play parents. This is not an inconvenience. At the very least, it is a challenge to accepted roles; at best, it arouses previously repressed memories or first insights into problems a helper may have failed to appreciate in people whose responsibilities they have never experienced themselves.

Examples of role-play scenarios

1 A mother returns from hospital where her husband is dying from injuries received in a road crash. She is faced with the decision of how to break the news to her children and whether to allow them to visit him. The youngest child, a boy of 7, has always had difficulty separating from mother; the eldest, 9, has always been 'daddy's girl'. The children's grandmother, who lost her own husband a few years before and has bottled up her grief, is concerned to spare the children 'any upset'. Their father's sister knows he was probably drunk again. She feels he has a right to see the children. Her husband would not want anyone to see him looking like that . . .

2 The 40-year-old managing director of a firm, who has been working flat out to prevent it going bust, has been told by his friend and GP that he has inoperable cancer and will probably die in about a year. Gradually losing touch with his wife because of his work, he cannot share this with her at all. Panic-stricken by her prompting, he begins to hit her around. His eldest son's exam work has begun to suffer as he feels himself responsible for sorting things out. His daughter thinks her father is going mad and accuses her mother of driving him to it. The GP feels a failure at not being able to cure his friend. His doubts about the wisdom of telling him the truth are not helped by his own wife, who tried to persuade him not to from the start. The managing

director attacks his wife, who rings in desperation for the friends to come around and rescue her . . .

3 A young, single girl, whose illegitimate spina-bifida baby died at six weeks old, feels the baby was punished for her own sins. She refused to go to the funeral, had not been to see her in the hospital and does not recognise her death in any way. She has gone back to live with her alcoholic, divorced mother who clings on to her 'baby', in the same way in which her daughter clings on to the idea of hers. The girl has become agoraphobic, despite the attempts of her father to get her out and about. A younger brother was once close to her, but cannot understand her attitude now. Father invites her elder sister to come round with her own, newborn, healthy baby to 'snap her out of it'. The sister's husband, who comes too, is not at all sure it was a good idea . . .

4 The father of a 4-year-old boy, twice operated on unsuccessfully and now dying at home of cardiac defects, is so devastated that he forbids talk of it with his wife, let alone with the son himself or his two older daughters. The elder daughter is brittlely bright. The younger daughter carries the guilt of her brother's sudden relapse on the one occasion she was allowed to visit him in hospital, the more so since she resented the attention he got and had sometimes secretly wished him dead. She has now become anorexic (mimicking the way her brother vomited after feeds when he was a baby). Once again there has been a battle over a meal. Her mother wants her referred for help. But her husband would never allow it . . .

5 The sudden death has just occurred of a grandmother who was the pillar of her family upon whom everyone leaned for support. Unable to accept being progressively crippled with rheumatoid arthritis, she took an overdose of painkillers and sleeping tablets. Her 'child-like' husband has been told it was accidental. Her son, already guilty because of long periods spent away in Saudi Arabia, feels it must have been suicide and wants it hushed up. His depressive wife, alternately grateful to her mother-in-law for helping with the kids and angry that she did it so well, wants things opened up to get back at her husband for 'deserting' her. Her eldest son is busy denying his grandmother's death means anything to him. The youngest son, who was very close to his grandmother, is on his way home from school and will be calling in on her as usual. Who is going to tell him, what and how? . . .

After 5 minutes or so, the scripts are retrieved by the organiser/observers and the role play is initiated at the flash-point involved. (It is important to collect the scripts. Some of the more anxious participants, who might otherwise discover surprising spontaneity within themselves, cling to them like drowning men to wreckage!) The role play is left to run for upwards of half an hour. Contrary to the participants' expectations, this never seems long enough. It does not have to come to any particular resolution, or any resolution at all. Real life is not so neatly packaged; there are no 'right' ways of doing it and no 'right' answers.

Building on the role plays

It has seemed valuable to have an initial discussion of the role play before de-roling so that each character may explain to the others how it felt from their point of view. They may be encouraged to illustrate this further by the non-verbal exercise of 'sculpting' the relationships as they saw them, using the other bodies as clay to move around nearer or farther from one another, looking away from or towards one another, standing above one another or sitting below, in front or behind, holding on to one another or pushing away. It is surprising how the physical tensions created in the pieces of the sculpture mirror the emotional tensions in the role-play relationships. Some positions which prove impossible to maintain physically were 'impossible' emotionally too.

De-roling

The role play is followed by an equally important de-roling exercise. This may be as simple as each member re-stating their real name and occupation. They may then go on to say how difficult or easy it was for them to 'play the role' assigned to them, thus being given an opportunity to distance themselves if they wish from anything they regarded as alien to them. The participants need to stick with the feelings the role play has aroused, but not with the particular part they have played, no matter how much of themselves it may have contained.

Discussing the role plays

After de-roling, the members may discuss how the characters they played related to their own personal experiences. In the original workshop format the sub-groups gathered together again in the main room to do this. If the role plays had been the same scenario for each group, this had the advantage of being able to compare the different ways the same scripts had been played and to relate this to the different personal backgrounds of the players as an illustration of how our conceptions of situations (and, therefore, of helping the dying and bereaved) are moulded by the experiences of our personal lives. If the whole group had stayed together throughout, using several members to role play while the rest divided into groups of observers who were asked to sculpt the role players afterwards, in turn, this allowed the group to see that different therapists will view the same family scenario in different ways. There can be no absolute objectivity. Empirically, however, it was felt that the advantages were outweighed by the unwieldiness of the larger group and the workshops stayed in the sub-groups for all discussion of their role plays. The players would in any case share their experiences over lunch, and this helped to maintain momentum and continuity between the morning and afternoon sessions.

Role of the observers

Being an 'observer' in the role plays is not a sinecure nor is it being a simple distributor and collector of scripts. Individual observers have played it many ways but it is at any rate an active role. The observer may be required to intervene if the role play gets irretrievably stuck – and to examine why it got stuck in terms of the 'stuck' feelings involved. He or she must interpret the dynamics as they see them and check them out with the individual players and the group as a whole in the discussion period. It is important to have two observers to each sub-group; observers themselves are subjective, and need to compare their observations with each other as they go along. They need to rescue each other from a sense of responsibility for how their sub-group's role play goes that might otherwise pressure them into intervening too obtrusively. Their combined presence, however they may keep to the background, serves to give the role players a link with reality and helps to contain the emotions released.

Reality and role play: links and dilemmas

The material for all of the role plays has been culled from the author's casework, with the names and some details altered to preserve confidentiality. In truth, they are such archetypal situations that they are instantly 'recognisable' by anyone working with the dying and bereaved. They will also come pretty close to the personal experiences of some of the helpers; sooner or later it is inevitable that one of the scenarios is a replica of what a participant has gone through or is going through. Since the whole point of the workshops is to work with feelings rather than avoid them, it would not generally be appropriate to 'tailor' the material to the particular members of a workshop, even if our knowledge of the applicants' background was good enough to allow it. We have criticised the medical profession too hotly for doing that by withholding information from the dying and their relatives. But the author did on one occasion drop the fourth role play (quoted above) when he learned at the start of the day that one of the members was struggling with the recently diagnosed, inoperable heart failure of her young son. Whether it was right to do so is a moot point. She had, after all, wanted to come to the workshop, and the general material of the day would in any case uncover the feelings that were so close to the surface and which she wanted to work on. But it was decided that the particular role play was so 'close to the bone' that it allowed her no room for emotional manoeuvre whatsoever. The author still has doubts whether that decision was taken to protect her or to protect the leader and the rest of the group. It is possible that we committed one of the errors we are trying to tackle in the workshops, but we are human. Perhaps that very dilemma should be used as a role play in a subsequent workshop to think about it further!

Afternoon session

The original plan: inter-agency exercises

In the first few workshops, the afternoon was designed to allow members to retreat into their professional roles to examine how the morning's feelings affect their attempts to help with the dying and bereaved – and in the process to encourage appreciation of the difficulties in professions other than their own. Participants were paired with someone from the same or analogous profession, and asked to draw up a list of the 'strengths' and 'weaknesses' of members of a completely different profession in dealing with death. The lists were then checked out with the self-conceptions of the other profession's representatives in large-group discussion afterwards. Not only do professionals become aware of how little they know of other agencies, but they may sometimes come up with surprisingly keen insights that the other agencies had been blind to in themselves. The whole group finished by working together on more effective communication and co-ordination, as a reflection of the inter-agency network necessary in work outside the workshop setting.

Later modifications: developing the feelings of the morning

Gradually, however, the afternoon session took on a much more experiential nature, in line with the events of the morning. The effect of the morning role play proved so deep that further space had to be carved out in the afternoon to work on the issues emerging from it; participants found it impossible to shift so suddenly (despite lunch intervening) from the emotional to the intellectual plane.

Many of the participants will have been in touch not only with experiences within their own families, but also with anxieties about their own death. The value of death-awareness exercises has been noted elsewhere (Hammer 1971). This can be built upon by guided fantasy work where the participants are asked to spread out and put themselves into comfortable positions, in which they are further relaxed by typical techniques.

They are encouraged to fantasise on their own death and the circumstances surrounding it: where it will take place, from what cause, when, who will be present, whether it is a painful or painless experience, whether life is 'complete' or whether there are regrets at things left undone, what things need to be done, and so on. The participants are brought back to the reality of the room at their own pace and instructed to share their experience in pairs and large-group discussion.

The links thus forged between the morning and afternoon exercises and jobs outside the workshops are no better illustrated than by the experience of one of the organisers attending the workshop as a consumer. His increasing difficulties in coping with a number of bereaved families in his job as a child and family psychiatrist were highlighted by the morning role play in which the pain of playing a child with a dying parent was intense. In the guided fantasy later, it became suddenly clear for the first time that his death would be full of regrets for the unresolved issues between himself and his father that had remained repressed since adolescence. Following the workshop he visited his father, about whom there were now serious health worries, and was able to cross some of the emotional and physical barriers that had divided them. Freed from the personal defences it carried, his professional work with the families in his care improved immediately.

This type of day has occasionally been ended by a set exercise like 'the Knot', in which the participants link hands in a chain, the first person of which winds in and out of the rest, tying the whole group in a tight heap which they must then disentangle by their co-operative effort – thus symbolising the freeing of the emotional knots that have been the main theme of the day. More often, however, the members of a group, between whom there are now intimate bonds of trust and familiarity, come together in a spontaneous physical and emotional huddle in the centre of the room with each of them in turn, when ready, making a statement of what they have got from the day.

CURRENT FORMAT

One of the clearest messages the workshops pass on to front-line contacts with the dying and bereaved is that they do have a relationship with their client that matters, and this is not necessarily related to the length of time for which they are in direct contact with them. People in crisis are maximally open to the influence of people around them. Individuals or families who pass only briefly through casualty or the labour ward on their way to longer-term involvement with an intensive-care unit or special-care baby unit remember everything about that first, crucial contact with the helping system. They will remember the exact words that people used and ponder over their significance; they remember what those people looked like and their names; above all, they remember every detail of how they behaved.

For the nurse, doctor or midwife on duty it may be the tenth accident or delivery they have handled that day; for the individual or family concerned it is their *only* one, and the experience will colour their memory of it and the helping context for ever. We have met parents of childhood cancer victims who remember the moment they first heard the news, after fifteen years' follow-up, as if it were yesterday. This responsibility sounds scary, but is partially relieved by the assurance of clients, questioned later, that far more 'damage' is done by those who are so terrified of making matters worse by saying or doing the wrong thing that they become frozen, aloof and do nothing at all, than those who roll up their sleeves, physically and emotionally, and do what they feel is right.

The relationship, then, is very important, and later workshops have recognised that by using the structure of a helping relationship as the backbone of the workshop day. Thus, there is a beginning (*joining*), in which worker and client are building trust between them, however telescoped that may become; there is a middle (*working through*), where the worker is trying to use knowledge and skills to help the client; and there is an end (*separation*), when they are saying goodbye, in itself a bereavement and needing to be respected as such.

The workshop examines each of these three phases and the issues peculiar to them. In the process, it reflects again the links between counselling itself and the training workshops – the workshop participants are also coming together in apprehension of what is to come, must learn to trust the occasion enough to expose some perhaps quite painful feelings and then say goodbye and separate at the end of the day!

Joining

The day begins with an ice-breaking exercise – a tactful fracture of the tension is as necessary in death education as it is with clients (Wojtowicz 1990) – followed by a discussion of the mechanics of the day. Knowing when the lunch and coffee breaks will take place is peculiarly comforting. Participants are reassured that no one has to drag themselves through any exercise they find too painful. Observing can be participating too. In fact, with this reassurance, the author has never known anyone totally unable to take part.

The day continues with an exercise designed to tap the feelings inside workers as they approach new clients by asking them to label themselves with a word or short phrase that describes the most uncomfortable, disturbing or distressing of these sensations and to circulate around the other participants, look at their labels and swap experiences. There is no way of doing this exercise quietly or sitting down!

Two things emerge. Firstly, there is much common ground; they are not alone in their feelings. In fact, most groups will come up with a fairly consistent list: hopelessness, helplessness, a sense of inadequacy, anger, guilt, not knowing what to say or do, the terror of being over-whelmed. Secondly, there is the realisation that dying people and their relatives would also come up with the same list. In other words, the feelings we have inside ourselves are roughly the same as those of the clients we are trying to help. This is what makes the job so difficult!

This leads naturally to discussion both of the mechanics of trust over a long period or breaking news in an emergency, and of where the feelings inside us come from – from our general humanity, our anxieties about our own mortality and (if we have been in the 'trade' long enough) from our own bereavement experiences. It is an obvious step to build on this exercise by asking each member to reflect on an actual loss in their personal or professional lives (or one which would be significant to them) and then to write down the bare details of what it was, what it felt like, why it was so crucial to them, how they were handled by family, friends and the system around them, for good or ill, and what they learned from it. They are then encouraged to share and discuss these further in smaller sub-groups.

This is an exercise that sounds deceptively simple, but can be very painful. It needs plenty of time. The group is brought together as a whole again, not to go over the more intimate details but common issues that have emerged. The group goes to coffee over a discussion of the necessity of support within hospital and community teams for the feelings of the counsellors if they are to handle their clients with the same sensitivity in turn, and of the nature of teamwork in general – the model we offer our clients of flexibility, sharing and co-operation.

Working through

After coffee, the group moves to examining some of the 'knowledge' involved in bereavement counselling, remembering always that these are rough guides only, within which all clients and their particular crises need to exert their personal, cultural and family individuality. The leader offers some skeleton thoughts about the cyclical nature of grieving, of the importance of anticipatory grief-work, of the different sorts of bereavement, of the normal irrationality of both the emotions and phenomena involved and of the essential non-resolution of grief, as opposed to any neatly packaged textbook theories. The group will flesh out the discussion with their own personal and professional experiences and it is important to let this sharing process develop, to listen and to facilitate the discussion just as the counsellor would with a client. Sharing is what we have to offer; exercises are merely a vehicle for it.

The group passes on to looking at families and the way they cope with crises, each in their own inimitable way. A role play may be used at this point – either one of the scripts (above) or a free 'invention' by half a dozen of the participants – with successive sculpting by several groups of observers. The role play is a springboard from which to begin thinking about the way bereavement affects family dynamics *in toto* and every-one's role in particular. Counsellors need to take account of possible resistances to the changes involved, starting from that family's rule-book of the way things are done, not the counsellor's own family background. Other groups may pass straight on to looking at what is perhaps the most controversial area of all – how we include children, or do not do so, in the information, rituals and emotions surrounding the death of adults in the family, siblings or themselves. This discussion has often been sparked by an exercise like 'Blind Killer' (Poulter 1987), which may reflect what it feels like to be a child, metaphorically in the dark in a family where awful things are happening but no one tells them what is going on.

There are many second-hand accounts of a death in the family (Stephany 1990), of the way the death of a grandparent may affect a child directly or through the maternal reaction (Vates 1989), of mother's, father's and child's reaction to the death of a sibling (Hogan 1990), of the grief of a bereaved twin (Woodward 1988), and of 'privileged communication' with dying children and adolescents themselves (Pazola 1990); but personal feelings are very different from theoretical stances. Many of the participants in the workshop will themselves be parents, with children of all ages, and will find their feelings challenged as such. There will be very strong reactions around; even those who thought they had 'settled' things in their mind may be very *un*settled by this bit of the workshop.

It is important to stress that they should continue to work out for themselves what they believe about child participation. They will be asked by parents in crisis how much to tell children, what language to use, whether they should take them on to the ward to see a dying relative, to see the dead body after death, to the funeral or cremation, and whether it is 'safe' for adults to cry in front of them. First-time contacts need to have thought about their own attitudes in advance. There are few generalisations to help, except of course to remember that children invariably know more than we think they do and may invent something far worse; they are often more curious than frightened by what they see, and find it a relief to see that it is permissible to show emotions openly.

This will take at least until lunch, if not beyond, and moves the group on to the question of skills. There is no way that a one-day workshop can 'teach' people how to counsel in one easy lesson, but thoughts can be provoked that participants can take away with them to practise under supervision elsewhere. Many staff groups follow up the workshops with a request for a series of skills days, and it is as well for the leader to be ready for that!

By this point, the participants have been asked to do much experiential work, exposing themselves bravely in the process. To return the compliment, and encourage the flagging, the author has laid himself on the line before the whole group by role playing a professional handling two of the participants themselves playing, for example, a couple coming up to hospital where a relative is dying or has died – firstly as badly as possible, secondly as sensitively as possible. Inevitably these role plays end up a mixture of the two. Amongst the horrified, amused and genuinely moved reactions emerge some crucial points about good and bad counselling, verbal and non-verbal techniques and a warning against any over-rigid adherence to a hierarchy of basic, intermediate and advanced level skills. Some of the basic skills (such as listening) are incredibly difficult; some of the rarefied ones (for example, self-disclosure) are called upon at first contact; some skills (like physical touch) are vital but do not appear in such hierarchies at all.

This exercise can be amplified and put to the test by dividing the whole group into sub-groups of three. Each sub-group is then given the same simple but distressing scenario for role playing simultaneously, with one member being client, one a helper and one an observer of their interactions. If three successive scenarios are used, with feedback in between, each member has a chance of filling all three roles. Examples of triangular role-play scenarios are as follows:

1 A doctor, uncertain of diagnosis, but convinced of a baby's handicap, is confronted by the mother who is equally sure that there is something wrong and wants to know exactly what – in a climate of growing suspicion.
2 A community nurse or health visitor, involved in the treatment of a dying teenager with parents who do not want anything talked about, is faced with a 5-year-old girl who is struggling to understand where her sister is, why her mother and father are always up at the hospital and what her next-door-neighbour meant about dying – in fear and confusion.
3 A voluntary worker agonises over how to discharge his responsibility to a suicidal, heavy-drinking client who feels she has little left to live for when her partner has left and all the children hate her – when she

won't let him near her emotionally and he is terrified that she might die on his 'patch'.

4 A casualty officer at 3 a.m. with a big accident on the way in and surrounded by emergencies, is asked to see the half-suspecting mother of a teenager who was brought in dead an hour ago as a result of an overdose – he, tired and angry that parents can be irresponsible; she, with her husband drunk again and a baby to look after.

5 A physiotherapist in the middle of chest physio with an 8-year-old child who is terminally ill with cystic fibrosis and who she has grown so fond of over the years of treatment, is suddenly asked by her if she is going to die.

6 A counsellor approaches a husband, married with children, with the news that he has AIDS.

Mindful of the time (and by this point it is clear that some things may have to be missed out to allow for relaxed, in-depth discussion periods), the facilitator may be able to set all this in the context of intra- and inter-agency co-ordination. All the empathy, knowledge and skills in the world will not rescue clients from a system that is pulling in several different directions at once. I have occasionally illustrated this by getting the whole group to role play some multi-layered bereavement crisis with different sub-groups playing family, school, hospital, community, social services, police and so on, giving them free rein to get in contact with any other group in whatever way they want and come up with a 'solution' to the situation in an impossibly short time.

Most groups will disintegrate rapidly into a rowdy chaos of conflicting meetings, case conferences, house-calls and police interventions, at which point the leader stops the role play. The participants are asked to sit in a circle around the central figure(s) of the main victim(s) of the scenario. Still in role, they can then say anything they like to anyone else, in role, in the circle – but to do so they must get into the middle, put their hands on the shoulders of the 'victim' and say it over the top of their head. At the end of it all, the players can explain their actions and learn especially what it felt like for the victim at the centre of the storm.

This again is a potentially painful experience. It needs time and should not be attempted if time is now short. It requires careful de-roling afterwards and a chance for the group, having learnt the lessons of a disintegrating system, more optimistically to draw upon their own experiences of good practice or think of ways in which helpers can integrate more successfully in the future.

Separation

The participants are reaching the end of a long day and with it the issues of parting in all senses – saying goodbye to clients and ending the workshop, with each reverberating with the original bereavements we are talking about in which the memories shared in 'last goodbyes' are so important (Justin 1989). They may discuss the importance of 'stage-managing' such separation and how to handle the inevitable final crises that are part and parcel of letting go, no matter how well it is done.

The day ends, as it began, with an exercise. Sometimes I have taken participants, through relaxation, to contemplation of their own experiences of saying goodbye, how painful or otherwise that is for them and why. In their own good time they come back to the present, choose the nearest partner, discuss their thoughts and simply say goodbye. This has the advantage of lowering the emotional temperature and sending participants away in a more relaxed and thoughtful mood. More often, either by 'the Knot' (see above) or group huddle, they prefer to share their learning in a more intimate, highly charged exchange, leaving in an excited if physically and emotionally exhausted state.

RESULTS

Size of the response

The workshops have had a large, continuing and wide-ranging response – so much so that they have taken up more and more of my time and I have had to cut back on them or risk becoming emotionally and physically 'played out'. I remain convinced that we can work constructively with the dying and bereaved, and with their helpers in turn, only by getting close to people emotionally and to our own feelings in the process. That being so, it is part of the job that at some time or other it all becomes too much to bear; helpers need maximum support from those around them or, preferably, a complete break from such work. It is part of the remit to relieve professional 'guilt' about that, but I have had to conquer my own guilt before deciding to tailor the number of workshops to resources and not the demand!

Are the workshops reaching those who really need them?

Despite this response, however, the workshops are open to the charge that they are only 'preaching to the converted' – and this on two levels: the particular professional groups, and the type of individuals within these groups who come to such workshops.

The groups who participate

It is reassuring to see the variety of groups represented at the workshops (from those front-line contacts one might have expected like social workers, teachers and nurses, to those one would never have considered, like the local government officers who have to hand out impersonal forms to the bereaved at a time of greatest distress and feel extraordinarily 'cut off' in the process). But it is true that there is great difficulty engaging two of the most important groups: general practitioners and the clergy. It is my experience that I am frequently invited to talk to GP special-interest groups on a variety of difficult subjects, including bereavement, but that it is quite another story to try and get GPs themselves to attend a workshop on anything. That experience seems to be a general one; GPs seem particularly resistant to exposing their own emotions to such an extent. Researchers have pointed out the need for greater training in counselling techniques and have been backed up by a demand for more courses at undergraduate or postgraduate level at medical school (Keane *et al.* 1983). But nowhere is it suggested that doctors, once in practice, need any further outlet to confront their own feelings. We can only hope that the talking we do to GPs, and the greater self-awareness built into their original training, might gradually erode their professional defensiveness.

Perhaps conflicting attitudes might have been anticipated from the clergy. On the one hand, it must be difficult for those who might be considered the natural 'experts' in the field to admit to any need for personal help; on the other hand, we might expect those who have had to struggle with painful insights during their professional training to be alive to the continuing need for self-examination. The two ministers who attended one of the workshops together illustrated the dilemma perfectly. Whereas one of them benefited enormously from the experience and was able to extend greater empathy to the rest of his group as a result, the second retreated into an archetypal religiose corner in which we were unable to reach him and from which he launched such swingeing attacks on those who could 'offer no hope' that we had to work hard both during and after the workshop to repair damage he had done to social workers already struggling with doubts about their effectiveness.

This should be set against one of my most recent experiences. I was asked to spend an afternoon talking about bereavement with a group of Nonconformist hospital chaplains, and worried all the way there about what I could 'teach' the 'experts'. Taking the bull by the horns, I told them of my feelings, that this was probably what everybody else thought of them and how paralysing that must be. I proposed, therefore, to treat them like ordinary people. With a combined sigh of relief, the chaplains settled to exposing just as painful emotions as everybody else!

It certainly does not seem to be those with the firmest religious beliefs and confirmed agnostics who are least troubled by death anxieties because they have the greatest sense of control and predictability (McMordie 1981). Believers have proved vulnerable; agnostics have been shaken in their disbeliefs.

Some of the greatest contributions have been made by those middle-of-the-road self-doubters whose beliefs are born of day-to-day work in other professional fields, where life and death does not obey neat, pre-conceived philosophies and the practitioners are constantly challenged in their beliefs.

The individuals who participate

Even within those groups who do come regularly to workshops, it is always possible that they net only those individuals who least need them – those who are open and aware enough to attend a workshop in the first place. Perhaps they might not be satisfying a hidden demand in everyone, but creating just another vehicle for the emotional groupie travelling from workshop to workshop in search of self-enlightenment without ever quite reaching it!

Experience over the years does not support such charges. Even if it were true that it is the least death-troubled who attend voluntary workshops (Telban 1981), it would be part of their strength that they recognise the need for continuing self-appraisal. Even if the workshops did attract the 'addicts', such attitudes are just one more form of defence, equivalent to those stuck in grief amongst the dying and bereaved they might have to help, whom we would feel appropriate to tackle in a workshop framework. In fact, the majority of those coming to the workshops have done so out of an uneasy awareness of their vulnerabilities, agonise over the decision to come, and work painfully but constructively through the feelings they knew would be aroused. The workshops accommodate people on widely different levels, but ultimately with the same need. If that is more difficult to handle, it is also more rewarding.

Arousal of feelings: constructive or destructive

The workshops have been accused, too, of deliberately causing pain rather than fulfilling professional responsibilities to relieve it. It could be pointed out, of course, that the workshops are voluntary and the people who attend have entered a contract, the terms of which were fully laid before them in the advance publicity. However, no matter how well the ground is prepared, the impact of the experiential techniques used is always a shock. If the only defence of what we do was that people ought to know what they are letting themselves in for, it would be unethical indeed.

The charge is a serious one and analogous to the bitter complaints often made amidst the anger, guilt and misery of bereavement itself, that those trying to work with those emotions rather than suppress them are making things worse, not better. The answer can only be empirical. The majority of 'pathology' presenting to us as helpers with the bereaved is a product of a grief repressed rather than grief experienced – no matter how painful the process in the short run. And so also with the workshops; their value is proved in the long-term increase in self-awareness of those attending them and their greatly increased ability to help the dying and bereaved that is the ultimate aim (see below).

It was to achieve this, and to increase the opportunities to work at the feelings involved, that I have made so many alterations to the original format of the day; in other words, I have resisted the temptation towards greater defences and have increased the experiential rather than the intellectual part of the programme.

Coping with 'casualties'

It is always difficult to assess where the necessary grief of the dying and bereaved slips over into 'pathology' – where defences become denial, healthy anger becomes generalised hostility, 'normal' guilt becomes self-persecution, physical reactions become psychosomatic 'illness', preoccupation becomes withdrawal from the world. So it is too with the emotions and behaviour of counsellors struggling with their own feelings in a workshop experience designed to arouse and explore them but not to leave the participants stuck in them without some resolution.

'Casualties' are likely to result from a combination of the process of group dynamics and the content of death under discussion. The point at which 'rescue' is needed and how it might be effected is a matter for the alertness, intuition and expertise of the group leaders within the flexibility of the day, but it is not only the leader's responsibility. This is, after all, a group experience, and the group itself can and should be used as a supportive medium. On occasions, it may even 'rescue' one of its own facilitators – as when, at the end of a particularly exhausting workshop, I became increasingly concerned about the trauma of separation until one of the participants suggested that perhaps we were dealing with the leader's anxieties more than the group's! Just so may children occasionally comfort grieving adults, and adults their professional helpers.

Frequently, it will become obvious that a role play, for example, has so re-triggered the unresolved personal experience of one of the participants that he or she needs extra attention to prevent them from being hurt by the day. The day's plan may be suspended temporarily to work with them on this by exploring the experience in further role play, sculpting and discussion. Although it would be wrong (both for the individual involved and the rest of the group) to let one person become 'spotlighted', it can also be very constructive for the group to see that these feelings can be contained and worked through. The individual, in a sense, becomes a 'champion' of the group's feelings, and I have seen the workshop experience helped immeasurably by the constructive exploration of something that would have led to casualties if repressed or ignored. As with helping the dying and bereaved themselves, we do more 'damage' by being paralysed into not doing anything than by opening things up.

More difficult to rescue, perhaps, are those individuals who become unwittingly the sink for one of the more unpalatable emotions aroused in all the participants – like anger or guilt – which the group is only too 'pleased' to split off from themselves and project on to them. The task for the leader is to relieve the 'victim' by getting all the participants to own their share of those feelings. It may be necessary to introduce an exercise centred on that particular emotion itself and what it means to every one of the participants.

Most difficult of all, I have found, are those individuals who become frozen by the experience and are unable to let out any emotions at all for fear of what 'may come out in the wash'. If the experiential nature of the workshop is made clear to would-be applicants and the workshop is run with empathy, these should be rare occurrences, but need careful handling in order not to scar the individuals and the watching group. The difficulty is not only how to cajole the individual out of their corner, but in deciding when to abandon this attempt and relieve the individual of the guilt (so often held by the bereaved surrounded by openly grieving others but temporarily blocked in their own feelings) of not being able to 'join in'. In many cases, that relief in itself is enough to allow them to come spontaneously out of the corner where greater efforts would have driven them further in; *sometimes* it is better to back off!

Having said that, I have found that casualties in general need to be 'chased' to some degree. We have seen how that may be done within the session; follow-up of casualties after the session is vital and in some cases will reveal a need for deeper and more prolonged help and counselling for the counsellors themselves and their families. One of the most striking results of the workshops I have run has been a number of self-referrals for therapy with their own unresolved bereavements from participants. 'Work', for the leader, does not stop at the end of the workshop, and it would be highly irresponsible to go into the 'business' expecting it to do so!

EVALUATION

What constitutes 'proper' evaluation, of course, is one of the perennial problems of any social intervention, and Murgatroyd's subject in Chapter 8. At the moment, evaluation of our workshops is wholly subjective. It relies on the reports of 'growth' in their own personal and professional lives from those who have taken part that are very much akin to the comments of nurses and other professionals recorded in many studies (Laube 1977):

> I think about my own feelings about death. . . . I allow myself to express my emotions more freely. . . . I share my experience with others in my work area. . . . I take time to listen to a patient . . . listen to that which is left unsaid . . . communicate with family members.

Sometimes the impact is immediate (Razavi 1988). I have begun to ask participants at the very start of a workshop to write down answers to a number of questions – what do they most want from the workshop, what do they fear most approaching it, what do they feel they have to give to other members of the group and what would they like to receive in return? – and to re-address them at the very end. I myself, and the workshop in general, are frequently judged by the excruciatingly detailed evaluation questionnaires prepared by the agencies involved. More often, the impact takes time to make itself felt and such snap judgements may not be valid.

Clinically, the initial result is an increased referral rate of families for grief work by professionals made more keenly aware of client difficulties than their own increased abilities to deal with them. Latterly, however, the demand has been for top-up sessions and continuing support with cases they retain in their care. There is less clinging to received expertise from workshop organisers and greater implementation of their own skills. They make strong calls for support from their own professional hierarchies that we would see as appropriate but which may come as a nasty surprise to those hierarchies concerned. It is perhaps significant that I am receiving increasing numbers of applications to join workshops from senior members of social work, health visitor and nursing administration and a scattering of paediatric consultants!

Whether we should have a more 'scientific' approach to evaluation is debatable (Warren 1988–89). Many people have tried it, but largely using criteria which do not seem valid measures of what such workshops set out to do. They do not set out to lower death anxieties, merely to acknowledge them as normal and healthy and, by providing an outlet for them, to decrease the need to defend against them in ourselves and, therefore, those we are trying to help.

I feel that we should not decry the value of subjective report. We are dealing with the arousal and working through of subjective feelings, and it is this awareness that is our aim. Nor, it would seem, is it particularly disturbing that what is learned is sustained for variable periods (Yarber *et al.* 1981). I would hope that the message to be gained from the workshops is not just that we need, as helpers, to be aware of our feelings about death and dying, but that we need to find continual means of sharing those feelings with our fellow professionals in order to prevent them interfering with the care of those we try to help. It is to be hoped that a rash of support groups appearing in such widely disparate contexts as hospices (Hover 1986) and colleges (Berson 1988) means that the message is getting through. I myself have been asked to facilitate such regular groups within paediatric units, special schools and social services.

THE FUTURE

Much future work, of course, will be in ironing out problems outlined above and in further refinement of techniques; but there are other directions beckoning too.

Workshops for target groups

I initially resisted taking into each workshop a sizeable block from one professional group as they tend to form a sub-group in themselves, are stronger in their resistances together and tend to dominate the workshop with their particular needs. In this, the workshops are no different from the ordinary principles of group work: blocks are blocks in all senses of the word. Nevertheless, I continue to receive mass applications from workers in particular professions or from their senior administrators on their behalf. As one possible way of dealing with this, I have run an increasing number of workshops aimed at specific target groups on request, in their own premises and directed to their own particular needs.

There are many dangers in this. Operating alone, with repeated 'performances', one is apt to become a travelling road-show bookable by widespread agencies with appropriate notice, peddling a slick star turn rather than true help. Every workshop needs to be just as carefully and individually thought out as the first; it needs to take account of the very particular needs of the particular branch of the particular professional group involved. Much of the material is applicable across the board, but people giving up a day or more for an intensive and painful experience need to know how they can apply what they have learned to their own work circumstances. They need just as much advance publicity and preparation and the opportunity afterwards to feed back what value or otherwise they feel the workshops have been to them. The itinerant workshop organiser needs close and continuing liaison with the group he is aiming at if he is not to become a hit-and-run merchant who at best achieves nothing and at worst leaves behind him a trail of personal damage and professional disillusionment.

Workshops for the bereaved

As a further development, I have begun to run workshops for the bereaved themselves. Experiences with voluntary helping agencies like Cruse, in which many of the workshop members were recently bereaved, has convinced me that there would be value in offering workshops to the bereaved as a group in addition to the individual and family support they might already have received. Not surprisingly, however, these workshops need very careful planning for adults (Yalom 1988) and especially children (Accelerated Development Inc. 1990). The defences against the emotions involved are more easily rather than less easily punctured, bonds formed are greater and the emotional discharge likely to be more intense.

I have found that they are best run on a two-day residential basis, which gives participants more time and space to work through their feelings with one another and the organiser alike. Break-times become as important a chance to share feelings as the programme itself, and I have spent exhausting nights continuing conversations begun in earlier whole-group discussions. I have modelled the general structure of these workshops on the stages of my grief work with families, with particular exercises devoted to joining, working through and separation, as above. The whole weekend becomes a microcosm of grief-work relationships, and leaves the participants in a closer supportive network of their own rather than mourning the loss of the organiser as a new bereavement to be added to the one with which they sought help.

Audit

In all this optimism, there is perhaps a note of caution; the spectre of evaluation casts a wider, more sinister shadow. All the caring services are now quite necessarily subject to regular audit. In a cost-conscious world, they must be shown to be effective and value for money. The choice of criteria used to examine their work, however, is crucial. Direct, face-to-face work with as many patients as possible per unit of time within a particular catchment area may be appropriate to operations for hip-replacement but not what the dying and bereaved require.

Bereavement counselling demands in-depth work over a prolonged period of time; it involves support work with staff groups too and liaison across geographical areas and units to draw together the threads of help and integrate the clients' sense of identity in the process. Whether such counselling is threatened in the modern economic climate we shall have to wait and see. So often the attitude towards training reflects and encourages the trend in field-work, in a positive or negatively vicious circle. There is already a pressure in some quarters to revert to short, 'punchy', seminar-based bereavement courses and away from more challenging but less 'economical' experiential techniques.

Follow-up: holding on or handing on

Finally, and appropriately so perhaps, there remains the question of follow-up. We tended to see the issue of follow-up in terms of the aftermath of particular workshops. I have agonised over how best to keep contact with those who attended such workshops and evaluate the personal impact on them; how best to sustain the co-ordinated effort of different professional groups that have found common ground in the intensity of the day. In truth, I think what we have really been after is something more: to hold on to the close individual relationships inevitably formed with those to whom we have exposed such intimate feelings and the group warmth of shared experience.

We cannot do so, nor would it be particularly appropriate. Just as those who work with the dying and bereaved have to let go of their clients, so workshop organisers have to let go of the helpers, too. The future of death education lies in the greater awareness of helpers with the dying and bereaved, once aroused by the workshops, that they must find support for within their own work circle.

We may bemoan a lack of 'quality control' (Crase 1980), but it should never become an excuse to hold on to the reins entirely ourselves. Death itself, the final emotional burial of the loved one by the bereaved, the first letting-go by those who help with the bereaved, the end of a workshop for those helping the helpers: separation is, perhaps, the hardest lesson of all for us to learn. But only by facing up to it may emotional energy be made free to invest in new relationships elsewhere.

REFERENCES

AARP A/V Programs (1991) *Spousal Bereavement and Primary Health Care*, Washington, DC.

Accelerated Development Inc. (1990) *Bereavement Support Group Program for Children*, Muncie, IN.

American Journal of Nursing Corporation (1991) *Bereavement Counselling: Theoretical and Clinical Perspectives*, New York: AJN video-discs.

Annual Reports of the Health Service Commissioner (1980–81, 1981–82, 1983–84), London: HMSO.

Aries, P. (1981) *The Hour of our Death*, London: Allen Lane.

Barnard, D. (1988) 'Love and death: existential dimensions of physicians' difficulties with moral problems', *Journal of Medical Philosophy*, 13 (4) (Nov): 393–409.

Barton, D. (1975) 'The use of role-playing techniques as an instructional aid to teaching about death, dying and bereavement', *Omega*, 6: 243–50.

Bass, D. M. (1990) 'The transition from care-giving to bereavement: the relationship of care-related strain and adjustment to death', *Gerontologist*, 30 (1) (Feb.): 35–42.

Berson, R. J. (1988) 'A bereavement group for college students', *Journal of American College Health*, 37 (3) (Nov.): 101–8.

Black, D. (1989) 'Educating medical students about death and dying', *Archives of Diseases in Childhood*, 64 (5) (May): 750–3.

Brammer, L. Y. (1990) *How to Cope with Life Transitions: the Challenge of Personal Change*, Bristol, PA: Hemisphere Publishing Corp.

British Medical Journal (1974) Editorial: Talking about Death, *British Medical Journal*, 2 (20 April): 131–2.

Bryant, C. M. (1989) 'Fathers grieve too', *Journal of Perinatology*, 9 (4) (Dec.): 437–41.

Clark, D. B. (1990) 'How physicians deal with their own impending death' (clinical conference), *Southern Medical Journal*, 83 (4) (April): 441–7.

Cordell, A. S. (1990) 'Fathers and grieving: coping with infant death', *Journal of Perinatology*, 10 (1) (March): 75–80.

Crase, D. R. (1980) 'The health educator as death educator – professional preparation and quality control', *Journal of School Health*, 50 (Dec.): 568–71.

——(1989) 'The imperative for a national initiative in death-related phenomena', *Journal of School Health*, 59 (2) (Feb.): 79–80.

——and Crase, D. C. (1974) 'Live issues surrounding death education', *Journal of School Health*, 44 (Feb.): 70–3.

Cullinan, Rev. A. (1991) 'An analysis of family change as a result of trauma and loss', Association for Death Education and Counselling, 13th Annual Conference, Duluth. Abstracts.

Davis, J. M. (1990) 'Hope or hopelessness', *Postgraduate Medicine*, 87 (8) (June): 22–3 and 26.

Detmer, C. H. and Lamberti, J. W. (1991) 'A model of family grief assessment and treatment', Association for Death Education and Counselling, 13th Annual Conference, Duluth. Abstracts.

Dickinson, G. E. (1981) 'Death education in US medical schools 1975–80', *Journal of Medical Education*, 56 (2) (Feb.): 111–14.

Di Mola, C. (1990) 'The role of volunteers in alleviating grief', *Journal of Palliative Care*, 6 (1) (Spring): 6–10.

Dugan, D. O. (1989) 'Symbolic expressions of dying patients: communications not hallucinations', *Nursing Forum*, 24 (2): 18–27.

Dupont, E. M. and Francoeur, R. J. (1988) 'Current stage of thanatology education in American health professions and an integrated model', *Loss, Grief and Care*, 2 (1 and 2): 33–8.

Durand, R. P. (1990) 'Family physicians' attitudes towards death and the terminally ill patient', *Family Practitioner Research Journal*, 9 (2) (Spring–Summer): 123–9.

Durlak, J. A. (1978) 'Comparison between experiential and didactic methods of death education', *Omega*, 9: 57–66.

Ebeling, C. (1988–90) 'When grief comes to school', video-recording, Bloomington, IN: Bloomington Educational Enterprises.

Evans, B. J. (1982) 'The death of a classmate: a teacher's experience of dealing with tragedy in the classroom', *Journal of School Health*, 52 (2) (Feb.): 104–7.

Field, D. (1984) 'Formal instruction in UK medical schools about death and dying', *Medical Education*, 18: 429–34.

Freud, S. (1917) 'Mourning and melancholia', in *Collected Papers* (1950) 4, pp. 152–72, London: Hogarth Press.

Gatcliff, E. D. (1988) *Death in the Classroom*, Cambridge: Epworth.

Gerber, L. A. (1990) 'Transformation in self-understanding in surgeons whose treatment efforts were not successful', *American Journal of Psychotherapy* 44 (1) (Jan.): 75–84.

Gilley, J. (1988) 'Intimacy and terminal care', *Journal of the Royal College of General Practitioners*, 38 (308) (March): 121–2.

Givelber, F. and Simon, B. (1981) 'A death in the life of a therapist and its impact on the therapy', *Psychiatry*, 44 (May): 141–9.

Glover, J. (1990) *Causing Death and Saving Lives*, Harmondsworth: Penguin Books.

Gray-Toft, P. and Anderson, J. G. (1986–87) 'Sources of stress in nursing terminal patients in a hospice', *Omega*, 17: 27–39.

Hagglund, R. B. (1981) 'The final stage of the dying process', *International Journal of Psychoanalysis*, 62 (1): 45–9.

Hammer, M. (1971) 'Reflections on one's own death as a peak experience', *Mental Hygiene*, 55: 264–5.

Herth, K. (1990) 'Fostering hope in terminally ill people', *Journal of Advanced Nursing*, 15(11) (Nov.): 1250–9.

Hinton, J. (1980) 'Whom do dying patients tell?', *British Medical Journal*, 281 (6251) (15 Nov.): 1328–30.

——(1981) 'Sharing or withholding awareness of dying between husband and wife', *Journal of Psychosomatic Research*, 25 (5): 337–43.

Hodgkinson, P. E. and Stewart, M. (1991) *Coping with Catastrophe: a Handbook of Disaster Management*, London: Routledge.

Hogan, N. S. (1990) 'Adolescent reactions to sibling death: perception of mothers, fathers and teenagers', *Nursing Research*, 39 (2) (March–April): 103–6.

Hover, D. (1986) 'Development of a hospice support group', *American Journal of Hospice Care* (Sept–Oct.): 38–41.

Humphrey, G. M. (1991) 'Facing the challenge: providing adolescent support groups within the school setting', Association for Death Education and Counselling, 13th Annual Conference, Duluth. Abstracts.

Hurtig, W. A. (1990) 'The effect of death education and experience in nursing students' attitude towards death', *Journal of Advanced Nursing*, 15 (1) (Jan.): 29–34.

Ilse, S. and Burns, L. H. (1985) *Miscarriage: a Shattered Dream*, Maple Plain, MN: Wintergreen Press.

Jeret, J. S. (1989) 'Discussing dying: changing attitudes amongst patients, physicians and medical students', *Pharos*, 52 (1) (Winter): 15–20.

Justin, R. G. (1989) 'Memories worth sharing: last goodbyes', *Postgraduate Medicine*, 86 (5) (Oct.): 85–6.

Kastenbaum, R. and Kastenbaum, B. (eds) (1989) *Encyclopaedia of Death*, Phoenix, AZ: Oryx.

Keane, W. G., Gould, T. A. and Millard, P. H. (1983) 'Death in practice', *Journal of the Royal College of General Practitioners*, 33 (251) (June): 347–51.

Knight, M. and Field, D. (1981) 'A silent conspiracy: coping with dying cancer patients on an acute surgical ward', *Journal of Advanced Nursing*, 6 (3) (May): 221–9.

Koocher, G. P. (1981) *The Damocles Syndrome*, New York: McGraw-Hill Inc.

Kowlerschke, K. (1989) 'When the doctor dies', *Texas Medicine*, 1985 (1) (Jan.): 64–8.

Kubler-Ross, E. (1969) *Death and Dying*, London: Tavistock Publications.

Lansdowne, R. (1989) 'The care of the child facing death', *Progress in Pediatric Surgery* (Berlin), 22: 64–8.

Laube, J. (1977) 'Death and dying workshop for nurses: its effect on their death anxiety level', *International Journal for Nursing Studies*, 14 (3): 111–20.

Leenaars, A. and Wenckstern, S. (1990) *Suicide Prevention in Schools*, Bristol, PA: Hemisphere Publishing Corp.

Letter Series (1990) 'Resuscitation of the terminal ill', *Canadian Medical Association Journal*, 142 (6) (15 March): 526 and at 530–3.

Lewis, E. (1979) 'Mourning by the family after a stillbirth or neonatal death', *Archives of Diseases in Childhood*, 54: 303–6.

McClam, T. (1980) 'Death anxiety before and after death education: negative results', *Psychological Report*, 46 (2) (April): 513–14.

McKee, C. M. (1988) 'Attitudes to a hospital-based terminal care scheme', *Postgraduate Medical Journal*, 64 (755) (Sept.): 678–80.

McMordie, W. R. (1981) 'Religiosity and fear of death: strength of belief system', *Psychological Report*, 49 (3) (Dec): 921–2.

Maguire, P. (1976) 'The psychological and social sequelae of mastectomy', in J. Howells (ed.) *Modern Perspectives in the Psychiatric Aspects of Surgery*, New York: Brunner/Mazel.

——(1988) 'Communication with cancer patients and handling uncertainty, collusion and denial', *British Medical Journal*, 297 (6654) (15 Oct.): 972–4.

Marin, P. (1989) 'Attitudes of hospital doctors in Wales to use of intravenous fluids and antibiotics in the terminally ill', *Postgraduate Medical Journal*, 65 (767) (Sept.): 650–2.

Marks, S. C. and Bertman, S. L. (1980) 'Experiences with learning about death and dying in the undergraduate anatomy curriculum', *Journal of Medical Education*, 55 (1) (Jan.): 48–52.

Mermann, A. C., Gunn, D. G. and Dickinson, C. E. (1991) 'Learning to care for the dying: a survey of medical schools and a model course', *Academic Medicine*, 65 (1) (Jan.): 35–8.

Metzgar, M. (1991) *Crisis in Schools: Is Your School Prepared? Workshop for Teachers, Administrators, Parents*, Workshop handbook, 1130/5th Ave NE, Seattle, WA.

Michels, N. (1988) *Helping Women Recover From Abortion*, Minneapolis: Bethany House.

Nuttall, D. (1977) 'Attitudes to dying and the bereaved', *Nursing Times*, 73 (4) (13 Oct.): 1605–7.

Oakley, A., McPherson, A. and Roberts, H. (1984) *Miscarriage*, London: Fontana.

Pacheco, R. (1989) 'Attitudes of medical personnel (doctors and nurses) towards informing the terminal patient', *Medical Law*, 8 (3): 243–8.

Page-Lieberman, J. (1990) 'How fathers perceive perinatal death', *American Journal of Maternal Child Nursing*, 15 (5) (Sept.–Oct.): 320–3.

Parkes, C. M. (1980) 'Bereavement counselling: does it work?', *British Medical Journal*, 281 (6232) (5 July): 3–6.

Pazola, K. J. (1990) 'Privileged communication – talking to a dying adolescent', *American Journal of Maternal Child Nursing*, 15 (1) (Jan.–Feb.): 16–21.

Pincus, L. (1974) *Death and the Family*, London: Faber.

Porter, R. (1982) 'Essay review: death and the doctors', *Medical History*, 26 (3) (July): 335–41.

Poulter, C. (1987) *Playing the Game*, London: Macmillan

Raimbault, G. (1981) 'Children talk about death', *Acta Paediatrica Scand.* 70: 179–82.

Rando, T. A. (1991) *Treatment of ·Complicated Mourning*, Champaign, IL: Research Press.

Raphael, B. (1977) 'Preventive intervention with the recently bereaved', *Archives of General Psychiatry*, 34: 1450–4.

Razavi, D. (1988) 'Immediate effectiveness of brief psychological training for health professionals dealing with terminally ill cancer patients: a controlled study', *Social Science and Medicine*, 27 (4): 369–75.

Redmond, L. M. (1989) *Surviving when Someone You Love was Murdered*, Clearwater, FLA: Psychological Consultation and Education Services Inc.

Rifkin, A. (1989) 'Should physicians always offer hope?' (letter), *Pharos*, 52 (3) (Summer): 38.

Riker, H. and Myers, J. E. (1989) *Retirement Counselling: a Handbook for Action*, Bristol, PA: Hemisphere Publishing Corp.

Saunders, C. (1972) 'A therapeutic community: St Christopher's Hospice', in B. Schoenberg, A. Catt, D. Perekz and A. Murscher (eds) *Psychological Aspects of Terminal Care*, New York: Columbia University Press.

Schachter, S. (1991) 'A descriptive study of adolescent bereavement experiences with the death of a peer', Association for Death Education and Counselling, 13th Annual Conference, Duluth. Abstracts.

Schmidt, T. A. (1990) 'Emergency physicians' responses to families following patient death', *Annals of Emergency Medicine*, 19 (2) (Feb.): 125–8.

Schonfeld, D. J. (1990) 'The impact of school-based education on the young child's understanding of death', *Journal of Developmental and Behavioral Pediatrics*, 11 (5) (Oct.): 247–52.

Scruby, L. S. (1989) 'Evaluation of bereavement intervention', *Canadian Journal of Public Health*, 80 (6) (Nov.–Dec.): 394–8.

Seravalli, E. P. (1988) 'The dying patient, the physician and the fear of death', *New England Journal of Medicine*, 319 (26) (29 Dec.): 1728–30.

Shooter, M. S. (1991) 'Conspiracies of silence', Opening address to the Second Annual Conference of the National Association of Bereavement Services on Unmentionable Losses, London: Regent's College.

——and Hobbs, T. (in preparation) 'A cyclical model of mourning'.

Silver, R. T. (1980) 'The dying patient: a clinician's view', *American Journal of Medicine*, 68 (4) (April): 473–5.

Sonstegard, L. (1976) 'Dealing with dying: the grieving nurse', *American Journal of Nursing*, 76 (9) (2 Sept.): 1490–2.

Stedeford, A. (1979) 'Psychotherapy of the dying patient', *British Journal of Psychiatry*, 135 (July): 7–14.

——(1981) 'Couples facing death II – unsatisfactory communication', *British Medical Journal* (Clinical Research), 283 (6299) (24 Oct.): 1093–1101.

Stephany, T. M. (1990) 'A death in the family', *American Journal of Nursing*, 90 (4) (April): 54–6.

Strange, G. R. (1989) 'Ethical considerations in emergency department management of terminally ill patients (clinical conference)', *Annals of Emergency Medicine*, 18 (2) (Oct.): 1085–8.

Stuart, M. (1991) *Are you listening/widows?* New York: Martha Stuart Communications Inc., 147 W. 22nd Street, New York.

Telban, S. G. (1981) 'Death anxiety and knowledge about death', *Psychology Report*, 49 (2) (Oct.): 648.

Tolle, S. W. (1989) 'A programme to teach residents humanistic skills for notifying survivors of a patient's death', *Academic Medicine*, 64 (9) (Sept.): 505–6.

Trent, N. (1988) 'A place for living, a place for dying', *Canadian Medical Association Journal*, 139 (9) (Nov.): 889–93.

University of Delaware (1989) 'Death – a personal encounter', IBM computer program.

Vaisrub, S. (1974) 'Dying is being worked to death' (editorial), *Journal of the American Medical Association*, 229 (30 Sept.): 1909–10.

Vates, B. T. (1989) 'Grandparents' deaths and severe maternal reaction in the etiology of adolescent psychopathology', *Journal of Nervous and Mental Disease*, 177 (11) (Nov.): 675–80.

Vienello, R. (1988) 'Children's understanding of death according to parents and paediatricians', *Journal of Genetic Psychology*, 149 (3) (Sept.): 305–16.

Wanzer, S. H. (1989) 'The physician's responsibility towards hopelessly ill patients: a second look', *New England Journal of Medicine*, 320 (13) (30 March): 844–9.

Ward, B. (1989) *Good Grief – Exploring Feelings, Loss and Death with Under 11's*, Luton, Beds: White Crescent Press.

Warren, W. G. (1988–89) 'Death education and research: critical perspectives', *Geriatric Education*, 9 (1–2): 1–200.

Wass, H. and Corr, C. (1984) *Childhood and Death*, Bristol, PA: Hemisphere Publishing Corp.

Watts, D. T. (1990) 'Physician–nurse conflict: lessons from a clinical experience', *Journal of the American Geriatric Society*, 38 (10) (Oct.): 1151–2.

Weisman, A. D. (1981) 'Understanding the cancer patient: the syndrome of the care-giver's plight', *Psychiatry*, 44 (May): 161–8.

Weisman, E. (1990) 'Counsellor humanizes hospital for dying patients' families', *Hospitals*, 64 (12) (20 June): 54–5.

Wells, R. (1988) *Helping Children Cope with Grief*, Sheldon Press, SPCK.

Wertheimer, A. (1991) *A Special Scar: the Experiences of People Bereaved by Suicide*, London and New York: Tavistock/Routledge.

Williston Park Group (1989) 'A prescription for peaceful death – a physicians' group examines care of the terminally ill', *Oncology*, 3 (6) (June): 38–9.

Wilson, V. C. (1990) 'How can we dignify death in the ICU?', *American Journal of Nursing*, 90 (5) (May): 38–42.

Witte, R. A. (1985) 'The psychological impact of a progressive physical handicap and terminal illness (Duchenne muscular dystrophy) on adolescents and their families', *British Journal of Medical Psychology*, 58: 179–87.

Wojtowicz, C. (1990) 'An ice-breaking introduction for death education', *Journal of School Health*, 60 (5) (May): 229–31.

Woodward, J. (1988) 'The bereaved twin', *Acta Geneticae Medicae et Gemellologial* (Rome), 37 (2): 173–80.

Woolley, H. (1989) 'Imparting the diagnosis of life-threatening illness in children', *British Medical Journal*, 298 (6688) (17 June): 1123–6.

Worden, W. J. (1989) *Grief Counselling and Grief Therapy*, London: Tavistock.

Yalom, I. D. (1988) 'Bereavement groups: techniques and themes', *International Journal of Group Psychotherapy*, 38 (4) (Oct.): 419–57.

Yarber, W. L., Gobel, P. and Rublee, D. A. (1981) 'Effect of death education on nursing students' anxiety and locus of control', *Journal of School Health* (May): 367–72.

Chapter 8

Evaluating change and development through workshops

Stephen Murgatroyd

At the end of a workshop the leader and the participants often engage in evaluative conversations. These are usually formative: they are concerned with general impressions, are unspecific and often concern the emotional tone of the experience. A variety of adjectives are used in such conversations – challenging, interesting, demanding, moving, disquieting, evocative, exhausting, instructive and surprising being amongst those heard at the end of one of the workshops on stress described earlier. Sometimes the leader may seek some more objective evaluation of the outcome of the workshop, a more summative evaluation. This may take the form of seeking to establish just what changes in attitudes, behaviours or emotions have occurred as a result of the workshop by means of interviewing, questionnaire, observation or some combination of these methods. In addition, the leader may seek to examine the quality of the workshop as a presentation so as to make changes to the format in the light of experience – Rhys has made specific reference to this in describing her health visitor workshops. These forms of evaluation are the concerns of this chapter. The aim is to examine the nature of changes that can be expected from workshops and to understand the ways in which such changes can be evaluated.

The chapter is not intended to be a comprehensive introduction to evaluation methods or to the technology of evaluation (but see Reason and Rowan 1981; Phillips 1983; Geber 1989; Brinkerhoff 1987); rather, it is an attempt to examine the issues which workshop leaders and participants need to consider when seeking to engage in evaluation tasks. It should be clear at the outset of this chapter that the contributors to this book feel strongly that workshops have a valuable place in the development of helping professionals: they provide opportunities for exposure to processes and tasks which are intended to affect directly the way helpers act, think and feel. It should also be clear that the outcomes of the workshops described here are intended to be at a variety of levels.

There are available some quantitative approaches to workshop and training evaluation. These range from methodologies for evaluating the extent to which a particular training event has had an impact on thinking, behaviour and competence to systematic methods for cost-benefit analysis of training investments (see especially Kearsley 1982 and also Spencer 1986). Some of these resources are reviewed in an accessible article by Gordon (1991).

One way of considering the question of evaluation is to look at four levels at which workshops and training events can be evaluated. The first level is to measure the reactions of participants. This usually occurs immediately after the workshop ends and can often involve a combination of rating scales and open-ended questions. Some consider these evaluations dubious – they can involve halo effects and often do not relate strongly to the subsequent behaviour of participants. None the less, evaluation at this level does involve feedback about the presentation quality, immediacy and felt-relevance of the workshop. At the second level the focus is upon measuring learning outcomes. This will often be measured sometime after the workshop and can involve on-the job evaluation by supervisors, self-report, demonstrating learning competencies through systematic testing, work sampling and peer evaluation (Rummler 1976). At level three the focus is upon sustainability: to what extent is the person using the knowledge, understanding and skills gained through a workshop consistently and repeatedly in their work or in other settings? Finally, the fourth level looks at consequences: what are the consequences of the learning for the professional development of the person and for their organisation? Different questions are being examined at each of these four levels and different tools are required for evaluation. A critical question for the workshop designer is: which of these levels will provide meaningful and efficient evaluation data, the collection of which will have an impact on the design and delivery of subsequent workshops?

For some of the workshops described in the volume it is intended that they lead mainly to direct changes in behaviour; that described by Hobbs is a clear sample of this. Others are intended generally to encourage further reflection and insight; those described by Shooter and Murgatroyd fall into this category. Yet others are intended to provoke some careful thought about the management and presentation of self whilst at the same time exploring attitudes, behaviours, beliefs and values; the workshops described by Pates, Woolfe and Rhys fall into this category. To some extent, each workshop will be offering a combination of these outcomes: they differ only in their intended emphasis. Whilst these are the outcomes intended by the workshop leader, participants may experience a great many other outcomes. These can include (amongst others) the following: a feeling of increased confidence, a strengthening of social support systems, a new insight into an old experience, a fresh look at the process of learning or a new understanding of the skills needed to achieve a particular goal. Given such a variety of levels of 'outcome' it is important to understand some of the dimensions of learning that might be amenable to evaluation before examining the evaluation process. The exploration of these dimensions in the sections which follow is intended to explore the extent to which different kinds of learning lead to different evaluation questions.

SOME DIMENSIONS OF WORKSHOP LEARNING

In considering the outcomes of a workshop experience (or any other learning experience, for that matter) it is important to have a clear understanding of the expectations that individuals bring to that learning. In looking at why attitude and behavioural change do not occur as a result of workshops, it is possible to use the findings of Baron (1968) and Kelman and Baron (1986) to suggest that key features of such non-learning are: (1) compartmentalisation – knowledge and experience have become compartmentalised and the person expects a workshop to maintain such compartmentalisation; (2) insulation – the person has become separated from their actions in such a way that learning about a subject (sex, death, stress, communication, counselling) has become divorced from learning about self – any workshop experience based upon linking self and subject becomes threatening and the person uses denial, distortion, rationalisation or derogation of the workshop as a means of defending their insulation; (3) ritualism – the person uses workshops to bolster their status or their previously held views and rejects experiences which challenge their status or views. These three mechanisms of non-learning – compartmentalisation, insulation and ritualism – are descriptions of three sets of expectations (learning 'sets') which predispose participants to want certain things from a workshop and to evaluate the workshop in terms of its success in minimising the challenges to their 'self' and skills.

As an example of this 'non-learning', consider the case of Sarah. She attended one of the stress workshops described earlier in this volume. For her, all stress was caused by other people, and she ritualistically blamed her parents for not helping her cope with people better. She saw all of her stress as resulting from things done to her; she was divorced from the way in which her own thoughts and actions contributed to her own stress. In this way, she insulated herself. Stress occurred for Sarah only at work (she said) and it did not affect her at home at all – she compartmentalised her experiences of stress. She was both rigid and dogmatic in expressing these views. The workshop leader had to work hard to encourage her to give herself permission to question these assumptions about herself and to learn.

The opposite of these three barriers to learning and change are more readily identifiable. Using some of the ideas developed by Rowan (1973) and derived from Fishbein (1967) and Abelson and Rosenberg (1958), those who expect to change and develop as a result of attending a workshop (albeit in a small but significant way) are those who (1) link the process of learning and the content of a workshop to positive values; (2) attach as much importance to feelings and experience as they do to thoughts and actions; (3) are able to make linkages both between the subject matter of a workshop and the processes of that workshop and between their experience at the workshop and previous experiences; (4) feel able during a workshop or shortly thereafter to explore previously suppressed values, beliefs or ideas; (5) are able to examine the ideas of others openly without undue defensiveness and with a view to integrating their ideas, thoughts and beliefs into their own thinking and experience; and (6) attend workshops because they see them as a means of opening themselves up to opportunities to learn rather than as being devices for confirming status and beliefs.

In describing these two sets of expectations and by describing them as non-learning and learning 'sets', it becomes clear that the way a participant approaches a workshop affects the outcome of the workshop for that person. Therefore, evaluation activities begin by exploring the different expectations that individuals have for the workshop that they are attending. This means that the process of evaluation begins as the ideas for the workshop are formulated: evaluation is not something simply completed at the end of the workshop but is an implicit feature of the workshop itself.

In several places in this collection of papers it has been noted that the organisers of workshops – those who contract our services – often make statements about the expectations of participants which are not then borne out by the statements made by the participants themselves. It has also been noted in several specific workshop descriptions (see especially those by Shooter, Pates and Rhys) that expectations about the kinds of learning from experience and reflection that can occur among the participants are varied.

In looking at the question of how expectations shape outcomes, it is important to look also at how the leader of a workshop looks at discrepancies and differences in expectations amongst those with whom he or she is working and to look at the use made of these differences throughout the workshop. A leader who ignores the fact that different participants in a workshop are seeking different outcomes may find that they are in conflict with one sub-group to such an extent that they are unable to meet the expectations of any group within the workshop. A leader who spends a considerable time negotiating and contracting with a group so as to overcome the process problems created by radically different expectations can so eat away into the time of the workshop that the subject matter of the workshop gets diluted and its purposes are lost. When looking at expectations, it is therefore important to understand not simply what they are but how they are used within the workshop to the benefit of all participants.

Formal measurement of learning development during a workshop is possible but not always desirable. Decisions need to be made about which of the four levels of measurement introduced on page 176 are appropriate and cost-effective. The key criteria for such a decision should focus upon the impact that evaluation data would have on the design and delivery of subsequent versions of the workshop.

LOCUS OF CONTROL

One dimension of learning which appears to tie strongly to expectations can be referred to as 'locus of control'. This refers to the extent to which a person feels that their thoughts and actions are responses to environmental situations in which others play a dominant role (external control), as opposed to feeling that they are very much in control of their own environments and that their thoughts and actions, whilst showing understanding of the views and actions of others, are very much their own (internal control).

The aim of all of the workshops described in this volume is to increase the extent to which the person is able to experience the world as something they themselves can shape and control (internal control), though recognising that there are a great many external forces and social conditions which make the exercise of that control difficult. One way of thinking about expectations is to think about the willingness of both participants and the leader to open themselves up to increasing the extent of their internal control of experiences. It follows from this that a task in evaluation is to explore the extent to which a particular workshop has increased the feeling of internal control amongst participants. Another way of describing the construct 'locus of control' is to think about workshops as aiming to increase the sense of personal autonomy which participants experience during the workshop and can carry from it (Hall *et al.* 1984). This also relates to the way in which participants show by their actions and expression that they accept responsibility for their own learning – a point explored fully in Chapter 1.

Whilst there are some objective measures of locus of control which could be used to examine changes occurring between the beginning and end of a workshop (see Lefcourt 1983; Hall *et al.* 1984), many of the changes that we have observed occur gradually rather than suddenly. Just as certain coping devices are summoned only when faced with a major stressor, so the experience of increased personal autonomy as a result of attending a stress workshop may only be apparent for some when a real and major stressor subsequently faces someone who was a participant at the stress workshops described by Woolfe and Murgatroyd. Measurements given as pre- and post-tests at a workshop may not, therefore, adequately reflect the extent of personally significant learning during that workshop (Collier 1977). In a formative evaluation, then, participants and leaders might usefully explore the extent to which this feature of learning has been experienced within the workshop.

DEVELOPMENTAL VERSUS IMMEDIATE LEARNING

The indication that some of the benefits of a learning experience may not become apparent until that learning is called out by some life event draws attention to another dimension of learning in workshops. It is that a great deal (though not all) of the learning that leaders hope will accrue from their work is developmental rather than immediate; it is a 'dripping tap' kind of change rather than the opening of a floodgate. This means that changes that occur during or as a result of a workshop are not generally intended to be immediate and observable (though Hobbs does expect direct behavioural outcomes from his training work) but are intended to stimulate the person in their own development towards greater personal autonomy and a greater sense of their own internal locus of control.

DEEP AND SURFACE LEARNING

At a minimum level, the changes which the workshops outlined in this volume are intended to encourage are related to increasing the participants' capacity for self-evaluation. This is achieved by encouraging self-disclosure, by active learning methods and by introducing new experiences (by means of role plays, games, simulations and direct teaching) and concepts. Enhanced self-evaluation coupled with increased awareness of the extent to which this can lead to better use being made of personal resources and relationships in a variety of settings leads to more opportunities for self-evaluation and for the exercise of personal autonomy. This 'deep-level' learning – 'deep' in the sense of its contribution to the ego development of the person and in terms of the kind of learning outcomes that it implies – underscores some of the surface learning outcomes that may be more readily observed; for example, the use of a technical language to describe stress or bereavement or the use of a particular skill such as dynamic meditation, systematic relaxation or assertiveness.

Let us examine this idea of deep and surface learning a little further. It is possible for a person to be taught the technical skills of writing – how to construct a paragraph, how to structure an article or a poem, how to make effective use of adjectives when conveying feelings. These are surface skills. For the person to show deep learning they need to use these skills to reveal some insights about themselves or others in their writing. That is to say, they express deeply held views or beliefs, and offer detailed observations in a way that is a risk to them. In terms of the workshop on sexuality described by Pates, some surface learning may occur about different sexual attitudes or behaviours. Deep learning would be indicated by a person genuinely and honestly exploring their own attitudes towards sexuality in a way that shows that they are open to new learning and development.

In evaluating a workshop in terms of both its processes and the outcomes, it is important to understand that different participants will experience different levels of learning at the deep and surface levels, and that not all of the learning that has taken place can be discerned from a careful study of the surface learning a person displays through their speech, attitudes and behaviour.

INDIVIDUAL VERSUS ORGANISATIONAL OUTCOME

A final dimension we consider important in the context of the workshops that we describe here concerns the extent to which outcomes are intended to be at the level of the individual (that is, relating to the individuals attending the workshop) and at the level of the organisation of which that individual is a part. For example, Murgatroyd describes a stress workshop which is in part intended to assist individuals cope with the stress they experience at work and in part to change those features of work experience that many find stressful. In evaluating this workshop it is necessary to look at outcomes, both in terms of the individual participants and in terms of the organisational consequences of the workshop. This also applies to some features of several of the workshops described here. To provide another example, Shooter describes death workshops which are intended to encourage greater self-awareness and reflection on the questions of death, dying, grief and bereavement. If this workshop is offered to a specific group of nurses working in a hospice, it might be expected to lead to some change in the practice of those nurses either in relation to grieving relatives or in relation to the grief nurses themselves experience when a patient dies. In evaluating this workshop it may be insightful to look at both the organisational as well as the personal outcomes. These might include changes in rota arrangements, in the provision of rest-room facilities or in the frequency of staff meetings or other organisational changes.

When considering this feature of the impact of workshops, some attention needs to be given to level 4 evaluation: systematically examining the impact of the workshop relative to the investment made. For example, one major oil company in Canada has invested approximately $2.6 million in stress management support systems and workshops during the last three years. The question for the management of the organisation is this: have we secured a good return on this investment? This is not the place to review in detail the statistical calculation methods needed to answer this question (but see Kearsley 1982), but two points do need to be made. Firstly, there needs to be some caution about the nature of causality assumptions being made in such studies. Only when the workshop design is intended to have concrete behavioural, attitudinal or organisational consequences can these calculations be made with confidence. Secondly, questions about return on investment are a function of time: when the question is examined will make a difference to the data. If the stress workshop described by Murgatroyd is subjected to a return on investment analysis two weeks after its completion, results will be very different from an evaluation conducted six months later. Durability and time-related objectives need to be specified ahead of time if such studies are to be valued.

This review of certain key dimensions of the learning experience in a workshop – expectations, locus of control, personal autonomy, developmental tasks and organisational change – leads now to questions about how to evaluate both the process and outcomes of workshops such as those described here.

EVALUATING LEADERSHIP

Hovland and his co-workers at Yale University (Hovland and Janis 1959; Hovland *et al.* 1953; Rosenberg and Hovland 1960) developed a programme of research which looked at the kind of facilitator styles which were most likely to have an impact on a group. They draw attention to the importance of credibility in the success of a leader in a group or workshop. They suggest that credibility consists of:

1 the ability to communicate a sense of competence in relation to the topic which provides the focus for the workshop activity – this competence can derive either from scholarship or experience or some combination of both;

2 being perceived as reliable as far as information sources are concerned – the extent to which workshop participants feel that the leader is dependable, predictable and consistent;

3 having one's motives clearly understood, especially in situations of conflict or when risks are being taken by participants;

4 being empathetic, warm and genuine in one's relations with participants;

5 the degree of dynamism or charisma displayed by the leader – indicated

by the control and activity-leadership displayed and the extent to which participants feel confident about the direction offered by the leader; and

6 majority opinion of the group – pressure towards conformity in workshops is high.

The display and communication of such qualities permits the leader to have a high level of influence upon the learning of workshop participants.

In some later development of this work, Janis (1982) developed a detailed check-list of those features of helping which maximised the helpers' ability to influence those with whom they worked. Amongst the influencing skills which he regards as critical are these:

(a) encouraging participants to make self-disclosures;
(b) giving positive feedback to participants and showing both acceptance and understanding of their feelings and thoughts;
(c) using helping skills to reshape thoughts presented by participants so as to encourage them to develop fresh insights;
(d) being concrete – making direct statements which endorse practical suggestions made by participants and which give direction to some workshop or helping activity;
(e) eliciting commitment to taking some action (for example, to read more, to discuss with a colleague some aspect of the workshop and so on) – encouraging participants to develop a self-contract for work as a result of the workshop process;
(f) showing that the ideas expressed by group members have antecedents in the work of other people – connecting 'naïve' ideas to bodies of research and/or theory;
(g) giving selective positive feedback so as to shape the direction of an individual's development during a workshop;
(h) undertaking direct training of a person or sub-group or group so as to give some practical skills;
(i) giving reassurances to individuals within the group that they are learning and developing;
(j) being explicit about the contract for the workshop and its termination;
(k) giving reminders as to the major features of learning that have occurred during the workshop; and
(l) building up the confidence of participants so that they can take some of the learning that has occurred during the workshop and apply it to situations which they encounter in the 'real' world.

These two lists of influencing skills are valuable when the workshop leader wishes to reflect on their own performance as a leader. They can be useful in exploring the style of leadership used and the extent to which any problems that emerged during the workshop can be related back to one or more of these features. Although not all of the items included in these two lists are relevant to all the workshops described in this volume, other workshops and other forms of training do involve these features.

These two lists are essentially concerned with three sets of leader characteristics. These are: (1) the disposition of the leader towards those who are to participate in the workshop – how he or she feels about the work they are to do and how he or she shows respect for the participants; (2) the attitudes that the leader encourages towards both the content of the workshop and the learning processes it involves; and (3) specific behaviours of the leader. The lists given above (and others that you might construct for yourself) all relate to these three features of leadership.

There are, of course, some objective measures of leadership qualities which can be completed by participants so as to reveal to the leader how he or she is perceived. Some of the leadership check-lists given in Woodcock (1979) can, if adapted, be useful for this purpose, as also are those in Davis (1975).

Rhys, in her contribution to this book, stresses the importance of the leaders as learners, both during and after the workshop they offer. This learning will take many forms, and it is important for some of the work of leadership to revolve around questions of influencing and supporting, since this is the implicit purpose of many of the workshops described here. All of the authors here give emphasis to the need for the leader to be aware of their own 'self' and the way that this 'self' and its expression influences others.

EVALUATING THE WORKSHOP AS A PRESENTATION

A workshop is intended to be a form of learning experience in which a leader seeks to facilitate the development of self-disclosure, self-awareness, opportunity awareness, transition learning and skill development. To do this he or she presents a learning experience. One way of evaluating this experience is in terms of the quality of the presentation.

Loughray and Hopson (1979) produce a very practical list of items to examine when considering presentation. This includes (1) staff assignments – about the number of leaders, the quality of administration of the workshop and about the support personnel (such as catering, registration, secretarial back-up and so on); (2) media – about the availability of hardware (like video, audio replay, or overhead and slide projectors) and how operable this was once it became available; (3) participant concerns – ensuring that comments from participants about rooms, meals, transportation or accommodation are borne in mind when arranging a subsequent workshop; and (4) facilities – were the coffee/tea, toilet and crèche arrangements satisfactory, and was there a range of furniture suitable for those with slight or serious disabilities? These sets of questions are useful in looking at the administration of a workshop.

However, questions of presentation go beyond these issues, as Loughray and Hopson (1979) acknowledge. There is also a need to ask some questions about goals. Which were achieved and which were not? How do you know that certain goals were achieved – what is the basis for your assumption? What are the most useful outcomes of this workshop – does the identification of these change the goals you might have for the next workshop of this kind? You might also want to examine the climate of the workshop: list the adjectives you think are appropriate in defining the climate of the workshop you have just completed. On the basis of this list, what might you change the next time you offer the workshop? Whereas not all of the workshops described here have such specific goals, some of these questions may still be relevant.

Hall *et al.* (1984) offer a detailed evaluation of a workshop they offered to experienced teachers. As a result of their evaluation, they conclude that 'it is impossible to predict which event will be most potent for any individuals'. This suggests that evaluation directed at presentation questions should examine the way the presentation impacted on different participants: what are the individual differences, were enough opportunities created during the workshop to encourage individual learning, and how did you as leader observe individual reactions and did you make adjustments to the programme because of them? These questions (and others you might generate) encourage reflection on the link between the design of a workshop and its outcome.

Because adult learners bring a great many unique experiences with them into a workshop (Eraut 1982), the way in which individuals are selected and grouped for workshops can be important in shaping reactions to the presentation (Collier 1977). In thinking about presentation issues it is important to ask questions about how participants were selected and what this selection leads to in terms of the design of the workshop: would it need to be different for different groups; what were the effects of participants' status positions within their profession upon their behaviour in the group; how did the selection of participants affect the group's dynamics? These questions help in planning subsequent workshops in which the leader can influence participant selection and grouping.

EVALUATING OUTCOMES FOR PARTICIPANTS

When evaluation questions focus upon the direct outcomes for participants in terms of attitudes, behaviours and feelings, the evaluation task is much more difficult. Indeed, those who offer workshops (both organisers and leaders) need to live with a great deal of uncertainty about the benefits of their work. This is because (1) the intended outcomes from many of the workshops described here are not amenable to direct observation or measurement; (2) some of the intended outcomes are long-term rather than short-term; (3) many of the intended outcomes relate to attitudes rather than to behaviour, so they are difficult to assess; and (4) the design of workshops seeks to maximise individual learning, so there is a need to see outcomes in terms of individual developments rather than in terms of the group's development of skill. Each of these factors make measurement of outcomes difficult, and this, therefore, created difficulties about the way in which workshops can be evaluated.

Some attempts have been made to overcome these difficulties. There are several studies of the effects of workshops on specific attitudes in which participants have been given attitude scales before, immediately after and some time after workshops so as to establish in some objective way the attitude changes that take place. One example of this is a study by Valerio and Stone (1982) of changes in attitudes as a result of an assertiveness training programme. There are a number of problems with such studies. The most significant problem is that it is not easy to establish just what impact the workshop itself has on attitude change over a long period (say, 6 to 12 months) because a variety of things happen to a person during this time which can also affect their attitudes. The second major problem is that the measuring instruments used – generally questionnaires – are not always designed to test for changes in the specific attitudes or behaviours for which the workshop is intended. None the less, it is possible to show that even brief learning experiences (6 to 10 hours) can have a significant impact on the attitudes of some participants.

Partly because of the technical difficulties and partly because of the feeling which many workshop organisers and leaders have that such objective evaluations become an intrusion into the workshop (see Hall *et al.* 1984), few workshops of the kind described here have been evaluated in the way just described. More common are quasi-objective evaluations. One exception to this general statement that concerns the workshops described here are those developed by Ivey (1971) and described above by Hobbs. These have been evaluated in a variety of studies, most notably by Kasdorf and Gustafsen (1978).

Quasi-objective evaluations take many forms. Rhys, in her contribution, refers to letters which she asks participants to write to themselves indicating what steps they are going to take to continue their learning following the workshop (see pages 101 and 108 above). Such letters provide some materials from which the leader is able to discern the kinds of experiences which participants have found valuable. There are other such devices. In some of the workshops on stress offered by Murgatroyd, participants have written self-contracts about their own stress-management strategies for display in their offices: these provide an indication of the skills to which individuals have attached importance as a result of attending the workshop. Others, such as Hall *et al.* (1984), have asked participants to participate in evaluative interviews shortly after the workshop, and these interviews have provided materials which indicate the value of the workshops in terms of individual learning. Other devices that have been used in this way include diaries completed before, during and after the workshops – a comprehensive example of the value of this process for evaluation is given in Ottaway (1966); video-recording of workshops which are then reviewed by participants (Breeze 1980; Wright 1980) and various forms of self-report (Bordin 1968).

Workshop leaders should recognise the worth of evaluative statements made by participants during the course of a workshop. In some of the workshops described in this volume (notably those offered by Woolfe, Rhys and Murgatroyd) participants are asked to make evaluations at various points in the workshop and to display these evaluations in the form of flip-chart comments sheets. These sheets, if reflected upon after the workshop, reveal many issues which are in the minds of participants at various stages in the course of a workshop, and can provide valuable clues as to how better to structure either particular activities or to the kinds of outcomes that can be expected to arise as a result of the kinds of thoughts which such recorded statements reveal. In addition, they provide valuable materials which can be useful for participants at other subsequent workshops. To some extent, evaluation is an implicit feature of the workshop, since almost all of the activities described in earlier chapters contain evaluative components. The kind of questions asked and the responses of participants to specific workshop activities constitute evaluations.

If these approaches to evaluation appear 'soft' rather than 'hard' in terms of their data quality, this reflects the 'softness' of the workshop objectives. In many cases only generalised outcomes are intended; in such cases only generalised evaluations can take place. Only if learning objectives become explicit and specific can 'harder' and more objective evaluations be attempted.

CONCLUSION

As several writers on workshop evaluation have commented (see Loughray and Hopson 1979 and Davis 1975, for example), it is far better to undertake some evaluation activity than simply to assume that all is well. However, the evaluations are likely to produce a variety of findings of different utility to the workshop leader. There are simply so many variables to be understood in the design and planning of a workshop and in determining outcomes that most evaluations are essentially formative rather than summative.

This observation leads to some comments about the nature of change that can be expected from a workshop. These comments are prompted by a review of our own evaluations of the workshops described in this book. First, the changes that some workshop participants report are not always obvious. For example, some of those who have attended the workshops described by Pates and Shooter indicate that the major outcome for them is an increase in their general social confidence – they feel more able to share their ideas in a group. In other cases, such as in the workshop described by Hobbs, the outcome for some has been increased awareness of the nature of communication in day-to-day life in addition to, generally, the development of particular communication skills. The development of increased confidence and awareness is not always something that is easy to observe.

A related point is that change is not always neat and tidy. A change in attitudes towards death or the development of a new skill in stress management may have effects on other aspects of a person's life that take time to 'sort out'. For example, one woman discovered her need to develop her assertiveness skills on a stress management course offered by Woolfe, which led her to seek further support because of the impact her assertiveness was having upon her husband. A change in one aspect of this person's life had consequences in another.

A third feature of change processes is that change is not always transferable. Murgatroyd (1985), looking at social skills training programmes, observes that it is not always possible to transfer skills learned in workshops into social situations. Indeed, a classical problem with all forms of training is the extent to which training is transferable from one setting to another – an issue examined extensively by Pribram (1964). If workshop leaders intend their participants to develop skills which are transferable to the social world or to a variety of planned situations, then the evaluation of these skills ought to reflect this assumption.

One final point about change. Change is not always permanent. Law (1977) observes that teachers on in-service training may develop new skills and attitudes during an intensive or long training programme which then are modified during their period of readjustment to the school or college. Indeed, in his study of the impact of counsellor education, he shows that teachers who trained as counsellors soon return to their former belief and value positions when working in schools, despite an initial change in these attitudes and values on leaving training (Law 1978). If workshops are intended to have both short- and long-term consequence for participants, then the process of evaluation ought to reflect this assumption.

In a chapter of this length it is not possible to examine all aspects of evaluation. The reader has already been referred to two sources of detailed comments about evaluation processes (see Reason and Rowan 1981; Bogdan and Taylor 1975). There is an excellent text devoted to assessment by Derek Rowntree (1977), which ends with the suggestion that all assessments of students should end with a government health warning: 'Relying too heavily on other people's opinions can damage your sense of reality' (p. 243). In the context of workshop evaluations, this text might be amended to read: 'Relying too heavily on measures of outcome can damage the quality of a workshop's progress and the value, extent and future impact of participants' learning.' For there is a danger in workshop evaluation that the quality of the learning experiences will be neglected in the pursuit of a larger number of discernible and permanent outcomes.

REFERENCES

Abelson, R. P. and Rosenberg, M. J. (1958) 'Symbolic psycho-logic: a model of attitudinal cognition', *Behavioural Science*, 3:16–21.

Baron, R. M. (1968) 'Attitude change through discrepant action – a functional analysis', in A. G. Greenwald, T. C. Broch and T. M. Ostrom (eds) *Psychological Foundations of Attitudes*, New York: Academic Press.

Bogdan, R. and Taylor, S. J. (1975) *An Introduction to Qualitative Research Methods: a Phenomenological Approach*, New York: Wiley.

Bordin, E. S. (1968) *Psychological Counselling* (2nd edn), New York: Appleton Century-Crofts.

Breeze, J. (1980) 'The use of video recordings in the training of counsellors', *New Era*, 61(5): 196–8.

Brinkerhoff, R. O. (1987) *Achieving Results from Training*, San Francisco: Jossey-Bass Publishers.

Collier, J. (1977) 'Research in small group methods in in-service work', *British Journal of In-Service Education*, 4(1): 74–7.

Davis, L. N. (1975) *Planning, Conducting and Evaluating Workshops*, Austin, Tex.: Learning Concepts.

Eraut, M. (1982) 'What is learned in in-service education and how? A knowledge use perspective', *British Journal of In-Service Education*, 9(1): 6–13.

Fishbein, M. (1967) *Readings in Attitude Theory and Measurement*, New York: John Wiley & Sons.

Geber, B. (1989) *Evaluating Training*, Minneapolis, MN: Lakewood Publications.

Gordon, J. (1991) 'Measuring the "goodness" of training', *Training*, 28(8) (Aug.): 19–25.

Hall, E., Woodhouse, D. A. and Wooster, A. D. (1984) 'An evaluation of in-service courses in human relations', *British Journal of In-Service Education*, 11(1): 55–60.

Hovand, D. and Janis, I. (1959) *Personality and Persuadability*, New Haven, CT: Yale University Press.

Hovand, D., Janis, I. and Kelley, H. (1953) *Communications and Persuasion*, New Haven, CT: Yale University Press.

Ivey, A. (1971) *Microcounselling: Innovations in Interview Training*, Springfield, IL: Thomas.

Janis, I. (1982) 'Helping relationships – a preliminary theoretical analysis', in I. Janis, (ed.) *Counselling on Personal Decisions*, New Haven, CT: Yale University Press.

Kasdorf, J. and Gustafsen, K, (1978) 'Research related to micro-training', in A. Ivey and J. Authier (eds) *Microcounselling – Innovations in Interviewing, Counselling, Psychotherapy and Psychoeducation*, Springfield IL: Thomas.

Kearsley, G. (1982) *Costs, Benefits and Productivity in Training Systems*, Reading, MA: Addison-Wesley Publishing.

Kelman, H. C. and Baron, R. M. (1986) 'Determinants of models of resolving inconsistency dilemmas: a functional analysis', in K. F. Abelson, J. B. Black and J. A. Galambas (eds) *Knowledge Structures*, New Jersey: Lawrence Erlbaum Associates.

Law, W. M. (1977) 'What do teachers learn from in-service guidance training?', *The Counsellor*, 2(2): 8–30.

——(1978) 'The concomitants of system orientation in secondary school counsellors', *British Journal of Guidance and Counselling*, 6(2): 161–75.

Lefcourt, H. (ed.) (1983) *Research Using the Locus of Control Concept*, New York: Academic Press.

Loughray, J. W. and Hopson, B. (1979) *Producing Workshops, Seminars and Short Courses – a Trainer's Handbook*, New York: Cambridge University Press.

Murgatroyd, S. (1985) *Counselling and Helping*, London: British Psychological Society/Methuen.

Ottaway, A. K. C. (1966) *Learning through Group Experience*, London: Routledge & Kegan Paul.

Phillips, J. J. (1983) *Handbook of Training Evaluation and Measurement Methods*, Houston, Tex.: Gulf Publishing.

Pribram, K. H. (1964) 'Neurological notes on the art of education', in E. R. Hilgard (ed.) *Theories of Learning and Instruction*, Chicago: University of Chicago Press.

Reason, P. and Rowan, J. (1981) *Human Inquiry – a Sourcebook of New Paradigm Research*, London: John Wiley.

Rosenberg, M. and Hovland, C. (eds) (1960) *Attitude, Organization and Change*, New Haven, CT: Yale University Press.

Rowan, J. (1973) *Psychological Aspects of Society – the Science of You*, London: Davis Poynter.

Rowntree, D. (1977) *Assessing Students – How Shall We Know Them?*, London: Harper & Row.

Rummler, G. A. (1976) 'The performance audit', in R. L. Craig (ed.) *Training and Development Handbook* (2nd edn), New York: McGraw-Hill.

Spencer, L. M. (1986) *Calculating Human Resource Costs and Benefits*, New York: John Wiley & Sons.

Valerio, H. P. and Stone, G. L. (1982) 'Effects of behavorial, cognitive and combined treatments for assertion as a function of differential deficits', *Journal of Counselling Psychology*, 29(2): 158–68.

Woodcock, M. (1979) *Team Development Manual*, London: Gower Press.

Wright, P. (1980) 'The use of video tape recordings in the training of counsellors', *New Era*, 6(5): 191–5.

Chapter 9

Practical guidelines for effective workshop practice

Tony Hobbs and Richard Pates

A wealth of comment, theoretical rationale and practical suggestion has been provided in the earlier chapters of this volume for those interested in training using an experiential approach. Here, in order to promote a high quality and professionalism of practice, we complement this by bringing together a range of specific factors for consideration and action both by those starting as trainers as well as those with more experience.

ENSURING COMPETENCE TO TRAIN OTHERS

There is an old adage: 'Those that cannot do the task teach it.' Although we accept that this is infrequently the case amongst teachers who choose a more traditional didactic approach, if this saying were to apply to any experiential trainer it would foretell a training disaster!

Key areas need to be focused upon in advance of setting out as a trainer of others. These are as follows.

Self-awareness

Those putting themselves forward as experiential trainers require a considerable degree of personal awareness. They need to be realistically aware of their own personal and professional strengths and limitations. They need to know how experiences which were formative for them bias their own attitudes, thoughts, emotions and reactions.

They need to be particularly knowledgeable about themselves in all areas in which they will be using this method of teaching. It is crucial that the trainer remains continually aware that apparently similar events happen to different people, yet the personal meaning of what has happened for each individual can be markedly different.

Whatever relevant life experiences the prospective trainers have had, it is strongly advisable for them to *make* appropriate opportunities to 'process' these sufficiently before making use of them in their experiential training work. This could be through active participation in somebody else's high-quality experiential workshop, or through personal counselling.

Professional ability

Knowledge

Trainers require a comprehensive *theoretical* knowledge of their selected topic, being sufficiently aware of the range of factual information, strengths and limitations of current theories, and key issues of debate available in the published literature.

They require extensive and varied *practical* experience of their area. This should be gained over a period of time, from comprehending and working with the 'live' issues for varied groups of people over a range of settings. Considerable breadth and depth of experience is what is valuable; only having had narrow exposure or minimal active participation does not enable the prospective trainer to achieve an adequate basis from which to do this work.

There is a growing, and worrying, tendency for some who are funded for brief training by their employers to do short 'taster' training courses (for example, two-day workshops in drug abuse management, or counselling), which include some theory but no practical experience with valid client groups. They then find themselves expected to be their organisation's expert immediately afterwards. Some others have been known to proclaim irresponsibly a level of expertise which is quite unfounded, offering 'therapy' and training to others. Such shamanistic entrepreneurs can be equipped with impressive jargon, but little else to support their claims. They do not have sufficient depth of knowledge or any real expertise as yet, and are dangerous.

Skills of working in groups

The trainer requires adequate knowledge of, and experience in working with, group processes and development. From a counselling perspective, development of such ability is best achieved via supervised practice during appropriate training. Such background knowledge and experience is necessary to ensure that the trainer is continually aware of the group processes influencing the nature of participants' learning throughout the workshop, and remains sensitive to specific needs developing in each individual's learning experience.

Trainers must possess the personal awareness and resilience to cope with confrontation and contentious group members. It is usually inappropriate for the trainers to become emotionally involved in contentious or heated debate; a position of emotional neutrality needs to be maintained.

However, it *is* their role to confront group members when avoidance of relevant issues is occurring.

Teaching ability

Ivey (1983: 307) refers to mastery of four levels of communication skill. Achieving mastery, or competence, at all levels results in a person's having achieved the ability to teach that skill to others successfully. Ivey identifies the initial level as that of identification; of being able to identify the skill being used when observing others, and appreciating the impact on the recipient. The second level, of 'basic mastery', is where the person can use that skill appropriately in a role play. Next comes the 'active mastery', as the person uses the new skill in 'live' situations to full effect. Finally, having achieved this theoretical and practical comprehension of the skill and its use, the person is in a position to teach others.

Similarly, a person is competent to teach using an experiential approach when they have achieved an appropriate integration of their own considerable self-awareness, theoretical knowledge and extensive practical experience of the topic area, and are skilled in working in groups.

Co-facilitation

Trainers who work together do so in order mutually to facilitate more effective learning for participants. It is important that co-workers know each other and their respective teaching styles well. At best, co-facilitators comprehend each other's intended direction, thoughts and feelings at any given moment in the training session and are able smoothly to interject with appropriate additional material in a manner which complements and does not disrupt the other's work. Such a close style as this can only arise as a result of time having been taken to develop an effective working relationship, based on knowledge of, and respect for, each other's values and style.

During the time of working together as experiential trainers it is crucial they hold frequent and uninhibited discussions regarding the nature and content of their work together. They must have freedom to speak bluntly to each other, knowing that no offence will be taken, in order to achieve their shared aim. Such 'no-holds-barred' discussions require time set aside for them; it is insufficient to expect this to occur adequately over a drink together at the end of a tiring working day.

Wherever possible, co-facilitators need to be mutually involved in all aspects of the preparation of the workshop, setting clearly realistic, concrete and well-defined objectives to be met during it. They need to be clear *why* they are offering such training. Afterwards, they need to review what happened – what was good and what was not – to talk over thoroughly together what each individual trainer did and did not do well, and to consider fully how well they worked together – what were their combined strengths and limitations, and whether the objectives were achieved. Considerable, and avoidable, difficulties can arise when two or more trainers attempt to work together without prior knowledge of each other; this situation should be avoided if at all possible.

ISSUES TO BE CONSIDERED PRIOR TO THE WORKSHOP

The context of training

Those responsible for organising and running the training sessions need to understand clearly why the training is being sought, and the value and practical utility it holds for those taking part and the organisations in which they work. This information will influence aspects of the focus and content of the training.

Trainers need to understand the intentions of those funding the training, whether they are funding it for themselves or for someone who works for them. Trainers need to comprehend the nature of the work in which participants are involved, how this training will be useful for them – both professionally and personally – and whether there are potential drawbacks for them in doing this.

'Boundaries' need to be made clear to all concerned. Such clarity helps ensure that incompatible aims or agendas are not held for the training. Funders, managers, organisers and trainers need to be clear about what and how much is being provided, to whom, how and why. This usually entails some explanation of the nature and rationale of experiential learning and mutual acceptance of aspects of the workshop 'rules'. For example, managers also need to recognise that all attending the workshop are expected to participate actively, that it is not possible for anyone to attend simply 'to observe', and certainly not sporadically to turn up unannounced to do this for a few minutes! Where the funders or managers themselves are to be participants in the workshop, they need to be quite clear that responsibility for its running is the trainers' and not theirs. It has been known for radical changes of remit to be attempted during the workshop!

Prior discussion of these issues enables the managers' detailed concerns to be clarified and responded to appropriately; it may be that they simply wish to know whether this training is worth providing for their staff, or they may be unclear about what they actually require.

Clarity is necessary regarding exactly what is being funded; for example, a series of training sessions plus follow-up meetings, or solely a 'one-off' session.

Ethical questions may need to be addressed. For instance, should a company which supports and promotes highly stressful working practices be able to buy a session on stress management, so as to mollify trade-union concern, when it is refusing to recognise it?

Practical issues

If pre-publicity material is used, it must be designed and distributed appropriately. Application and selection procedures need to be finalised.

The format of training needs to be decided. With the need for flexibility of content in mind, a plan for training can be drawn up ensuring that there will be adequate material and exercises to promote the intended learning during the sessions. Agreement needs to be reached regarding whatever 'ground-rules' are deemed necessary. Trainers need to check that the aims they hold for the training will be met by the selected content and training format.

Potential participants and relevant others (for example, their management) need to be given instructions by means of publicity material that they will be requested not to go in to work when they are scheduled to attend the workshop sessions. The knowledge that they are not expected at work can clear their minds and promote their ability to concentrate fully on the workshop. Pre-occupying them with work tasks or problems dilutes the learning potential available to the whole group. The knowledge that they are due to go to work after the training session has the same effect. They also need to be informed, prior to the workshop, that they must arrange not to be interrupted during sessions, and that in many instances late-comers will not be admitted.

The venue needs to be selected carefully. Rooms for use in workshop sessions need to be private, interruption-free, of adequate size, well ventilated, sufficiently warm and comfortable without being sleep-inducing, and with access to toilets, refreshments and possibly a telephone during breaks. Ideally, the setting will be well away from participants' normal place of work or training; this particularly helps where the experiential approach to learning is alien to the group's usual training methodology. Where sessions are run on participants' 'home' territory where they are used only to didactic forms of teaching, and practised in presenting their relatively invulnerable, competent selves in that setting, they can experience difficulty.

The availability of necessary teaching aids and materials needs to be checked. Trainers should ensure that they know how to work the equipment, and should check that it is in full working order.

THE TRAINING SESSIONS

Arrival

Trainers should ensure that they arrive early to check the current acceptability of the venue (for example, its cleanliness and seating arrangements), and that any teaching aids which may have been requested have indeed been provided, in working order. From the moment the first participant arrives the trainers are at work. Participants will be making their decisions about whether this is an acceptable forum for them to work in, and anything that trainers do at this stage is influential in this process.

Introduction and 'rules' agreement

This process of welcoming the participants becomes more formalised in the trainers' introduction to the workshop. The importance of this section of the workshop cannot be overstated. It enables people to arrive 'psychologically' – to stop travelling, wondering what is to happen, or thinking about what they had been doing and so on. It continues, in a more direct manner, the trainers' work of establishing a prerequisite sense of safety for participants to be their vulnerable selves, prepared to share some aspects of their professional and personal experiences and concerns, strengths and limitations.

The introduction needs to be delivered in a calm, relaxed, yet quietly assertive manner to instil confidence in participants that these people are strong enough to work with. This needs to be done at a time when the trainers too are feeling anxious; it helps for them to acknowledge this. Part of the introduction needs to acknowledge the participants' existing competencies, and that the sessions will be at times particularly enjoyable and fun.

The requisite 'ground-rules' need to be clearly stated, and explicit agreement sought. It should be made plain, though not in a heavy-handed manner, that if any person is unable to agree to abide by these rules, they must leave before the workshop goes further. Should this happen, and it is rare, the issue of their departure must be directly addressed within the group; the need for respect for personal privacy is crucial to the learning process. Consideration must be given to suitability of advance publicity, application and selection later.

An additional focus is required where staff of different ranks are present, and in management relationships with one another. In such instances, it is necessary to clarify that people are attending the training to participate as the individuals they are, and not in the role which they fulfil at work. It can help to request that first names only are used throughout the training and not, for example, 'Sister A' or 'Mr B', the title which might be used to refer to that person at work.

The training sessions

The first exercise should be introduced with confidence, even if the trainers are feeling uncertain about how safe they feel with this new group of people. A suitable analogy is that of a duck which is swimming on a lake and which manages to appear calm and unruffled on the surface, even though paddling frantically under the surface of the water. Trainers do need to maintain participants' confidence in them. Previous chapters have consistently pointed out that this does not preclude their also being seen as vulnerable too. It is a sign of strength to acknowledge one's own vulnerability in a constructive manner.

Depending on the nature of the workshop, it is sometimes advisable for the first exercise to be one which elicits participants' expectations, anxieties or concerns regarding the workshop. This also helps to begin to draw out any private or previously 'hidden' agendas people may have. It is also necessary for trainers to participate fully in this first exercise, thereby modelling a degree of personal risk taking and disclosure.

If the trainers do not make their own personal experiences and vulnerabilities available to the group, nor will the other participants. This is a *powerful* challenge *each* time, involves genuine risk and trust in the group, and demands a considerable degree of personal strength and resilience in the trainers in addition to their personal awareness. It is also draining of energy. It is partly for this reason that trainers must take care not to run too many workshops in a given period. Their quality will deteriorate, as will the trainers' own comfort and health. Trainers need to be sensitive to the group process and the individual experience of participants at all times. This is wearing, and is one reason why the help and support of a co-worker is necessary.

Scheduled breaks in the training programme, arranged with flexibility of exact timing, need to be used appropriately. They are often not breaks for the trainers, as individual participants will request discussion time, or co-workers will need to meet to discuss workshop progress.

Where role plays are being conducted, it helps for their introduction to be succinct and brief; the role play should begin as soon as possible after it is announced, in order to avoid participants' performance anxieties having too long to incubate! The introduction should include a brief rationale (if relevant), but avoid participants switching into an 'intellectualising' mode. The role-play structure should be described, participants should assume their roles and the action should be started clearly. Observation needs to be non-intrusive yet effective. The role play should be brought to an end in a definite manner, discussion with players still in role take place if relevant, and then players adequately de-roled (see Chapter 7, page 151). It may be necessary to re-check that de-roling has been effectively achieved at the end of the session or day.

At the end of each day it is important to check whether any person is concerned with 'unfinished business'. The final few minutes of the day – earlier and for longer if it is the end of the training – can be set aside for reflecting on the experiences of that training day. Participants can be invited to make statements regarding any aspect of the training with which the person feels 'unfinished'. It should be made clear these statements are *not* for discussion. It is simply a way for participants to acknowledge current concerns and, in so doing, to attempt to leave them in the training setting rather than be unduly bothered by them away from the work setting.

Before they make any offers of 'follow-up' contacts after the workshop is over, trainers are well advised to ascertain that such offers can and will be adhered to by them. For example, one workshop leader suggested that participants write their plans of intended action as a letter to themselves and place it in a stamped and self-addressed envelope which she undertook to post in six months. None of the envelopes ever arrived!

EVALUATION

After each completed training workshop, a period of evaluation is necessary. One way of doing this is to request written comments at the end of the workshop; these can be in response to a list of provided questions. A second way is to write to participants after a certain time has elapsed, such as three or six months, and ask appropriate questions. The first method, coming as it does at the end of what has hopefully been a predominantly enjoyable as well as constructive time spent together, is frequently influenced by the warm glow of the social facilitation effect. Trainers must not allow themselves to be unduly swayed by this. The second method can ascertain whether real change has occurred. Both methods yield information of different utility and quality. Murgatroyd, in Chapter 8, has reviewed several methods for evaluation of these training workshops.

An essential aspect of the evaluation is that the co-trainers take time to discuss in depth their mutual and differing perceptions of the sessions, to achieve an honest and accurate appraisal of the strengths and limitations of their partnership, and any other relevant aspect of their work together.

Participant feedback forms may have been utilised, requesting comments and ratings of different aspects of the sessions, trainers' style, venue and so on. Follow-up evaluation measures may be used, delivered to participants at a specific time after the training and returned. The parent organisation of the participants, if one exists and is approachable, could provide their perception of the impact of the course on their staff. If this source of evaluative information is to be tapped, arrangements for so doing should be agreed before the training takes place.

Whatever form of evaluation is used, any information collected needs to be made use of, either to improve subsequent workshops or to demonstrate their efficacy. It can be helpful to record lists of 'learning points' and 'actions taken' as a result of evaluation.

REFERENCE

Ivey, A. E. (1983) *Intentional Interviewing and Counselling*, Monterey, CA: Brooks-Cole.

Name index

Subject index